SAT II WRITING

Dr. Leo Lieberman

Prof. Jeffrey Spielberger

Department of English
Bronx Community College
City University of New York

MACMILLAN • USA

Third Edition

Macmillan General Reference
A Prentice Hall Macmillan Company
15 Columbus Circle
New York, NY 10023

An Arco Book

MACMILLAN is a registered trademark of Macmillan, Inc.
ARCO is a registered trademark of Prentice-Hall, Inc.

Library of Congress Cataloging-in-Publication Data

Lieberman, Leo.
SAT II Writing / Leo Lieberman, Jeffrey Spielberger.—3rd ed.
    p.   cm.
  ISBN 0-671-86400-9
Previously published as College Board Achievement Test: English composition.
    1. English language—Composition and exercises—Examinations,
questions, etc. 2. Scholastic assessment test—Study guides.
I. Spielberger, Jeffrey. II. Title. III. Title: SAT 2 writing.
LB1631.L43   1993   93-17593
428'.0076—dc20   CIP

Manufactured in the United States of America

10 9 8 7 6 5 4 3

CONTENTS

Introduction to the Writing Test

In 1993–1994, The College Entrance Examination Board and Educational Testing Service introduced a revised SAT testing program. This new program consists of two major components designated SAT I and SAT II. The old SAT verbal and mathematical sections were reconfigured to become SAT I: Reasoning Tests; the old Achievement Tests have become SAT II: Subject Tests.

A major feature of SAT II is the brand-new Writing Test, which replaces the old Achievement Test in English Composition. The Writing Test, offered five times a year, includes both multiple-choice questions and a writing sample. This book is designed to familiarize students with the Writing Test and to help them score high on this important new college entrance exam.

Answers to Frequently Asked Questions About the Writing Test

Q: What is the format of the Writing Test?
A: SAT II Writing is a one-hour test divided as follows:

Writing Exercise	20 Minutes	1 Essay
Multiple-Choice Questions	40 minutes	60 questions

    Usage—30 questions
    Sentence Correction—18 questions
    Revision-in-Context—12 questions

Q: When is the Writing Test offered?
A: The Writing Test is offered five times a year, in January, May, June, November, and December.

Q: Who should take this test?
A: Some colleges require Writing Test scores; others allow students to choose among the subject tests. It is up to you to check the requirements of each college to which you expect to apply.

Q: How is the Writing Test scored?
A: Score reports for SAT II Writing will include scores for each multiple-choice question type and for the writing sample. For the multiple-choice questions, students will be given the number of right, wrong, and omitted responses and a raw score.

Writing samples are scored holistically by experienced high school and college English teachers. Each essay is scored by two different readers. Since each reader assigns a score between 1 and 6, the actual essay score ranges from 2 to 12, the sum of the two individual scores. Essay and multiple-choice scores are then combined and reported on a scale of 200 to 800.

Q: How do I register for the Writing Test?
A: You can obtain Registration Bulletins from most guidance offices, or you can write to request one from:

> College Board ATP
> P.O. Box 6200
> Princeton, NJ 08541-6200

Q: What's the best way to prepare for the Writing Test?
A: The Practice Tests in this book are patterned on the actual test. Take as many of them as you can to build the test-taking confidence you need to do your best. The Guide to Good Writing provides a concise and practical review of English grammar and usage. Use it to strengthen any weaknesses and to help boost your test scores.

Suggestions for Successful Studying

1. Do not depend on last-minute cramming to prepare for a test. Although a review of material directly before a test is valuable, this should not be the sole form of studying. It is better to combine several weeks of study periods with a more intensive review prior to the test to reinforce material.

2. Take good notes. Note-taking that is disorganized, illogical, and confused may hurt more than it helps. Instead of copying material word for word, rephrase important ideas in your own way. Rewriting material that you don't understand serves little purpose. It is better to attempt to understand an idea first and then to write it in such a way that it will be clear as it is reviewed.

3. Concentrate on the material you are studying and try to avoid distractions. Watching television or listening to the radio or the stereo can hurt your concentration, as can telephone interruptions and visits from friends. It is hard enough to keep your mind from wandering as you study. Don't add to the problem by providing intrusions. If you don't have a quiet place to study at home, consider using the library at school or in your neighborhood.

4. Study at a table or desk with all the necessary material clearly and neatly organized. Lounging in bed while studying seldom helps you stay alert, and facing a window or door may be distracting. Having your books and materials in front of you is far better than interrupting your study to find a piece of paper or a pen.

5. Eighteen hundred years ago, wise people wrote, "Set a fixed time for study." Their words are appropriate today. It is better to study an hour a day for ten days than to study five hours a day for two days. Also, try to study when you are alert and not overly tired. Set realistic study requirements. Don't be overambitious. Study at a regular time and place.

6. As you review material, determine the important ideas and the major points of each section.

7. Keep your study area free of tempting magazines and foods.

8. Use the library—it is an excellent study resource because you can borrow books.

9. Study at a desk with indirect lighting. This will avoid a glare that will tire your eyes.

10. Good ventilation will keep you alert.

Test-Taking Tips

1. Get to the room at least 10 to 15 minutes before exam time. Allow yourself ample time to settle down so that you are familiar with the environment and relatively comfortable.

2. Bring all necessary equipment with you. This includes identification, pen, pencils, and a watch.

3. Make certain that the test conditions are favorable. If there are distractions or any adverse conditions, inform the proctor. Don't be a martyr. The test will require all your energy. Don't be distracted unnecessarily.

4. Follow all the directions given by the proctor. If you do not understand what to do or are uncertain how to proceed, don't hesitate to ask for assistance.

5. Budget your time wisely. Be certain you understand the directions for your examination. Don't spend too much time on any one question. Proceed from question to question without worrying about how you answered a previous question. If a question thoroughly confuses you, omit that question and move on to the next one.

6. If you find yourself becoming tense, a few deep breaths will help. Some people find it helpful to close their eyes for two or three seconds and then continue to work.

7. It is better not to answer a question than to take a wild guess. But an educated guess is better than a complete omission.

8. For the essay section, you will have only 20 minutes to write a composition. You should allow yourself two or three minutes to proofread your paper, but you will probably not have enough time to rewrite the entire essay.

9. The answer sheet has a pre-printed grid. Completely blacken the space containing the letter of your answer choice. Do not make any unnecessary marks on the answer sheet as this will confuse the marking and may result in penalties. Each question must have only one answer. If you change your mind, be certain you have completely erased your previous response.

10. If you have used this book wisely, you will be at ease with the general format of the exam and the types of questions asked. As a result, there will be no surprises for you and you will be free to concentrate on giving correct responses. This is one of the major values of this book and one of the reasons for reading each section thoroughly and completing all exercises.

Relaxation Techniques for Test Taking

It is perfectly normal to be tense before a test. In fact, a little tension can prove helpful because it sets the adrenalin flowing and "peps" you up before the test. But too much anxiety can block your thoughts and interfere with the thinking process. If you become extremely tense, then a little relaxation prior to the exam may help you achieve a higher score.

First, arrive at the examination room at least 15 minutes before the exam is scheduled to begin. Choose a seat that you feel is best for you—up front, near a window, away from the door—wherever you are most comfortable. Then try one of these two relaxation techniques.

Relaxation Technique One

1. Place your chin on your chest and raise it slowly while *breathing in.*
2. Roll your head to one side, allowing it to fall sideways and down as you exhale.
3. Pause briefly, then repeat three to six times, allowing your head to fall on alternate sides.

Relaxation Technique Two

1. Sit quietly, feet flat on the floor, arms hanging loosely with hands on lap, palms facing down, eyes closed.
2. Focus on breathing through your nose and say silently to yourself, "in, out . . . one; in, out . . . two; in, out . . . one," etc. Continue this until you are aware of your *natural breathing rhythm.*
3. Starting at your feet, *contract* (hold for 3 seconds) and then *release* the muscles of your body in the following order: feet, lower legs, thighs, buttocks; stomach, chest; hands (make a fist); arms; shoulders; upper back; jaws (clench your teeth); cheeks; eyes (squeeze shut); eyebrows; forehead and scalp.

   Here are three hints to help you stay relaxed:

1. Take advantage of the quiet environment of the room in which the test is being given.
2. Pay attention to the normal rhythm of your breathing; start with deep breathing.
3. Sit in a comfortable position to eliminate undue muscular tension.

Practice these relaxation techniques at home prior to the day of the test. If you wish to read more about relaxation techniques, the following two books may be helpful:

Benson, Herbert, M.D. *The Relaxation Response.* New York: William Morrow & Co., 1976 (Books on Tape edition, 1986).

Selye, H. *Stress Without Distress.* Philadelphia: J.B. Lippincott, 1975.

Analyzing the Writing Test

Multiple-Choice Questions

SAT II Writing consists of three types of multiple-choice questions. First is the *usage question*. Here, you are given a sentence that may or may not contain an "error"—that is, a part not expressed in standard written English. Four different portions of the sentence are underlined; each underlined segment is labeled with a letter, A–D. You are to find which underlined segment is an "error" and mark its letter on your answer sheet. Or, if there is no error—if none of the underlined parts is "non-standard English"—then you mark E on your answer sheet. Two sample usage questions follow.

Sample Usage Questions

Directions: The sentences below contain errors in grammar, usage, word choice, and idiom. Parts of each sentence are underlined and lettered. Decide which underlined part contains the error and circle its letter. If the sentence is correct as it stands, circle E under "No error." No sentence contains more than one error.

1. Our blue team competed <u>with</u> our white team
                                          A
<u>for</u> five years, but the white team was <u>best</u>
  B   C   D
every time. <u>No error</u>
                        E

Answer:

(D) Should be *better*. In cases of comparison of two things, the comparative form of the adjective must be used. Only where there are three or more things being compared should the superlative form be used.

2. From the <u>shards</u> of glass <u>laying</u> <u>all over</u> the
                            A   B   C
living room, we hastily <u>inferred</u> that there
                                               D
had been an implosion brought on by the

cyclone. <u>No error</u>
                        E

Answer:

(B) Should be *lying*. *Laying* is the present participle of *lay* ("to put in place," "to set, as a table"). *Lying* is the present participle of *lie* ("to recline," "to remain in position," "to remain motionless").

The second type of question on the Writing Test is the *sentence correction* question. Here, the task is to rewrite the underlined portion of a sentence so that it is as representative as possible of "correct" standard written English: The punctuation must be right, the rules of grammar must be followed, and "awkwardness" or "long-windedness" must be avoided. You are writing awkwardly when your reader knows what you mean, but wishes you had said it more simply and directly. You are long-winded if you take fifty words to state what you could have said in ten. Sample sentence correction questions follow.

Sample Sentence Correction Questions

Directions: The sentences below contain problems in grammar, sentence construction, word choice, and punctuation. Part or all of each sentence is underlined. Select the lettered answer that contains the best version of the underlined section. Answer (A) always repeats the original underlined section exactly. If the sentence is correct as it stands, select (A). Circle the letter that appears before your answer.

1. The reason we stopped fishing was <u>because the fish had already stopped biting</u>.

   (A) because the fish had already stopped biting
   (B) because the fish had all ready stopped biting
   (C) that the fish had already stopped biting
   (D) that the fish had all ready stopped biting
   (E) because the fish had stopped biting already

Answer:

(C) The conjunction "because" makes no sense following "reason." A subordinate conjunction like "that" or "why" makes better logic. (D) is wrong because "all ready" is not an adverb.

2. Ignorance of the law does not <u>preclude you from being arrested</u> for a misdemeanor.

   (A) preclude you from being arrested
   (B) prevent you from being innocent
   (C) preclude you from being innocent
   (D) prevent your being acquitted
   (E) preclude your being arrested

Answer:

(E) "Preclude" should not be confused with "prevent." The idea of preventing something from happening *in advance* differs from mere prevention "on the spot." (D) is correct usage since the genitive *your* precedes the participle *being*, but (D) changes the meaning of the original sentence.

The third type of multiple-choice question is called *revision-in-context*. This section consists of a passage that is an early draft of a student's essay followed by questions about revising and improving the draft. The questions may relate to individual sentences or to the essay as a whole. You may be asked to examine sentence structure, diction, usage, or organization and development of the essay as a whole. Your task is to choose the answer that makes the meaning clear and that follows the conventions of standard written English. A sample passage and questions follow.

Sample Revision-in-Context Questions

Directions: Questions 1–3 are based on a passage that might be an early draft of a student's essay. Some sentences in this draft need to be revised or rewritten to make them both clear and correct. Read the passage carefully; then answer the questions that follow it. Some questions require decisions about diction, usage, tone, or sentence structure in particular sentences or parts of sentences. Other questions require decisions about organization, development, or appropriateness of language in the essay as a whole. For each question, choose the answer that makes the intended meaning clearer and more precise and that follows the conventions of standard written English.

(1) Is television an enhancer of or a deterrent to education? (2) Some educators feel that, properly managed, television can open up educational vistas to children and expose them to ideas; others say that television stifles activity and makes children into passive creatures.

(3) Certainly most people will agree that television is here to stay and that parents must accept the fact that their children are going to watch programs and they will have to deal with it. (4) By this, they must learn first of all what kind of programs are available and also the time schedule. (5) Perhaps they will have to preview programs. (6) Then parents must decide which programs will be beneficial for children.

1. In relation to the entire passage, which of the following best describes the writer's intention in sentence (2)?

   (A) To evaluate an opinion set forth in paragraph two
   (B) To point out a difference of opinion regarding the opening sentence
   (C) To restate the opening sentence
   (D) To provide examples
   (E) To summarize contradictory evidence

Answer:

(C) The first sentence, phrased as a question, presents the two opposing views of television vis-à-vis education. The second sentence rephrases this by using the two camps of educators, the first viewing television as an enhancer and the second viewing it as a deterrent to education. Thus, sentence (2) restates the first sentence and choice (C) is correct.

2. Which of the following is the best revision of the underlined portion of sentence (3) below?

   Certainly most people will agree that television is here to stay and that parents <u>must accept the fact that their children are going to watch programs and they will have to deal with it</u>.

   (A) will have to deal with their children's television watching
   (B) will as a result be forced to accept their children as they watch television
   (C) must accept and deal with their children if they watch television
   (D) must accept this, children will watch television and this must be handled
   (E) will have to deal with their children since they will watch television

Answer:

(A) The portion underlined is awkward and wordy, and it ends with a pronoun whose antecedent is not clear. Choice (A) corrects these weaknesses. Choices (B), (C), and (E) change the meaning of the sentence, and choice (D) is grammatically incorrect.

3. Which of the following is the best way to combine sentences (4), (5), and (6)?

   (A) Parents will have to learn time schedules, programs, and how to evaluate television.
   (B) The availability of programs as well as the time schedule will help parents to evaluate programs beneficial to children.
   (C) Subject matter of programs, time scheduling, and even actual previewing are factors that help parents decide on the suitability of television for children.
   (D) In order to decide on what programs are beneficial for their children, parents will have to develop criteria.
   (E) It is up to parents to evaluate programs for their children.

Answer:

(C) Only choice (C) takes in all the ideas expressed in sentences (4), (5), and (6)—kinds of programs available, time schedules, previewing, and deciding which programs are beneficial—and combines them in a grammatically correct sentence. Choice (A) is awkward and changes the intended meaning. Choices (B), (D), and (E) omit much of the original meaning.

The Essay Question

The essay section of the Writing Test allows you 20 minutes to plan and write an essay on an assigned topic. The essay topic will not require any specific subject-matter knowledge. Only one topic is offered, and you must fulfill the requirements of the assignment in your essay.

Each essay is evaluated by experienced high school and college English teachers who assign a rating to the essay based upon its overall effect. The prime objective of your essay is to demonstrate to the reader that you can develop a thesis, support it with appropriate facts or illustrations, and come to a conclusion in a clear, well-written, well-organized composition. A sample essay question follows.

Sample Essay Topic

Directions: You will have 20 minutes to plan and write an essay on the topic given below. Make certain that you do not stray from the topic, that you give specific details as supporting evidence, and that you organize your ideas logically.

Topic: Some people criticize city life for being dangerous, expensive, and noisy. Others describe country living as dull, culturally empty, and narrow.

Assignment: Write an essay in which you take a stand on the issue of city versus country living. Support your opinions with specific examples from your personal experience, your observations of others, or your reading.

Guidelines for Essay Writers

Aim for:

1. Originality of approach
2. Clarity of organization
3. Freshness of expression
4. Logical development
5. Variety of sentence patterns

Avoid:

1. Technical errors in sentence structure, spelling, grammar, and usage
2. Poor paragraphing
3. Unnecessary repetition of material
4. Substandard level of English—illiteracies, mixed metaphors, trite expressions, overuse of colloquialisms
5. Stylistic problems such as oversimplification, incoherent writing, wordiness

Suggestions for Writing a Successful Essay

Do:

1. Take a minute or two (but no more) to read the question, to underline important phrases, and to consider the implications of the statement or quotation.

2. Plan on writing a three- or four-paragraph essay containing an introduction, a development, and a conclusion.

3 Use supporting details to back up your ideas.

4. Keep your writing clear and relevant.

5. Spend the full 20 minutes on the essay. If possible, use the last minute or two to proofread your work and correct mistakes.

Do not:

1. Attempt to produce a sophisticated outline.

2. Plan on rewriting the entire essay.

3. Write so quickly that your handwriting becomes illegible.

4. Write notes or incomplete sentences hoping the examiner will understand what you have *not* written.

5. Spend more than 20 minutes on the essay. When time is called, go on to the multiple-choice questions.

Diagnostic Test

The Diagnostic Test that follows is designed to help you discover your strengths and weaknesses. It is modeled after the SAT II Writing Test, but it contains fewer questions. This is not a timed test. Following the essay question and the 20 multiple-choice questions are an answer key and an explanation of the answers, including two sample essay responses that have been annotated to indicate errors and analyzed for content and style.

If you carefully examine each part of the Diagnostic Test, you will see where your particular problems lie. Then, as you study the Guide to Good Writing, you can concentrate on those areas in which you are most in need of help.

Part A: Essay Section

Directions: You have 20 minutes in which to plan and write the essay assigned below. Make certain that you do not stray from the topic, that you give specific details as supporting evidence, and that you organize your ideas logically. Remember to proofread carefully to be certain that you have expressed your ideas in standard written English.

Topic: Computers, word processors, and other modern technological devices make it unnecessary for people to know how to write well in their everyday lives.

Assignment: Do you agree or disagree with this statement? Write an essay in which you support your opinion with specific examples from your personal experiences, your observations of others, or your reading.

Part B: Multiple-Choice Section

Usage

Directions: Some of the sentences below contain an error in grammar usage, word choice, or idiom. Other sentences are correct. Parts of each sentence are underlined and lettered. The error, if there is one, is contained in one of the underlined parts of the sentence. Assume that all other parts of the sentence are correct and cannot be changed. For each sentence, select the one underlined part that must be changed to make the sentence correct and mark its letter on your answer sheet. If there is no error in a sentence, select answer E. No sentence contains more than one error.

	Example	**Sample Answer**
	<u>Being that</u> <u>it's</u> such a lovely day, we A B	● Ⓑ Ⓒ Ⓓ Ⓔ
	<u>are having</u> a difficult time C	
	<u>concentrating</u> on our assignment. D	
	<u>No error</u> E	

1. <u>According to</u> Thoreau, Walden was the
   A
   <u>deepest</u> pond in the area and the last
   B
   <u>to freeze</u> every <u>winter</u>. <u>No error</u>
   C   D   E

2. He was <u>shocked</u> by the <u>students</u> outburst
   A   B
   when the professor reprimanded the boys
   <u>who</u> <u>had arrived</u> a few minutes before the
   C   D
   test was over. <u>No error</u>
   E

3. <u>I'm</u> not surprised that my brother always
   A
   eats twice as much as I do <u>since</u> he is so
   B
   much bigger <u>than</u> <u>me</u>. <u>No error</u>
   C   D   E

4. You <u>would of been</u> able to go to the theater
   A
   with <u>us</u> <u>if</u> you had purchased <u>your</u> ticket in
   B C   D
   advance. <u>No error</u>
   E

5. Everyone in both groups <u>except</u> for John
   A
   and <u>me</u> <u>were</u> amazed when the <u>contest's</u>
   B   C   D
   results were announced. <u>No error</u>
   E

6. <u>There was</u> scarcely <u>no</u> possibility that we
   A   B
   would be able <u>to go</u> to the beach with
   C
   <u>them</u>. <u>No error</u>
   D   E

7. The <u>assent</u> of Mount Everest <u>brought</u>
   A   B
   <u>lasting</u> fame <u>to</u> Sir Edmund Hillary.
   C   D
   <u>No error</u>
   E

8. Because the moon rotates on <u>its</u> axis <u>at the</u>
   A
   <u>same rate</u> as <u>revolving</u> around the earth,
   B   C
   only one side of the lunar surface
   <u>is ever visible</u> to us. <u>No error</u>
   D   E

Sentence Correction

Directions: The sentences below may contain problems in grammar, usage, word choice, sentence construction, or punctuation. Part or all of each sentence is underlined. Following each sentence you will find five ways of expressing the underlined part. Answer choice (A) always repeats the original underlined section. The other four answer choices are all different. You are to select the lettered answer that produces the most effective sentence. If you think the original sentence is best, choose (A) as your answer. If one of the other choices makes a better sentence, select the letter of that choice. Do not choose an answer that changes the meaning of the original sentence.

Example

I have always enjoyed <u>singing as well as to dance</u>.
(A) singing as well as to dance
(B) singing as well as dancing
(C) to sing as well as dancing
(D) singing in addition to dance
(E) to sing in addition to dancing

Sample Answer

Ⓐ●ⒸⒹⒺ

---

9. The textbook was poorly written, outdated, and <u>with errors</u>.
   (A) with errors
   (B) with mistakes
   (C) factually incorrect
   (D) showing errors
   (E) being erroneous

10. Someone <u>has taken the book off of</u> the shelf.
    (A) has taken the book off of
    (B) has took the book off
    (C) took the book off of
    (D) has taken the book off
    (E) has taken the book off from

11. <u>Unlike football</u>, baseball fields can vary somewhat in size and shape.
    (A) Unlike football
    (B) Not like in football
    (C) Contrary to football fields
    (D) Unlike football fields
    (E) Contrary to football

12. I hope you don't feel <u>too badly about</u> coming late to the meeting.
    (A) too badly about
    (B) to badly about
    (C) too bad when
    (D) too badly when
    (E) too bad about

13. Sunshine, good soil, <u>and caring continually</u> will almost always result in beautiful house plants.
    (A) and caring continually
    (B) and caring on a continual basis
    (C) and continual care
    (D) and care that is continuing
    (E) and care which can be continuous

14. <u>The pump having been repaired,</u> my cousin could turn on the heating system once again.
    (A) The pump having been repaired,
    (B) Because the pump is repaired,
    (C) The pump's having been repaired,
    (D) The pump has been repaired so that
    (E) Having the pump repaired,

15. She jumped out of bed as soon as the alarm rang <u>and races to be the first in the shower</u>.
    (A) and races to be the first in the shower
    (B) and she races to be the first in the shower
    (C) and raced to be first in the shower
    (D) and raced first to the shower
    (E) then she raced to be first in the shower

16. She has stopped eating <u>bread and pasta. In an effort to test</u> whether she is allergic to glutin.
    (A) bread and pasta. In an effort to test
    (B) bread and pasta, a testing of
    (C) grains, in an effort to test
    (D) bread and pasta in an effort to test
    (E) bread and pasta in order to make a test

Revision-In-Context

Directions: Questions 17–20 are based on a passage that might be an early draft of a student's essay. Some sentences in this draft need to be revised or rewritten to make them both clear and correct. Read the passage carefully; then answer the questions that follow it. Some questions require decisions about diction, usage, tone, or sentence structure in particular sentences or parts of sentences. Other questions require decisions about organization, development, or appropriateness of language in the essay as a whole. For each question, choose the answer that makes the intended meaning clearer and more precise and that follows the conventions of standard written English.

(1) The question of if ordinary citizens should own handguns has been asked for many years. (2) It used to be a fairly "intellectual" exercise to discuss individual rights versus the right of society to control citizens. (3) But recently the problem has taken on a very "practical" aspect. (4) More and more people, according to newspaper articles and news magazines, are carrying guns, for protection and, incredible as it may seem, to make a fashion statement as well.

(5) Just the other day a study appeared; it concerned the desire of the police to be allowed to carry 9 mm. guns, as opposed to the .38 or .45 caliber weapons they now possess. (6) Police organizations feel that in order to keep up with criminals, they need more modern and sophisticated weapons, with the ability to fire more bullets more rapidly. (7) To worsen things many average law-abiding citizens, especially living in urban centers, are already carrying the newer guns. (8) If owners are trained in proper handling and shooting techniques, that may be one thing. (9) If not, that may be another.

(10) Then there's the problem of fashion. (11) Many people carry unlicensed guns just to be "cool" and in style. (12) Do you want a silver gun? (13) A rosewood and metal gun? (14) A small beauty with mother of pearl handle? (15) No problem. (16) They are all available for a price. (17) And many ordinary citizens are paying that price for protection and fashion.

17. Which of the following is the best revision of the underlined portion of sentence (1) below?

The question of <u>if ordinary citizens should own handguns</u> has been asked for many years.

(A) ordinary citizens who own handguns
(B) if ordinary citizens should own handguns or not
(C) whether ordinary citizens should own handguns or whether not
(D) whether ordinary citizens should own handguns
(E) ordinary citizens owning their own handguns

18. Which of the following is the best revision of the underlined portion of sentence (4) below?

<u>More and more people, according to newspaper articles and news magazines, are carrying guns,</u> for protection and, incredible as it may seem, to make a fashion statement as well.

(A) More people, according to newspaper and news magazine articles, are carrying guns,
(B) More and more people are carrying guns according to newspaper articles and news magazines,
(C) According to newspaper articles and news magazines, more and more people are carrying guns
(D) According to newspaper articles and news magazines, recently more people are carrying guns
(E) More and more people, in accordance with newspaper articles and news magazines, are carrying guns

19. Which of the following is the best revision of the underlined portion of sentence (7) below?

   To worsen things many average law-abiding citizens, especially living in urban centers, are already carrying the newer guns.

   (A) To worsen things, many average law-abiding citizens, especially in urban centers,
   (B) To make matters worse, many average law-abiding citizens, especially those living in urban centers,
   (C) Even worse, many average law-abiding citizens, especially urban-centered,
   (D) To make things worse, most law-abiding citizens, especially those living in urban centers,
   (E) To make matters worse, the law-abiding citizens in urban centers

20. Which of the following is the best way to combine sentences (12), (13), and (14)?
   (A) If a person wants a silver gun?; a rosewood and metal gun?; a small beauty with mother of pearl handle?
   (B) Do you want a silver gun?, a rosewood and metal gun?, a small beauty with mother of pearl handle?
   (C) Want a silver gun, a rosewood and metal gun, a small beauty with mother of pearl handle?
   (D) Do they want a silver, rosewood and metal, small beauty with mother of pearl handle gun?
   (E) Do they want a silver gun, a rosewood and metal gun, or a small beauty with mother of pearl handle?

Sample Essay Responses

Now that you have written your own essay responding to the Diagnostic Test topic, you should examine the two sample responses. Evaluate each one in terms of content and written expression. Then turn to the annotated responses, noticing the errors made and the suggested corrections. Finally, read the summary analysis of each response.

Sample Essay A

Its not important to be a good writer today as it use to be. In the past people didn't have telephone and computer and telegraph and etc. Whereas today we have all those thing, so we don't worry about writing. We can always just push a button and turn on t.v. or radio or make a call and say hello to a friend. So we won't have to write letters if we don't want.

Also, we won't have to write reports if we don't want. it depends on your job or occupation. Teachers and lawyers will of course have to write good essays but its not important for nurses and mechanical and computer occupations to be able to express theirselves in writing.

In conclusion, students should be able to study what their interested in instead of practicing to write better in the future.

Sample Essay B

Certainly modern technological advance have provided us with significant ways of improving our life style and I do not think that there are many clear thinking people who would want to get rid of the computer or word processor. Still there is no substitute for personal contact in the exchange of ideas and the written word provides us with exactly this sort of contact.

Letter-writing is an effective way of staying in touch with friends and cementing good professional relationships. Writing can avoid the coldness of a computer print-out and the warmth of the human voice on the telephone cannot be forgotten. There is simply no substitute for a good letter which can be re-read from time to time. Business firms often keep letters on file and refer to them when appropriate; and the sentiment of holding on to notes from a relative or friend can be a very meaningful and important part of our private life.

The well-rounded individual should seek to utilize all means to develop his power to communicate effectively and to present himself in the best possible light.

Writing clearly, coherently, and carefully will help to fulfill these objectives. Writing well should not be a lost art, part of the past, but rather a very important aspect of our daily lives.

Annotated Sample Essay A

1   Its not important to be a good writer today as it use to be. In the

2   past people didn't have telephone and computer and telegraph, and

3   etc. Whereas today we have all those thing, so we don't worry about

4   writing. We can always just push a button and turn on t.v. or radio or

5   make a call and say hello to a friend. So we won't have to write letters

6   if we don't want.

7   Also, we won't have to write reports if we don't want it depends on

8   your job or occupation. Teachers and lawyers will of course have to

9   write good essays, but its not important for nurses and mechanical and

10 computer occupations to be able to express theirselves in writing.

11   In conclusion, students should be able to study what their interested

12 in instead of practicing to write better in the future.

Analysis of Sample Essay A

Essay A is very weak; it is poorly written and developed in a sketchy manner. Among the flaws: fragments (lines 2, 3), punctuation problems (lines 1, 2, 7), lack of clarity or precision (lines 3, 4, 6, 8, 11), word-ending errors (lines 1, 2, 3).

As the suggested revision indicates, a good deal of work is necessary if the essay is to convey its thoughts effectively. In addition to correcting the aspects as noted, the writer would also want to develop the content more fully, to explain and support the few points made in the essay.

Annotated Sample Essay B

1   Certainly modern technological advance have provided us with

2   significant ways of improving our life-style and I do not think that

3   there are many clear-thinking people who would want to get rid of the

4   computer or word processor. Still there is no substitute for personal

5   contact in the exchange of ideas and the written word provides us

6   with exactly this sort of contact.

7   Letter-writing is an effective way of staying in touch with friends

8   and cementing good professional relationships. Writing can avoid the

9   coldness of a computer print-out and the warmth of the human voice

10   on the telephone cannot be forgotten. There is simply no substitute

11   for a good letter which can be reread from time to time. Business

12   firms often keep letters on file and refer to them when appropriate;

13   and the sentiment of holding on to notes from a relative or friend can

14   be a very meaningful and important part of our private life.

15   The well-rounded individual should seek to utilize all means to

16   develop his power to communicate effectively and to present himself

17   in the best possible light.

18   Writing clearly, coherently, and carefully will help to fulfill these

19   objectives. Writing well should not be a lost art, part of the past, but

20   rather a very important aspect of our daily lives.

Analysis of Sample Essay B

Essay B is written in a mature style and conveys its message effectively and clearly, for the most part. It is generally well organized, progressing from an introductory statement of specific examples to a summation that reinforces the writer's views.

As the suggested revision indicates, the essay might be enhanced by a few changes to improve punctuation (lines 1, 2, 4) and clarity (lines 2, 11, 13). The comment concerning "the human voice on the telephone" (lines 9–10) might be utilized more properly in another part of the essay, or reworded to fit more coherently with the context of the paragraph. Nevertheless, the essay succeeds in conveying its point to the reader.

Answer Key to Diagnostic Test

1. **E**	5. **C**	9. **C**	13. **C**	17. **D**
2. **B**	6. **B**	10. **D**	14. **A**	18. **C**
3. **D**	7. **A**	11. **D**	15. **C**	19. **B**
4. **A**	8. **C**	12. **E**	16. **D**	20. **E**

Explanatory Answers to Diagnostic Test

1. **(E)** The sentence is correct.

2. **(B)** The correct word is *students'* or *student's* since the possessive form is required.

3. **(D)** The nominative *I* following the comparative *bigger than* is required.

4. **(A)** The correct verb form is *would have been.*

5. **(C)** The singular *was*, agreeing with the singular subject *everyone*, is required.

6. **(B)** Since *scarcely no* is a double negative, the correct phrase is *scarcely any.*

7. **(A)** *Assent* means agreement. The word needed here is *ascent*, meaning climbing or scaling.

8. **(C)** The idea calls for parallel structure: "Because the moon rotates on its axis at the same rate as *it revolves* around the earth. . . ."

9. **(C)** *Factually incorrect* is needed to parallel *poorly written* and *outdated.*

10. **(D)** The correct phrase is *taken off*, not *taken off of.*

11. **(D)** Sentences (A), (B), and (E) improperly contrast an entire sport (*football*) with one aspect of another sport (*baseball fields*). (B), (C), and (E) are also unidiomatic. Only (D) corrects the sentence logically and idiomatically.

12. **(E)** The correct word is *bad,* since the adjective, not the adverb, is required after the verb *feel.*

13. **(C)** To maintain parallelism, the third item must also be a noun.

14. **(A)** The sentence is correct.

15. **(C)** The original (A) is inconsistent in tense, starting in the past (*jumped, rang*) and then switching to the present (*races*). (B) exhibits the same problem. (C), (D), and (E) all supply the required past tense, but (D) changes the meaning of the original sentence and (E) is a run-on sentence.

16. **(D)** The sentences should be combined to eliminate the fragment beginning with *in an effort.*

17. **(D)** Choice (A) distorts the question; choice (B) asks *if*, which should be used in a conditional statement; choices (C) and (E) contain repetitious wording. Choice (D) is best.

18. **(C)** Choice (A) attempts to be concise but changes the sense of the statement and is awkward; choices (B), (D), and (E) change the sense of the statement. Choice (C) is best; it moves the subject and verb closer together.

19. **(B)** In choice (A), *to worsen things* is ungrammatical; in choice (C), *urban-centered* is poor phrasing; in choices (D) and (E), *most* and *the* make the statements statistically inaccurate. Choice (B) is best.

20. **(E)** In choices (A) and (B), the punctuation after the question marks is incorrect; in choice (C), the tone is too casual and informal; choice (D) is confusing. Choice (E) is best.

Part I

Guide to Good Writing

The first part of this Guide is devoted to the rules of English grammar. Simply-stated rules are followed by examples to illustrate their application and by frequent drills to assess mastery of the material covered. Correct answers are provided for all drills so that you can check your work and review any points you missed.

The second part of the Guide covers the rules of punctuation that every college-bound student should know. Presented alphabetically from apostrophe to semicolon, each punctuation mark is explained and thoroughly illustrated. Drills reinforce correct usage of each punctuation rule.

The final section of the Writing Guide tackles the subject of usage and diction—choosing and using the right words in the right places. It includes two glossaries: one of words that look or sound alike yet have distinct and different meanings; the other of words that are similar in meaning and yet have clear-cut differences in usage. In addition, there are helpful discussions of language to avoid—clichés, incorrectly-used idioms, and mixed metaphors—to increase your awareness of these potential writing problems.

Basic Rules of Grammar

Agreement

Basic Rule: A *verb* agrees in *number* with its subject. A singular subject takes a singular verb. A plural subject takes a plural verb.

Examples.
The boy is studying.

The teacher was dozing while his students were studying.

Choose the correct verb: (is, am, are) John, Mary, Bill, and I *are* going to spend the summer together.

Explanation: Remember that the verb must agree with the subject. Since the subject is plural—subjects joined by *and* are plural—a plural verb is needed. The correct response therefore should be:

John, Mary, Bill, and I *are* going to spend the summer together.

►**Caution!** Sometimes the subject comes after the verb, but the rule still applies.

Choose the correct verb: (is, are) There *are* three more items on the agenda.

Explanation: *Are* is correct since the subject *three more items* is plural and requires a plural verb.

►**Caution!** There is one major exception to this rule. When the sentence is introduced by the word *there* and the verb is followed by a compound (double) subject, the first part of the subject dictates whether the verb should be singular or plural.

Example: There *is one woman* in the living room and four women in the kitchen.

When compound subjects are joined by *either-or* or *neither-nor,* the verb agrees with the subject closest to the verb.

Examples: Neither the young man nor *his friends have had* much practice.
Neither you nor *I am* willing to serve as chairperson.

Explanation: In the first example, *friends* (plural) is closest to the verb; in the second example *I* (singular) is closest to the verb.

►**Caution!** Sometimes a word or a group of words may come between the subject and the verb. The verb still must agree with the simple subject and the *simple subject is never part of a prepositional phrase.*

22

Example: The *author* of the three books *is* well known.
The simple subject is *author,* a singular noun. The verb must be *is.*

Choose the correct verb: (was, were) The causes of the war~~were~~ not known.

Explanation: The simple subject is *causes; of the war* is a prepositional phrase. Since the subject is plural, the plural verb *were* is required.

Correct: The *causes* of the war *were* not known.

Basic Rule: A pronoun agrees with the word it refers to (the *antecedent*) in both person and number.

Example: They deposited their money in the bank since they were afraid they might lose *it.*

Explanation: The pronoun *it* refers to *money,* the antecedent.

▶**Caution!** Remember to use a singular pronoun when you refer to words such as *everyone, everybody, each, every, anyone, anybody, nobody, no one, one, each, either, neither.*

Examples: *Everyone* should take *his* coat (not *their*).
Each *woman* brought *her* child (not *their*).
We heard that *none* of the men neglected to bring *his* ticket (not *their*).

▶**Caution!** Collective words present special problems. A collective names a group of people or things. Although usually singular in form, it is treated as either singular or plural according to the sense of the sentence:

Singular when members of the group act, or are considered as a *unit:*

The junior *class is sponsoring* the fund drive.

Plural when the members act, or are considered, individually:

The jury *are* unable to agree on a verdict.

Common collectives include:

assembly, association, audience, board, cabinet, class, commission, committee, company, corporation, council, counsel, couple, crowd, department, family, firm, group, jury, majority, minority, number, pair, press, public, staff, United States

The following short words—though seldom listed as collectives—are governed by the rule for collectives. They are singular or plural according to the intended meaning of the sentence.

all, any, more, most, none, some, who, which

Drill I: Try the following drill to see if you understand the basic principles of agreement. Answers are on page 41.

Choose the correct word for each blank.

1. (is, are) Bill and Jean _are_ going to the game tomorrow.

2. (have, has) Either Jay or his friends _have_ the answer key.

3. (was, were) There _were_ several students absent last week.

4. (his, their) I hope that no one has left _his_ homework at home.

5. (her, their) Each of the sisters celebrated _her_ birthday at the Plaza.

6. (is, are) The music of Verdi's operas _is_ filled with dramatic sweep.

7. (his, their) All the musicians tuned _their_ instruments.

8. (know, knows) Neither Mark nor the twins _know_ the correct answer.

9. (go, goes) Either Mrs. Martinez or Carlos _goes_ to church each week.

10. (is, are) However, neither the seller nor the buyers _are_ satisfied with the arrangement.

If you achieved a perfect score, you may wish to go directly to the next area. If not, review this section carefully and then try the following drill.

Drill II: In the following paragraph, there are ten words underlined. If the word is grammatically correct, write C in the margin; if a change is necessary, indicate the change and give a grammatical reason for it. Do not make unnecessary changes. Answers are on page 41.

Joseph, one of my best friends, <ins>are</ins> [1 _is_] planning to be a doctor. He and I <ins>feel</ins> [2 C] that medicine, of all the professions, <ins>are</ins> [3 _is_] one of the most exciting. He has asked each of his friends to give <ins>their</ins> [4 _his_] opinion and everyone stated what <ins>they</ins> [5 _he_] thought was most valid. Then Joseph asked his parents what they <ins>think</ins> [6 C] he should do. It seems that his friends and his mother <ins>is</ins> [7 _are_] in agreement but his father <ins>do</ins> [8 _does_] not agree. His father strongly feels that the medical profession, unlike other professions, <ins>requires</ins> [9 C] too much study and will be too taxing. There <ins>is</ins> [10 _are_] always several considerations that must be examined before making a choice.

Capitalization

The use of capital letters is a convention of language and culture. There are languages that do not even have capital letters, such as many mid-Eastern and Oriental languages. In standard written English, you must capitalize:

1. The first word of a sentence.

   Example: With cooperation, a depression can be avoided.

2. All proper names, as well as a word used as part of a proper noun.

   Examples: William Street is now called Morningside Terrace.
   (but We have a terrace apartment.)
   America, General Motors, Abraham Lincoln

3. Days of the week and months.

   Examples: The check was mailed on Thursday.
   Adam's birthday is in July.

4. The word *dear* when it was the first word in the salutation of a letter.

   Example: Dear Mr. Jones: (but My dear Mr. Jones:)

5. The first word of the complimentary close of a letter.

   Example: Truly yours, (but Very truly yours,)

6. The first, last, and all other important words in a title

   Example: The Art of Salesmanship

7. Titles, when they refer to a particular official or family member.

   Examples: The report was read by Secretary Marshall.
   (but Miss Shaw, our secretary, is ill.)
   Let's visit Uncle Harry.
   (but I have three uncles.)

8. Points of a compass, when they refer to particular regions.

   Example: We're going South next week.
   (but New York is south of Albany.)

   ▶Note: Write the Far West, the Pacific Coast, the Middle East.

9. The first word of a direct quotation.

   Example: It was Alexander Pope who wrote, "A little learning is a dangerous thing."

   ▶Note: When a direct quotation is broken, the first word of the second half of the sentence is not capitalized.

   "Don't phone," Irene told me, "because they're not in yet."

10. Adjectives derived from the names of religions, countries, languages.

    Examples: Jewish, Protestant, South American, Spanish.

Drill III: Rewrite the following sentences on another sheet of paper, changing lowercase letters to capital letters wherever needed. Answers are on page 41.

1. we took a trip to the city of tuscaloosa in the south last june.

2. *"my brother was an only child* is a very catchy title and should interest all people," said bob smith.

3. my uncle lives on allendale boulevard near the red apartment house.

4. we will see doctor arnold next wednesday when we attend the meeting of the modern language association in Albany.

5. your aunt is a bit older than cousin betty.

Comparisons

Basic Rule: When two things are being compared, the comparative form of the adjective is used. The comparative is formed in one of two ways: (1) Adding *er* to the adjective; (2) placing *more* before the adjective.

Examples:	He is *more* educated than his brother.
	She is *prettier* than her sister.

▶**Note:** Do not use *both* of the above methods.

Not:	Jeremy is *more wiser* than we know.
But:	Jeremy is wiser (or *more wise*) than we know.

Basic Rule: When three or more things are compared, the superlative form of the adjective is used. The superlative is formed in one of two ways: (1) adding *est* to the adjective; (2) placing *most* before the adjective.

Examples:	Of all the books, this one is the *most* difficult.
	Which is the *shortest* of all of Shakespeare's plays?

Error:	Mary is the *shorter* of all of her friends.
Correct:	Mary is the *shortest* of all of her friends.

▶**Note:** Do not use both of the above methods.

Not:	This is the *most sharpest* knife I have.
But:	This is the *sharpest* knife I have.

▶**Note:** Some modifiers are compared by changes in the words themselves. A few of these irregular comparisons are given below; consult your dictionary whenever you are in doubt about the comparisons of any adjective or adverb.

Positive	Comparative	Superlative
good	better	best
well	better	best
bad (evil, ill)	worse	worst
badly (ill)	worse	worst
far	farther, further	farthest, furthest
late	later, latter	latest, last
little	less, lesser	least
many, much	more	most

▶**Caution:** Some adjectives and adverbs express qualities that go beyond comparison. They represent the highest degree of a quality and, as a result, cannot be improved. Some of these words are listed below.

complete	deadly	immortally
correct	exact	infinitely
dead	horizontally	perfect
perfectly	secondly	totally
perpendicularly	square	unique
preferable	squarely	uniquely
round	supreme	universally

▶**Note:** The use of the comparative in such an expression as *This thing is better than any other,* implies that *this thing* is separate from the group or class to which it is being compared. In these expressions a word such as *other* or *else* is required to separate the thing being compared from the rest of the group of which it is a part.

Not: Our house is cooler than any house on the block. (The mistake here is not separating the item being compared— *house*—from the group to which it is being compared.)

But: Our house is cooler than any *other* house on the block. (Our house is one of the houses on the block.)

Not: He has a better record than any salesman in our group.

But: He has a better record than any *other* salesman in our group. (He himself is one of the salesmen in the group.)

▶**Caution!** Be careful of incomplete comparisons. The result is illogical and confusing.

Error: The plays of Shakespeare are as good as Marlowe.

Correct: The plays of Shakespeare are as good as *those* of Marlowe.

Error: His skill in tennis is far better than other athletes his age.

Correct: His skill in tennis is far better than *that* of other athletes his age.

Error: His poetry is as exciting, if not more exciting than, the poetry of his instructor.

Correct: His poetry is as exciting *as,* if not more exciting than, the poetry of his instructor.

Fragments

Basic Rule: Every sentence must have a complete subject and verb and express a full idea. There are three ways to correct incomplete sentences:

1. Add the fragment to the sentence that precedes it.

2. Add the fragment to the sentence that follows it.

3. Add a new subject and verb to the fragment.

Incorrect: My uncle is a very unusual person. A man fluent in several languages.

Correct: My uncle is a very unusual person, a man fluent in several languages.

Explanation: The fragment is added to the sentence that precedes it.

Incorrect: Worrying about how to prepare for the examination. I finally decided to set up a conference with my instructor to ask for advice.

Correct: Worrying about how to prepare for the examination, I finally decided to set up a conference with my instructor to ask for advice.

Explanation: The fragment is added to the sentence that follows it.

Incorrect: Slipping on the ice.

Correct: Slipping on the ice, the elderly woman lost her balance and fell.

Explanation: A new subject and verb are added to the fragment.

▶**Caution!** Do not use a phrase as a sentence.

Incorrect: To walk down the street.

Incorrect: Walking down the street.

Incorrect: By walking down the street.

Correct: By walking down the street, you will pass many places of interest.

Incorrect: In the afternoon.

Incorrect: By mid-day.

Correct: We will see you sometime in the afternoon.

▶**Caution!** If a sentence begins with a subordinating conjunction such as *If, When, Since, Because, Although,* a comma usually comes after the dependent clause and is followed by a main clause.

Incorrect: Although she is young. She is weary and aimless.

Incorrect: Although she is young she is weary and aimless.

Correct: Although she is young, she is weary and aimless.

Drill IV: Read the following pairs of sentences carefully. Decide which sentence of each pair is correctly punctuated. Answers are on page 41.

1. (A) Late registration, at best, is always a difficult experience; especially since so many sections are no longer available.
   (B) Late registration, at best, is always a difficult experience, especially since so many sections are no longer available.

2. (A) We try to arrive on time, feeling this is crucial to the whole process.
   (B) We try to arrive on time. Feeling this is crucial to the whole process.

3. (A) Usually, the night before we review all the courses we should like to take. Making out a schedule which we feel would be desirable.

   (B) Usually, the night before, we review all the courses we should like to take, making out a schedule which we feel would be desirable.

4. (A) If we are fortunate. We move through the lines quickly; if not, we see what changes must be made to avoid conflicts.
   (B) If we are fortunate, we move through the lines quickly; if not, we see what changes must be made to avoid conflicts.

5. (A) It is helpful to keep a sense of humor and two aspirins with you on the day of registration. I certainly do.
   (B) It is helpful to keep a sense of humor and two aspirins with you on the day of registration. As I do.

Modifiers

Basic Rule: Modifiers should be placed as closely as possible to the words they modify. This is true whether the modifier is a single word, a phrase, or a clause.

Incorrect: I bought a piano from an old lady with intricate carvings.
Correct: Who or what had the carvings? It would be better to write: I bought a piano with intricate carvings from an old lady.

Incorrect: I read about the destruction of Rome in my history class.
Correct: In my history class, I read about the destruction of Rome.

▶**Note:** The word *only* often causes confusion. Examine the following sentences.

> Only he kissed her.
> He only kissed her.
> He kissed only her.

All three sentences are possible, but a different meaning is conveyed in each, depending on the positioning of the word *only*.

▶**Caution:** Sometimes a problem is created by the placement of a participle phrase.

Example: Answering the doorbell, the cake remained in the oven. (The *cake* answered the doorbell?)

Correct this sentence by adding a subject to which the phrase can refer:

Answering the doorbell, *we* forgot to take the cake from the oven.

Incorrect: Falling on the roof, we heard the sound of the rain.
Correct: We heard the sound of the rain falling on the roof.

Drill V: Rewrite the following sentences so that the word being modified is clear. Answers are on page 41.

1. He tripped on a crack in the pavement going to school.

2. Mary only failed the test.

3. Did you see the film about the five on the boat on television?

4. The police officer ordered the man to stop in his patrol car.

5. Upon picking up the phone, the noise became muted.

6. While swimming, a fish nibbled on my toe.

7. He went to the old church to pray for the people on Cemetery Hill.

8. Of all his admirers, his wife only loved him.

9. Upon entering the class, the blackboard came into view.

10. The baby was pushed by his mother in a stroller.

Parallel Structure

Basic Rule: In a sentence in which there are two or more elements of equal importance in function and content, they must be alike in grammatical construction.

Incorrect: He spends his time playing cards, swimming, going to the theater, and at school.

Analysis: *At school* is incorrect since a gerund is required to be parallel with *playing, swimming, going*.

Correct: He spends his time playing cards, swimming, *going* to the theater and *going* to school.

Incorrect: He manages his business affairs with knowledge, with ease, and confidently.

Analysis: *Confidently* is incorrect since it lacks parallelism with the prepositional phrases *with knowledge* and *with ease*.

Correct: He manages his business affairs with knowledge, with ease, and *with confidence*.

Incorrect: He was required by the instructor to go to the library, to take out several books on the Vietnam War, and that he should report to the class on what he had learned.

Analysis: The clause *that he should report* is incorrect since it is not parallel with the infinitives *to go* and *to take out*.

Correct: He was required by the instructor to go to the library, to take out several books on the Vietnam War, and *to report* to the class on what he had learned.

Pronouns

Pronouns substitute for nouns.

Examples: Helen is my sister; *she* is older than my brother.
Bill just purchased a new wristwatch; *it* keeps perfect time.

The following *Pronoun Chart* may prove helpful:

Number	Person	Subjective Case	Objective Case	Possessive Case
Singular	1st person	I	me	mine
	2nd person	you	you	yours
	3rd person	he, she, it, who	him, her, it, whom	his, hers, whose
Plural	1st person	we	us	ours
	2nd person	you	you	yours
	3rd person	they, who	them, whom	theirs, whose

Basic Rule: The subject of the sentence is in the subjective case. The subject of each verb is in the subjective case. If the pronoun is used as an appositive to the subject or as a predicate nominative, the pronoun is kept in the subjective case.

Incorrect: John and *him* were chosen.
Correct: John and *he* were chosen. (*He* is the subject of the verb; we certainly would not say that *Him* was chosen.)

Incorrect: It was *her* who was chosen.
Correct: It was *she* who was chosen.

Incorrect: *Us* students were chosen.
Correct: *We* students were chosen.

Incorrect: He is as witty as her.
Correct: He is as witty *as she.*

Incorrect: I will give the book to *whomever* comes first.
Correct: I will give the book to *whoever* comes first.
(Don't be fooled by the preposition *to;* we would say *who comes* since *who [or whoever]* is the subject of the verb *comes.*)

Basic Rule: If a pronoun is the object of a verb or preposition, it is placed in the objective case.

Incorrect: They accused Tom and *he* of stealing.
Correct: They accused Tom and *him* of stealing.
(Him is the object of the verb *accused;* they accused *him,* not *he.)*

Incorrect:	The tickets were given to the instructor and *I*.
Correct:	The tickets were given to the instructor and *me*.
	(*Me* is the object of the preposition *to;* the tickets were given to *me*, not to *I*.)

Incorrect:	*Who* did you see?
Correct:	*Whom* did you see?
	(*Hint:* Make this a declarative sentence: You saw *him*.)

Basic Rule: A pronoun that expresses ownership is in the possessive case.

Personal pronouns that express ownership never require an apostrophe.

Incorrect:	This book is *your's*, not *her's*.
Correct:	This book is *yours*, not *hers*.

A pronoun that precedes a gerund is usually in the possessive case.

Incorrect:	He rejoiced at *him* going to the party.
Correct:	He rejoiced at *his* going to the party.
	(In this sentence *going* is a gerund, a verbal ending in *ing* used as a noun.)

Drill VI: Some of the following sentences contain misused pronouns. Make all corrections. If the sentence is correct, indicate by marking with a C. Answers are on page 42.

It may be helpful to refer to the Pronoun Chart as you do the drill.

1. We are happy that Bob, Bill, and he are going to be there.

2. I know that us men will be able to complete the job by next week.

3. Whoever is here will see Mr. Smythe and me.

4. They objected to them taking the exam late.

5. He is more intelligent than her.

6. He is not as good a runner as Mary or her.

7. He will change the sweater for her.

8. He laughed at me addressing such a prestigious group.

9. If you get here before John or me, please tell the director that the poor roads may have caused John and me to drive slowly.

10. Who are you thinking about, John or me?

Basic Rule: Do not use forms of the same pronoun to refer to different antecedents.

Not:	The teacher told John that *he* thought *his* work was improving. (Does the teacher think that his own work is improving, or that John's work is improving?)
But:	John was told by *his* teacher that *his* work was improving.

Basic Rule: Place the pronoun as close as possible to its antecedent to avoid ambiguity or confusion.

Not: The letter is on the desk *that* we received yesterday.
But: The *letter that* we received yesterday is on the desk.

▶**Caution!** Be sure that the reference to an antecedent is specific.

Not: When you have finished the book and written your summary, please return *it* to the library. (What are you returning? The book or the summary?)
But: When you have finished the book and written your summary, please return *the book* to the library.

▶**Note:** The impersonal use of *it, they,* and *you*—tends to produce vague, wordy sentences.

Not: In the Manual *it* says to make three copies.
But: The manual says to make three copies

Not: *They* say we are in for a cold, wet winter.
But: The almanac predicts a cold, wet winter.

The Run-On Sentence

To confirm what I have now said and further to show the miserable effects of a confined education I shall here insert a passage which will hardly obtain belief in hopes to ingratiate myself farther into his Majesty's favour I told him of an invention discovered between three and four hundred years ago to make a certain powder into an heap of which the smallest spark of fire would kindle the whole in a moment although it were as big as a mountain and make it all fly up in the air together with a noise and agitation greater than thunder that a proper quantity of this powder rammed into an hollow tube of brass or iron according to its bigness would drive a ball of iron or lead with such violence and speed as nothing was able to sustain its force.

—From *Gulliver's Travels* by Jonathan Swift

The paragraph cited above appears to be a jumble of ideas because there are no punctuation marks to help set off thoughts. Indeed, all ideas run into each other. In order to make sense out of the paragraph, we need to use end-stop punctuation to divide complete thoughts or suitable connectors (conjunctions) to join two ideas.

Basic Rule: Do not carelessly run main clauses together without appropriate punctuation or connectors. Correct run-on sentences in one of the following ways:

Method 1. The most common way to correct a run-on sentence is to divide the sentence using end-stop punctuation.

Run-on:	The lecture was dull you almost fell asleep.
Correct:	The lecture was dull. You almost fell asleep.

Run-on:	Was the lecture dull you almost fell asleep.
Correct:	Was the lecture dull? You almost fell asleep.

Run-on:	The lecture was incredibly dull you almost fell asleep.
Correct:	The lecture was incredibly dull! You almost fell asleep.

▶**Note:** When end-stop punctuation is used, the new thought begins with a capital letter.

In the above three corrections, three different end-stop marks were used:

1. The period (.)
2. The question mark (?)
3. The exclamation point (!)

▶**Caution!** The comma is not an end-mark. It cannot be used by itself to separate two sentences.

Incorrect:	Close the window, there is a draft in the room.
Correct:	Close the window. There is a draft in the room.

Method 2. Sometimes two sentences are very closely related in meaning and full end-stop punctuation may seem too strong. A semicolon can then be used to divide the two sentences. If a semicolon is used, do *not* use a capital letter to begin the word following the semicolon, unless the word normally begins with a capital letter.

Run-on:	It was a beautiful day there was not a cloud in the sky.
Correct:	It was a beautiful day; there was not a cloud in the sky.

Method 3. A third way to correct the run-on is to use a connector (conjunction) such as *and, but, for, or,* and *nor* if the two sentences are equal in importance. *It is usually advisable to place a comma before these connectors.*

Run-on:	I like to ski, my friend prefers to sit by the fire.
Correct:	I like to ski, but my friend prefers to sit by the fire.

▶**Note:** Some problem words that may cause run-ons are *however, therefore, consequently,* and *moreover.* These words are not sentence connectors, and when they follow a complete thought, they should be preceded by either a period or semicolon.

Drill VII: Examine the following word groups. Wherever you believe a sentence ends, put in the correct punctuation mark and capitalize the next word. Do this only where you feel that punctuation is necessary. Indicate a correct sentence by C̲. Sometimes it is helpful to read the word groups aloud. Answers are on page 42.

1. It was an exhausting day we could hardly wait to get home.

2. The house was completely empty, no one came to the door.

3. Where had everyone gone all the lights were off.

4. We entered slowly, almost afraid.

5. Suddenly I felt that something was going to happen my heart began to beat furiously.

Verb Tense

Basic Rule: Use the same verb tense whenever possible within a sentence or paragraph. Do not shift from one tense to another unless there is a valid reason.

> *Incorrect:* Joan *came* home last week and *goes* to her home in the country where she *spends* the last weekend of her vacation.
>
> *Correct:* Joan *came* home last week and *went* to her home in the country where she *spent* the last weekend of her vacation.

Principal Parts of Verbs

We indicate tense by changing the verb itself or by combining certain forms of the verb with auxiliary verbs. The verb tenses from which we derive every form of a verb are called the *principal parts*. The principal parts of a verb are:

1. The Present Tense: talk, write

2. The Past Tense: talked, wrote

3. The Present Perfect: have talked, has written

Verbs are classified as *regular* (or *weak) and irregular* (or *strong*), according to the way in which their principle parts are formed. Regular verbs form their past tense and present perfect tense by the addition of *-ed* to the infinitive:

Present Tense	Past Tense	Present Perfect Tense
talk	talked	has (have) talked
help	helped	has (have) helped
walk	walked	has (have) walked

The principal parts of irregular verbs are formed by changes in the verb itself:

Present Tense	Past Tense	Present Perfect Tense
see	saw	has (have) seen
say	said	has (have) said
go	went	has (have) gone

Principal Parts of Common Irregular Verbs

Present	Past	Past Participle
arise	arose	arisen
be	was, were	been
bear	bore	borne
become	became	become
begin	began	begun
bid	bade	bid, bidden
blow	blew	blown
break	broke	broken
bring	brought	brought
build	built	built
buy	bought	bought
catch	caught	caught
choose	chose	chosen
cling	clung	clung
come	came	come
cut	cut	cut
do	did	done
draw	drew	drawn
drink	drank	drunk
drive	drove	driven
eat	ate	eaten
fall	fell	fallen
feed	fed	feed
feel	felt	felt
fight	fought	fought
find	found	found
flee	fled	fled
fling	flung	flung
fly	flew	flown
forget	forgot	forgotten
forgive	forgave	forgiven
freeze	froze	frozen
get	got	gotten
give	gave	given
go	went	gone
grow	grew	grown
hang (a person)	hanged	hanged
hang (an object)	hung	hung
hear	heard	heard
hide	hid	hidden
hold	held	held
hurt	hurt	hurt
keep	kept	kept
know	knew	known
lay	laid	laid
lead	led	led
leave	left	left
lend	lent	lent
lie	lay	lain
light	lit, lighted	lit, lighted

Present	Past	Past Participle
lose	lost	lost
make	made	made
meet	met	met
ride	rode	ridden
ring	rang	rung
rise	rose	risen
run	ran	run
see	saw	seen
send	sent	sent
shake	shook	shaken
shoot	shot	shot
shrink	shrank, shrunk	shrunk, shrunken
sit	sat	sat
slay	slew	slain
sleep	slept	slept
slide	slid	slid
speak	spoke	spoken
spend	spent	spent
spin	spun	spun
spring	sprang, sprung	sprung
stand	stood	stood
steal	stole	stolen
sting	stung	stung
strive	strove	striven
swear	swore	sworn
swim	swam	swum
swing	swung	swung
take	took	taken
teach	taught	taught
tear	tore	torn
tell	told	told
think	thought	thought
throw	threw	thrown
wake	waked, woke	waked, woken
wear	wore	worn
weave	wove	woven
win	won	won
wring	wrung	wrung
write	wrote	written

Drill VIII: Choose the correct form of the verb. Answers are on page 42.

1. (hanged, hung) The picture was _____ on the wall nearest the bay window.

2. (sown, sewed) She has _____ the hem on the skirt perfectly.

3. (frozen, friezed, froze) The water has not _____ on the pond sufficiently.

4. (lent, loaned) The bank _____ him the required money.

5. (drank, drunk) He _____ all the poison from the vial.

6. (flang, flinged, flung) He _____ the papers on the desk and ran out of the room.

7. (lieing, lying, laying) You have been _____ on the beach for over two hours.

8. (losed, lost) He had to pay a fine because he _____ the book.

9. (hanged, hung) The outlaw was _____ in the town square.

10. (rang, rung) They _____ the bell so softly that we did not hear it.

Drill IX: Write the correct form of the verb. You may wish to refer to the verb chart on pages 36 to 37. Answers are on page 42.

1. (come) A gentleman has _____ to see you.

2. (suppose) Bill was _____ to telephone you last night.

3. (begin) My friend has _____ to get impatient.

4. (catch) He has _____ a serious cold.

5. (sing) He could _____ before large groups, if he were asked to.

6. (sing) She has _____ before large groups several times.

7. (go) They have already _____ to the theater.

8. (give) He has _____ me excellent advice.

9. (devote) He is _____ to his parents.

10. (build) The engineer has designed and _____ his own home.

When to Use the Perfect Tenses

Basic Rule: Use the *Present Perfect* for an action begun in the past and extended to the present.

Example: I am glad you are here at last; I *have waited* an hour for you to arrive.

Explanation: In this case, *I waited* would be incorrect. The action *have waited* (present perfect) began in the past and extended to the present.

Basic Rule: Use the *Past Perfect* for an action begun and completed in the past before some other past action.

Example: The foreman asked what *had happened* to my eye.

Explanation: In this case, *what happened* would be incorrect. The action *asked* and the action *had happened* (past perfect) are used because one action (regarding the speaker's eye) is "more past" than the other (the foreman's asking).

Basic Rule: Use the *Future Perfect* for an action begun at any time and completed in the future.

> *Example:* When I reach Chicago tonight, my uncle *will have left* for Los Angeles.
> *Explanation:* In this case the action *will have left* is going to take place before the action *reaches,* although both actions will occur in the future. When there are two future actions, the action completed first is expressed in the future perfect tense.

Drill X: In the following sentences, select the correct verb tense. Answers are on page 42.

1. (cheer, have cheered, cheered) When he spoke, all the people _____ him.

2. (is, was, be) Since he _____ late, he didn't receive a gift.

3. (had completed, have completed) I am told that you _____ the job.

4. (had completed, have completed) I was told that you _____ the job.

5. (are, were) We were taught that vitamins _____ important for our well-being.

The Subjunctive Mood

Basic Rule: The subjunctive expresses a condition contrary to fact, a wish, a supposition, or an indirect command. Although it is going out of use in English, the subjunctive can still be seen in the following forms:

1. To express a wish not likely to be fulfilled or impossible to be realized.

   I wish it *were* possible for us to approve his transfer at this time.
   (It is *not* possible.)

2. In a subordinate clause after a verb that expresses a command, a request, or a suggestion.

   He asked *that* the report *be* submitted in duplicate.
   It is recommended *that* this office *be* responsible for preparing the statements.
   We suggest *that* he *be* relieved of the assignment.

3. To express a condition known or supposed to be contrary to fact.

   If I *were* in St. Louis, I should be glad to attend.
   If this *were* a simple case, we would easily agree on a solution.
   If I *were* you, I should not mind the assignment.

4. After *as if* or *as though*. In formal writing and speech, *as if* and *as though* are followed by the subjunctive, since they introduce as supposition something not factual. In informal writing and speaking, the indicative is sometimes used.

He talked *as if* he *were* an expert on taxation. (He's not.)
This report looks *as though* it *were* the work of a college freshman.

▶**Caution!** Avoid shifts in mood. Once you have decided on the mood that properly expresses your message, use that mood throughout the sentence or the paragraph. A shift in mood is confusing to the listener or reader; it indicates that the speaker or writer himself has changed his way of looking at the conditions.

Not: It is requested that a report of the proceedings *be* prepared and copies *should be* distributed to all members. (*Be* is subjunctive; *should be*, indicative.)

But: It is requested that a report of the proceedings *be* prepared and that copies *be* distributed to all members.

▶**Caution!** We have seen that a verb must agree with its subject. A special case is the *third person singular* of most verbs in the present tense. Study the following chart:

Present Tense Verb: To Speak

	Singular	Plural
1st person	I speak	we speak
2nd person	you speak	you speak
3rd person	he speaks	they speak
	she speaks	
	it speaks	

▶**Note:** The third person singular subject of the present tense ends in *s*.

Fill in the correct form for each of the following verbs in the present tense:

1. (to laugh) He _____

2. (to jump) She _____

3. (to hurt) It _____

4. (to see) The man _____

5. (to walk) The child _____

The subject of each of the above is the third person singular, and each of the verbs conforms to the rule: laugh*s*, jump*s*, hurt*s*, see*s*, walk*s*.

▶**Caution!** With certain verbs (*go, do*), the third person singular in the present tense ends in *es* (*goes, does*).

Answer Key for Grammar Drills

Drill I:

1. **are** The subject, *Bill* and *Jean*, is plural.

2. **have** The verb must agree with the word closest to it, in this case a plural, *friends*.

3. **were** The subject, *students*, is plural.

4. **his** The antecedent is *no one*, which requires the singular, *his*.

5. **her** The antecedent, *each*, requires the singular pronoun.

6. **is** The subject of the verb is singular, *music*.

7. **their** The antecedent of the pronoun is *musicians*, a plural.

8. **know** In a *neither-nor* construction, the verb is governed by the closest subject, *twins*.

9. **goes** The verb is governed by *Carlos*, a singular noun.

10. Look back at number 8. Did you have the correct answer? The correct answer is *are*.

Drill II:

1. **is** The subject, *Joseph*, is singular.

2. **C** The subject, *He and I*, is plural.

3. **is** The subject, *medicine*, is singular.

4. **his** The antecedent *each* governs the singular pronoun his.

5. **he** The antecedent *everyone* governs the singular pronoun *his*.

6. **C**

7. **are** The plural subject *his friends and his mother* governs the plural verb are.

8. **does** Since the subject, *father*, is singular, a singular verb is required.

9. **C**

10. **are** The subject, *considerations*, a plural, requires a plural verb.

Drill III:

1. We took a trip to the city of Tuscaloosa in the South last June.

2. *"My Brother was an Only Child* is a very catchy title and should interest all people," said Bob Smith.

3. My uncle lives on Allendale Boulevard near the red apartment house.

4. We will see Doctor Arnold next Wednesday when we attend the meeting of the Modern Language Association in Albany.

5. Your aunt is a bit older than Cousin Betty.

Drill IV:

1. **B**

2. **A**

3. **B**

4. **B**

5. **A**

Drill V:

1. Going to school, he tripped on a crack in the pavement.

2. Only Mary failed the test.

3. Did you see the film on television about the five on the boat?

4. The police officer in his patrol car ordered the man to stop.

5. When we picked up the phone, the noise became muted.

6. While I was swimming, a fish nibbled on my toe.

7. He went to the old church on Cemetery Hill to pray for the people.

8. Of all his admirers, only his wife loved him.

9. When we entered the class, the blackboard came into view.

10. The baby was in a stroller pushed by his mother.

Drill VI:

1. **C**

2. I know that *we* men will be able to complete the job by next week.

3. **C**

4. They objected to *their* taking the exam so late.

Drill VII:

1. It was an exhausting day. We could hardly wait to get home.

2. The house was completely empty. No one came to the door.

3. Where had everyone gone? All the lights were off.

Drill VIII:

1. hung
2. sewed
3. frozen
4. lent

Drill IX:

1. come
2. supposed
3. begun
4. caught

Drill X:

1. cheered
2. was
3. have completed

5. He is more intelligent than *she*.

6. He is not so good a runner as Mary or *she*.

7. **C**

8. He laughed at *my* addressing such a prestigious group.

9. **C**

10. *Whom* are you thinking about, John or me? (*Hint:* You are thinking about *me;* both pronouns require the objective case.)

4. **C**

5. Suddenly I felt that something was going to happen. My heart began to beat furiously. (You might have inserted an exclamation point in place of the final period.)

5. drank
6. flung
7. lying
8. lost
9. hanged
10. rang

5. sing
6. sung
7. gone
8. given
9. devoted
10. built

4. had completed

5. are (When you are expressing a permanent fact, the *present tense* is used.)

Proper Punctuation

Although punctuation is stressed less than other aspects of writing on the multiple-choice part of the examination, the careful writer must be aware of the principal rules governing punctuation. Certainly a knowledge of proper punctuation is essential for the essay part of the exam. The following section is not intended to give a definitive set of rules but rather only to provide a basic framework for the writer.

The Apostrophe

The apostrophe usually is either misused or omitted because of the writer's failure to proofread his paper or because he is not certain about its use. The apostrophe is used:

1. To indicate the possessive case of *nouns.* (It is not used with possessive pronouns, since such pronouns as *yours, hers, our, theirs,* and *whose* indicate possession already.)

2. To indicate a *contraction*—the omission of one or more letters.

3. To indicate *plurals* of letters, abbreviations, and numbers.

To form the possessive of a noun: If the noun does not end in *s*—whether singular or plural—add an *'s;* if the noun ends in *s* simply add the '. (Some writers like to add *'s* to all nouns, even those that already end in *s.*)

Examples:　the children's teacher
the teacher's children
Keats' poetry (or Keats's poetry)

Drill I: In each of the following sentences, decide if an apostrophe is needed in the underlined words. Answers are on page 50.

1. The *boys* hand was injured.

2. He went to the *doctors* office.

3. The *rooms* were painted bright green.

4. The *colors* were muted by the *suns* rays.

5. The *teachers* had a meeting in the *principals* office.

To form a contraction: Place the apostrophe exactly where the missing letters occur.

Examples: can't = can not
it's = it is

Drill II: Are the following underlined words contractions? If so, what letter(s) are missing? Answers are on page 50.

1. *Its* my book.

2. *What's* the matter?

3. I *won't* let him take the test.

4. The cat placed *its* paw in the milk.

5. This book is *hers,* not *yours.*

To form plurals of letters, abbreviations, and numbers: Usually the apostrophe is used to form the plurals of lower-case letters (a's, b's, c's, etc.) plurals of abbreviations with periods (Ph.D.'s, R.N.'s), and numbers (3's, 6's). With capital letters, abbreviations without periods, and even with numbers when no confusion results, you have a choice. In either case, the writer should be consistent in his or her style.

Drill III: Circle the correct spelling in the following sentences. Answers are on page 50.

1. The (boys, boys') books were stolen.

2. (Mary's, Marys', Marys) hat is new but (its, it's) slightly soiled.

3. (Whose, Who's, Whoses's) class are you in?

4. There are two (C.P.A.S., C.P.A.'s) working for the firm.

5. He is a member of the (Diner's, Diners) Club.

6. The (ladies, ladies', ladie's) department is on the second floor.

7. The (instructor's, instructors) comments were worthwhile.

8. There are two 6's and three (sevens, 7s, 7's) on the paper.

9. Spell the word with two (t's, T S, Ts) and one r.

10. Is the hat (hers, her's, hers'); (it's, its, its') certainly not (Joans, Joans', Joan's).

The Colon

The colon is used to precede a list of three or more items or a *long quotation.*

Examples: There are four different types of political systems:
The mayor made the following statement:

▶**Caution!**   Avoid using the colon directly after a verb. Avoid using the colon to interrupt the natural flow of language.

Poor: We purchased: apples, pears, bananas, and grapes.
Better: We purchased apples, pears, bananas, and grapes.

The Comma

The comma is used:

1. To set off words in a series. Use a comma between words in a series when three or more elements are present. The elements may be words, phrases, or clauses. (Notice the use of the commas in this last sentence.)

   Examples: He hopped, skipped, and jumped.
   She is certainly a good student, a fine athlete, and a willing worker.
   I will not listen to, follow, or obey your instructions.

   ▶**Note:** It is acceptable to omit the comma before *and* or *or*. However, the writer should be consistent in his choice.

2. Before coordinating conjunctions *(and, but, nor, or, for)* that join two independent clauses.

   Examples: Joe has been very diligent about completing his work, *but* he has had many problems concerning his punctuality.

   I sincerely hope that these exercises prove of assistance to you, *and* I believe that they will help you to make a better showing on your examinations.

   ▶**Note:** If the independent clauses are short, you may omit the separating comma.
   Example: I saw him and I spoke to him.

3. To set off nonrestrictive, parenthetical, and appositive elements. A nonrestrictive element supplies material not essential to the sentence and, if removed, will not change the meaning of the original sentence.

   Example: Millie, who is a fine student, has a perfect attendance record.

   A parenthetical element is one that is added to the sentence without changing the sentence's meaning. Some common parenthetical elements are: *to tell the truth, believe me, it appears to me, I am sure,* and *as a matter of fact.*

   An appositive element describes a noun or pronoun but is not grammatically necessary for the sentence.

   Examples: Bob, an industrious and hard-working student, will run for class treasurer.
   Shrill and loud, her voice grated on our ears.

   ▶**Note:** In the first example the appositive phrase follows the noun it describes *(Bob);* in the second, the appositive phrase precedes the noun it describes *(voice).*

4. To set off introductory clauses and phrases.

> *Examples:* When you come home, please ring the bell before open-
> ing the door.
> Forcing back his tears, he embraced her warmly.

5. To separate two coordinate adjectives that precede the noun they
   describe. (Coordinate adjectives are adjectives of equal importance.)

> *Examples:* He is a wise, charming man.
> She is a slow, careful reader.
>
> In both these examples *and* can be substituted for the
> comma. But if you cannot substitute *and* without chang-
> ing the meaning, the adjectives are not coordinate, and no
> comma is needed.
> *Example:* He is a charming young man.

6. To set off nouns in direct address. The name of the person addressed
   is separated from the rest of the sentence by commas.

> *Examples:* Bob, please close the door.
> I think, José, that you are the one who was chosen.

7. With dates and addresses: The different parts of a date and an
   address are separated by commas, including a comma after the last
   item.

> *Examples:* The train will arrive on Friday, February 13, 1992, if it is
> on schedule.
>
> My daughter traveled from Cambridge, Massachusetts, to
> Albany, New York, in three hours.
>
> ▶**Note:** Using a comma where it is not needed is as confusing as
> omitting one when it is required.

Drill IV: Check the seven rules for using the comma and then decide when commas are required in the following paragraph. Answers are on page 50.

It was a cold blustery day and the temperature was hovering at twenty degrees. Although the calendar indicated that the month was October we felt that we were experiencing December weather. Bill Smith the newly appointed professor was arriving by plane from Seattle Washington and we had arranged to have a group welcome him at the airport. To tell the truth I was happy that I was not chosen to be part of the committee since I knew how windy the airport could be. But events that took place on that fateful day of October 15 1990 proved that I was more than lucky.

The Dash

A dash is used:

1. Before a word or word group which indicates a summation or reversal of what preceded it.

   Examples: Patience, sensitivity, understanding, empathy—these are the marks of a friend.

   To lose weight, set yourself realistic goals, do not eat between meals, eat only in the kitchen or dining room, avoid resturants—and then go out and binge.

   ▶**Note:**   The material following the *dash* usually directs the attention of the reader to the content preceding it.

2. Before and after abrupt material of a parenthetical nature.

   Example: He was not pleased with—in fact, he was completely hostile to—the take-over.

End-Stop Punctuation

There are three types of punctuation used to end a sentence: the period, the question mark, and the exclamation mark.

1. A period is used at the end of a sentence that makes a statement.

   Examples: He is my best friend.
   There are thirty days in September.

2. A question mark is used after a direct question. A period is used after an indirect question.

   Examples: *Direct Question*—Did you take the examination on Friday?
   Indirect Question—The instructor wanted to know if you took the examination on Friday.

3. An exclamation mark is used after an expression that shows strong emotion or issues a command. It may follow a word, a phrase, or a sentence.

   Examples: Wonderful! You won the lottery!
   Oh, no! I won't go!
   Do it!

Drill V: Add the necessary punctuation to these sentences. Answers are on page 50.

1. He was not aware that you had lost your wallet

2. Did you report the loss to the proper authorities

3. I suppose you had to fill out many forms

4. What a nuisance

5. I hate doing so much paper work

6. Did you ever discover where the wallet was

7. I imagine you wondered how it was misplaced

8. Good for you

9. At least you now have your money and your credit cards

10. What will you do if it happens again

The Hyphen

The hyphen is used with a compound modifier that precedes the noun.

> *Examples:* There was a sit-in demonstration at the office. (but We will sit in the auditorium.)
> I purchased a four-cylinder car. (but I purchased a car with four cylinders.)

The hyphen also is used with fractions that serve as adjectives or adverbs.

> *Example:* The optimist feels that his glass is one-half full; the pessimist feels that his glass is one-half empty.

Drill VI: Rewrite the following sentences, inserting all <u>necessary</u> punctuation marks. Answers are on page 51.

1. Bob read Tennyson's "Ulysses" to the class everyone seemed to enjoy the reading.

2. He ordered a set of books several records and a film.

3. He has forty-three thousand dollars to spend however once that is gone he will be penniless.

4. The careless student may write dont in place of does not.

5. Before an examination do the following review your work get a good nights sleep eat a balanced breakfast and arrive on time to take the test.

Quotation Marks

Quotation marks are used:

1. To enclose the actual words of the speaker or writer.
2. To emphasize words used in a special or unusual sense.
3. To set off titles of short themes or parts of a larger work.

> *Examples:* Jane said, "There will be many people at the party."
> He kept using the phrase "you know" throughout his conversation.
>
> The first chapter of *The Scarlet Letter* is "The Custom House."

> ▶**Caution!** Do not use quotation marks for indirect quotations.
> *Incorrect:* He said that "he would be happy to attend the meeting."
> *Correct:* He said that he would be happy to attend the meeting.
> *Or:* He said, "I would be happy to attend the meeting."

> ▶**Caution!** Do not use quotation marks to justify your own poor choice of words.

> ▶**Note:** The period and comma are placed *inside* the quotation marks; the colon and the semicolon are placed outside the quotation marks.

> *Examples:* My favorite poem is "My Last Duchess," a dramatic monologue written by Robert Browning.
> My favorite poem is "My Last Duchess"; this poem is a dramatic monologue written by Robert Browning.

The Semicolon

A semicolon may be used to separate two complete ideas (independent clauses) in a sentence when the two ideas have a close relationship and they are *not* connected with a coordinating conjunction.

> *Example:* The setting sun caused the fields to take on a special glow; all was bathed in a pale light.

The semicolon is often used between independent clauses connected by conjunctive adverbs such as *consequently, therefore, also, furthermore, for example, however, nevertheless, still, yet, moreover, otherwise.*

> *Example:* He waited at the station for well over an hour; however, no one appeared.
> (Note the use of the comma after the conjunctive adverb.)

▶**Caution!** Do *not* use the semicolon between an independent clause and a phrase or subordinate clause.

Drill VII: Decide whether the semicolons are correctly placed in the following sentences or whether another mark of punctuation would be preferable. Answers are on page 51.

1. He is an excellent student and a fine person; as a result, he has many friends.

2. Because he is such an industrious student; he has many friends.

3. We tried our best to purchase the books; but we were unsuccessful.

4. The rebuilt vacuum cleaner was in excellent condition; saving us a good deal of expense since we didn't have to purchase a new one.

5. Marie has a very soft voice; however, it is clear and distinct.

6. Don't open the door; the floor is still wet.

7. Don't open the door; because the floor is still wet.

8. We worked for three days painting the house; nevertheless, we still needed more time to complete the job.

9. The telephone rang several times, as a result; his sleep was interrupted.

10. Peter was chosen recently to be a vice-president of the business; and will take over his duties in a few days.

Answer Key to Punctuation Drills

Drill I:

1. *boy's* (Since we are speaking of the hand *of the boy*, we add *'s* to *boy*.
2. *doctor's* (We are speaking of the office *of the doctor;* therefore, we add *'s* to *doctor*.)
3. *rooms* (This is a simple plural, so no *'s* is needed.)

4. Only *sun's* requires the apostrophe since we are speaking of the *rays* (plural) *of the sun; colors* is a simple plural.
5. Since *teachers* is a simple plural, no apostrophe is required; but it is the office *of the principal,* so we write *principal's* office.

Drill II:

1. *It's = It is,* so the apostrophe is needed.
2. *What's = What is,* so the apostrophe is correct.
3. *won't = will not,* so the apostrophe is needed. (You might look up *wont* in the dictionary and discover the meaning.)

4. No apostrophe is called for. This is a pronoun in the possessive case and no letters are missing.
5. See the explanation for #4. It applies for *hers* and *yours*.

Note: Formal writing tends to avoid the use of contractions. In a formal essay it is preferable to spell out all words.

Drill III:

1. boys'
2. Mary's, it's
3. whose
4. C.P.A.'s
5. Diner's
6. ladies'
7. instructor's
8. 7's (Be consistent!)
9. t's
10. hers, it's, Joan's

Drill IV:

It was a cold blustery day, and the temperature was hovering at twenty degrees. Although the calendar indicated that the month was October, we felt that we were experiencing December weather. Bill Smith, the newly appointed professor, was arriving by plane from Seattle, Washington, and we had arranged to have a group welcome him at the airport. To tell the truth, I was happy that I was not chosen to be part of the committee, since I knew how windy the airport could be. But events that took place on that fateful day of October 15, 1990, proved that I was more than lucky.

Drill V:

1. He was not aware that you had lost your wallet.
2. Did you report the loss to the proper authorities?
3. I suppose you had to fill out many forms.
4. What a nuisance!
5. I hate doing so much paper work!
6. Did you ever discover where the wallet was?
7. I imagine you wondered how it was misplaced.
8. Good for you!
9. At least you now have your money and your credit cards.
10. What will you do if it happens again?

Drill VI:

1. Bob read Tennyson's "Ulysses" to the class; everyone seemed to enjoy the reading.

2. He ordered a set of books, several records, and a film.

Drill VII:

1. Correct.
2. Substitute a comma for the semicolon.
3. Substitute a comma for the semicolon.
4. Substitute a comma for the semicolon.
5. Correct.
6. Correct.
7. Delete the semicolon.

3. He has forty-three thousand dollars to spend; however, once that is gone, he will be penniless.

4. The careless student may write "don't" in place of "does not."

5. Before an examination, do the following: review your work, get a good night's sleep, eat a balanced breakfast, and arrive on time to take the test.

8. Correct.

9. The telephone rang several times; as a result, his sleep was interrupted. (Note the two punctuation changes. The semicolon is placed in front of the conjunctive adverb and the comma after it.)

10. Delete the semicolon; no punctuation is necessary in its place.

Usage and Diction

The section that follows is not an English textbook; it is simply a guide. It has been carefully prepared to help the student who is about to take the SAT II Writing Test, and it should also prove of great value to the college freshman who wants to gain better knowledge of standard English.

Do not try to master all the information at once. Study one section at a time. At the end of each section there is a practice drill. See how well you do on the drill by checking your answers against the key provided. If you do well, go on to the next part. If you find that you have made a number of errors, review the section. It is important that you master each section before moving on to the next and that you do not skip any section.

A thorough mastery of this guide will result in higher scores on the Achievement Test, better grades in college English courses, and increased ability to write clear and effective essays.

Levels of Usage

Diction concerns choosing the right word to express a thought most effectively. The successful writer selects words that are appropriate and correct for his purpose. It is important for the writer to know the essential difference between standard and nonstandard English.

Standard English is acceptable for most educated writers and speakers. It is used to convey precise or exact meaning. This is the level of writing that the college student is expected to manage with ease. Basically, standard English is the language of instruction, scholarship, and public address.

Nonstandard English is unacceptable for formal writing and speaking. Because nonstandard English includes illiteracies, ungrammatical constructions, slang, jargon, and obsolete words, you should avoid using nonstandard English unless you are aware that you are using a word or phrase that will not be acceptable or understood by a majority of readers. Colloquialisms are sometimes called informalisms, and while they may be appropriate to relaxed conversation, they usually should be avoided in writing.

Most tests measure the student's ability to recognize the difference between standard and nonstandard writing. Nonstandard forms should be avoided in formal essay writing.

Confusing Word Groups I

a is used before words that start with a consonant sound
an is used before words that start with a vowel sound

> Please give the baby *a* toy.
> He is *an* only child.
> We put up *a* united front. (*United* begins with a consonant sound—*y.*)
> We spent *an* hour together. (*Hour* begins with a vowel sound, since the *h* is silent.)

and is used to join words or ideas

> We enjoy shopping *and* sightseeing.
> She is a very serious student, *and* her grades are the best in the class.

accept means *to receive* or *to agree to* something
except means *to exclude* or *excluding*

> I'll *accept* the gift from you.
> Everyone *except* my uncle went home.
> My uncle was *excepted* from the group of losers.

advice means *counsel* (noun), *opinion*
advise means *to offer advice* (verb)

> Let me give you some free *advice*.
> I'd *advise* you to see your doctor.

affect means *to influence* (verb)
effect means *to cause* or *bring about* (verb) or *a result* (noun)

> The pollution *affected* our health.
> Our lawsuit *effected* a change in the law.
> The *effect* of the storm could not be measured.

all ready means *everybody* or *everything ready*
already means *previously*

> They were *all ready* to write when the test began.
> They had *already* written the letter.

all together means *everybody* or *everything together*
altogether means *completely*

> The boys and girls stood *all together* in line.
> His action was *altogether* strange for a person of his type.

desert (DEZZ-ert) means an *arid area*
desert (di-ZERT) means *to abandon*, or a *reward or punishment* (usually plural)
dessert (di-ZERT) means the *final course of a meal*

> I have seen several movies set in the Sahara *desert*.
> The soldier was warned not to *desert* his company.
> We're certain that execution is a just *desert* for his crime. He received his just *deserts*.
> We had strawberry shortcake for *dessert*.

in is used to indicate *inclusion, location, or motion within limits*
into is used for *motion toward* one place *from* another

> The spoons are *in* the drawer.
> We were walking *in* the room.
> I put the spoons *into* the drawer.

it's is the contraction of *it is* or *it has*
its is a possessive pronoun meaning *belonging to it*

> *It's* a very difficult assignment.
> *It is* a very difficult assignment.
> We tried to analyze *its* meaning.

lay means *to put*
lie means *to recline*

To lay:

(present)	I lay	
(past)	I laid	} the gift on the table.
(present perfect)	I have laid	

To lie:

(present)	I lie	
(past)	I lay	} on my blanket at the beach.
(present perfect)	I have lain	

lets is third person singular present of *let*
let's is a contraction for *let us*

> He *lets* me park my car in his garage.
> *Let's* go home early today.

loose means *not fastened or restrained,* or *not tight-fitting*
lose means *to mislay, to be unable to keep, to be defeated*

> The dog got *loose* from the leash.
> Try not *to lose* your umbrella.

passed is the past tense of *to pass*
past means *just preceding* or *an earlier time*

> The week *passed* very quickly.
> The *past* week was a very exciting one.

principal means *chief* or *main* (adjective), or *a leader,* or *a sum of money* (noun)
principle means *a fundamental truth or belief*

> His *principal* support comes from the real estate industry.
> The *principal* of the school called a meeting of the faculty.
> He earned 10% interest on the *principal* he invested last year.
> As a matter of *principle,* he refused to register for the draft.

quiet means *silent, still*
quit means *to give up* or *discontinue*
quite means *very* or *exactly, to the greatest extent*

> My brother is very shy and *quiet.*
> I *quit* the team last week.
> His analysis is *quite* correct.

raise means *to lift, to erect*
raze means *to tear down*
rise means *to get up, to move from a lower to a higher position, to increase in value*

> The neighbors helped him *raise* a new barn.
> The demolition crew *razed* the old building.
> The price of silver will *rise* again this month.

set means *to place something down* (mainly)
sit means *to seat oneself* (mainly)

To set:

(present)	He sets	
(past)	He set	} the lamp on the table.
(present perfect)	He has set	

To sit:

(present)	He sits	
(past)	He sat	} on the chair.
(present perfect)	He has sat	

stationary means *standing still*
stationery means *writing material*

> In ancient times, people thought that the earth was *stationary*.
> We bought our school supplies at the *stationery* store.

suppose means *to assume* or *guess*
supposed is the *past tense* and also *past participle* of *suppose*
supposed also means *ought to* or *should* (when followed by *to*)

> I *suppose* you will be home early.
> I *supposed* you would be home early.
> I had *supposed* you would be there.
> I am *supposed* to be in school tomorrow.

than is used to express *comparison*
then is used to express *time* or a *result* or *consequence*

> Jim ate more *than* we could put on the large plate.
> I knocked on the door, and *then* I entered.
> If you go, *then* I will go too.

their means *belonging to them*
there means *in that place*
they're is the contraction for *they are*

> We took *their* books home with us.
> Your books are over *there* on the desk.
> *They're* coming over for dinner.

though means *although* or *as if*
thought is the past tense of *to think*, or *an idea* (noun)
through means *in one side and out another, by way of, finished*

> *Though* he is my friend, I can't recommend him for this job.
> I *thought* you were serious!
> We enjoyed running *through* the snow.

to means *in the direction of* (preposition); it is also used before a verb to indicate the
  infinitive
too means *very, also*
two is the numeral 2

> We shall go *to* school.
> We shall go, *too*.
> It is *too* hot today.
> I ate *two* sandwiches for lunch.

use (yōōz) means *to employ, put into service*
used is the past tense and the past participle of *use*

> I want to *use* your chair.
> I *used* your chair.

used (yōōsd), meaning *in the habit of* or *accustomed to,* is followed by *to*
used (yōōsd) is an adjective meaning *not new*

> I am *used* to your comments.
> I bought a *used* car.

weather refers to *atmospheric conditions*
whether introduces a *choice;* it should not be preceded by *of* or *as to*

> I don't like the *weather* in San Francisco.
> He inquired *whether* we were going to the dance.

were is a past tense of *be*
we're is a contraction of *we are*
where refers to *place* or *location*

> They *were* there yesterday.
> *We're* in charge of the decorations.
> *Where* are we meeting your brother?

who's is the contraction for *who is* (or *who has*)
whose means *of whom,* implying ownership

> *Who's* the next batter?
> *Whose* notebook is on the desk?

your is a possessive, showing ownership
you're is a contraction for *you are*

> Please give him *your* notebook.
> *You're* very sweet.

Drill I: Underline the correct choice. Answers are on page 91.

1. He is the (principal, principle) backer of the play.

2. I hope your company will (accept, except) our offer.

3. We hope to have good (weather, whether) when we are on vacation.

4. Put the rabbit back (in, into) the hat.

5. The attorney will (advice, advise) you of your rights.

6. She is far taller (than, then) I imagined.

7. Are they (all ready, already) to go?

8. She answered the letter on shocking pink (stationary, stationery).

9. What is the (affect, effect) you are trying to achieve?

10. I want to (set, sit) next to my grandfather.

11. He's going to (lay, lie) down for a nap.

12. I'm (all together, altogether) tired of his excuses.

13. He saluted when the flag (passed, past) by.

14. I'd like another portion of (desert, dessert).

15. Try not to (loose, lose) your good reputation.

Drill II: Check [✔] the space provided if the sentence is correct; if there is an error, write the correct form. Answers are on page 91.

1. How much will the final examination effect my grade? _____

2. What is it your trying to suggest? _____

3. If it's a clear day, let's go sailing. _____

4. I don't have too much money with me. _____

5. She's not use to such cold weather. _____

6. He ate a apple before lunch. _____

7. The cost of the coat will raise again. _____

8. They are all though with the task. _____

9. Who's basketball are we using? _____

10. We live in a clean and quite neighborhood. _____

11. You are suppose to be home at six o'clock. _____

12. Where are their knapsacks? _____

13. Her cat ran straight for it's bowl of food. _____

14. Are they leaving when we're leaving? _____

15. Have their been any calls for me? _____

Confusing Word Groups II

allusion means an *indirect reference*
illusion means an *erroneous concept* or *perception*

> The poem contains an *allusion* to one of Shakespeare's sonnets.
> The mirror created the *illusion* of space in the narrow hall.

allude means *to make a reference to*
elude means *to escape from*

> In his essay, he *alludes* to Shakespeare's puns.
> The burglar *eluded* the police.

angel is a *heavenly creature*
angle is a *point at which two lines meet,* or an *aspect seen from a particular point of view*

> She has been an *angel* in these difficult times.
> A line perpendicular to another line forms a right *angle*.

ante is a prefix meaning *before*
anti is a prefix meaning *against*

> The *ante*chamber is the smaller room just before the main room.
> He is known to be *anti*-American.

breath means an *intake of air*
breathe means *to draw air in and give it out*
breadth means *width*

> Before you dive in, take a very deep *breath*.
> It is sometimes difficult to *breathe* when you have a bad cold.
> The artist's canvas was twice greater in length than in *breadth*.

build means to *erect, construct* (verb), or the *physical makeup* of a person or thing (noun)
built is the past tense of *build*

> I want to *build* a sand castle.
> She has a very athletic *build*.
> We *built* a moat around the sand castle.

buy means *to purchase*
by means *near, by means of,* or *before*

> I want *to buy* a new tie.
> He comes to school *by* public transportation.

capital refers to the *place of government* or to *wealth*
capitol refers to the *building* which houses the state or national legislatures

> Paris is the *capital* of France.
> It takes substantial *capital* to open a restaurant.
> Congress convenes in the *Capitol* in Washington, D.C.

cease means *to end*
seize means *to take hold of*

> Please *cease* making those sounds.
> *Seize* him by the collar as he comes around the corner.

choice means *a selection*
choose means *to select*
chose is the *past tense of choose*

> My *choice* for a career is teaching.
> We may *choose* our own advisors.
> I finally *chose* my wedding dress.

cite means *to quote*
sight means *seeing, what is seen*
site means *a place where something is located or occurs*

> He enjoys *citing* Shakespeare to illustrate his views.
> The *sight* of the accident was appalling.
> We are seeking a new *site* for the baseball field.

cloth is *fabric* or *material*
clothe means *to put on clothes, to dress*

> The seats were covered with *cloth,* not vinyl.
> Her job is *to clothe* the actors for each scene.

coarse means *vulgar* or *harsh*
course means *a path* or *a plan of study*

> He was shunned because of his *coarse* behavior.
> The sandpaper was very *coarse.*
> The ship took its usual *course.*
> How many *courses* are you taking this term?

complement means *a completing part*
compliment is an *expression of praise or admiration* (something given without charge is *complimentary*)

> His wit was a *complement* to her beauty.
> He received many *compliments* for his fine work.

conscience refers to the ability to *recognize the difference between right and wrong*
conscious means *aware*

> The attorney claimed that the criminal lacked a *conscience*.
> He was *conscious* that his action would have serious consequences.

consul means a *government representative*
council means an *assembly that meets for deliberation* (councilor)
counsel means *advice* (counselor)

> Americans abroad should keep in touch with their *consuls*.
> The student *council* met to discuss a campus dress code.
> The defendant heeded the *counsel* of his friends.

decent means *suitable*
descent means *going down*
dissent means *disagreement*

> The *decent* thing to do is to admit your error.
> The *descent* into the cave was dangerous.
> Two of the justices filed a *dissenting* opinion.

farther is preferred to express *distance*
further is preferred to express *time or degree*

> John ran *farther* than Bill walked.
> Please go no *further* in your argument.

fine means *good, well, precise,* or *a penalty*
find means *to locate*
fined means *penalized*

> He is a *fine* cook.
> Can you *find* the keys?
> The judge *fined* him twenty dollars.

knew is the past tense of *know*
new means of *recent origin*

> I *knew* her many years ago.
> I received a *new* bicycle for my birthday.

know means *to have knowledge or understanding*
no is a *negative* used to express *denial* or *refusal*

> I *know* your brother.
> There are *no* more books available.

later means *after a certain time*
latter means the *second of two*

> I'll see you *later*.
> Of the two speakers, the *latter* was more interesting.

mine is a possessive, showing ownership
mind means *human consciousness* (noun) or *to object, to watch out for* (verb)

> Use your own sled; that one is *mine*.
> Make up your *mind* which record you want.
> We don't *mind* if you bring a friend.

moral means *good or ethical* (adjective) or *a lesson to be drawn* (noun)
morale (more-AL) means *spirit*

> The administrator of the trust had a *moral* obligation to the *heirs*.
> The *moral* of the story is that it pays to be honest.
> The *morale* of the team improved after the coach's half-time speech.

personal refers to an *individual's character, conduct, private affairs*
personnel means an *organized body of individuals*

> The professor took a *personal* interest in each of his graduate students.
> The store's *personnel* department is on the third floor.

seem means *to appear*
seen is the past participle of *see*

> He *seems* to be sleeping.
> Have you *seen* your sister lately?

Drill III: Underline the correct choice. Answers are on page 91.

1. Are you (conscience, conscious) of what you are doing?

2. It will (seen, seem) that we are afraid.

3. His essays are filled with literary (allusions, illusions).

4. This wine will be a good (complement, compliment) to the meal.

5. It's (later, latter) than you think!

6. My cousin has a swimmer's (build, built).

7. I never (knew, new) him before today.

8. She asked her a (personal, personnel) question.

9. The golf (coarse, course) was very crowded.

10. The costume was made from old (cloth, clothe) napkins.

11. The ballcarrier was trying to (allude, elude) the tacklers.

12. There are (know, no) more exhibitions planned.

13. I'll wait for you in the (ante, anti) room.

14. Her (moral, morale) is very low.

15. Begin the sentence with a (capital, capitol) letter.

Drill IV: Check [✔] the space provided if the sentence is correct; if there is an error, write the correct form. Answers are on page 92.

1. I don't mind letting her come with us. _____

2. He looks for the best angel in every business arrangement. _____

3. They will want to fined the answers to the crossword puzzle. _____

4. Isn't her picture a pretty site? _____

5. I was happy to get such a great compliment. _____

6. After racing around the block, he stopped to catch his breathe. _____

7. I choose the blue umbrella when I went to the store yesterday. _____

8. His counsel is highly respected. _____

9. They are very descent people. _____

10. She swam much further than I did. _____

11. I went out to buy you a birthday gift. _____

12. He helped the police cease the suspect. _____

13. Have you seem anyone you know here? _____

14. His daughter loves to cloth her baby brother. _____

15. You are to cite at least four critics in your research paper. _____

Confusing Word Groups III

accede means *to agree with*
exceed means *to be more than*
concede means *to yield* (not necessarily in agreement)

> They will *accede* to your request for more information.
> Unfortunately, her expenditures now *exceed* her income.
> To avoid delay, they will *concede* that more information is necessary.

access means *availability*
excess means the *state of surpassing specified limits* (noun) or *more than usual* (adjective)

> The lawyer was given *access* to the grand jury records.
> Expenditures this month are far in *excess* of income.
> The airline charged him fifty dollars for *excess* baggage.

adapt means *to adjust or change*
adept means *skillful*
adopt means *to take as one's own*

> Children can *adapt* to changing conditions very easily.
> Proper instruction makes children *adept* in various games.
> The war orphan was *adopted* by the general and his wife.

adverse means *unfavorable*
averse means *having a feeling of repugnance or dislike*

> He was very upset by the *adverse* decision.
> Many writers are *averse* to criticism of their work.

assistance is the *act of assisting, aid*
assistants are *helpers, aides*

> I needed his *assistance* when I repaired the roof.
> The chief surgeon has four *assistants*.

canvas is a *heavy, coarse material*
canvass means *to solicit, conduct a survey*

> The *canvas* sails were very heavy.
> The local politicians are going *to canvass* our neighborhood.

carat is a *unit of weight*
caret is a *proofreading symbol*, indicating where something is to be inserted
carrot is a *vegetable*

> The movie star wears a ten-*carat* diamond ring.
> He added a phrase in the space above the *caret*.
> Does he feed his pet rabbit a *carrot* every other day?

click is a *brief, sharp sound*
clique is an *exclusive group of people*, a *circle* or *set*

> The detective drew his gun when he heard the *click* of the lock.
> In high school, I was not part of any *clique*.

confidant is *one to whom private matters are confided* (noun)
confident means *being sure, having confidence in oneself* (adjective)
confidence is a *feeling of assurance* or *certainty, trust* (noun)

>His priest was his only *confidant.*
>Her success in business has given her a very *confident* manner.
>The ballplayer is developing *confidence* in his fielding ability.

disburse means *to pay out*
disperse means *to scatter, distribute widely*

>This week the bank has *disbursed* a million dollars.
>The defeated army began *to disperse.*

discomfit means *to upset*
discomfort means *lack of ease*

>The general's plan was designed *to discomfit* the enemy.
>This starched collar causes *discomfort.*

dual means *double*
duel means a *contest between two persons or groups*

>Dr. Jekyll had a *dual* personality.
>Aaron Burr and Alexander Hamilton engaged in a *duel.*

elicit means *to draw forth, evoke*
illicit means *illegal, unlawful*

>Her performance *elicited* tears from the audience.
>He was arrested because of his *illicit* business dealings.

emigrate means *to leave a country*
immigrate means *to enter a country*

>The Norwegians *emigrated* to the United States in the nineteenth century.
>Many of the Norwegian *immigrants* settled in the Midwest.

eminent means *of high rank, prominent, outstanding*
imminent means *about to occur, impending*

>He was the most *eminent* physician of his time.
>His nomination to the board of directors is *imminent.*

epitaph is a *memorial inscription on a tombstone or monument*
epithet is a *term used to describe or characterize the nature of a person or thing*

>His *epitaph* was taken from a section of the Bible.
>The drunk was shouting *epithets* and being abusive to passersby.

expand means *to spread out*
expend means *to use up*

>As the staff increases, we can *expand* our office space.
>Don't *expend* all your energy on one project.

fair means *light in color, reasonable, pretty*
fare means a *set price*

>   Your attitude is not a *fair* one.
>   The *fare* is reduced for senior citizens.

faze means *to worry* or *to disturb*
phase means an *aspect*

>   I tried not to let his mean look *faze* me.
>   A crescent is a *phase* of the moon.

formally means *in a formal way*
formerly means *at an earlier time*

>   he was dressed *formally* for the dinner party.
>   he was *formerly* a delegate to the convention.

fort means a *fortified* place
forte (fort) means a *strong point*
forte (for-tay) is also a musical term that means *loudly*

>   A small garrison was able to hold the *fort*.
>   Conducting Wagner's music was Toscanini's *forte*.
>   The final movement of the musical composition was meant to be played *forte*.

idle means *unemployed* or *unoccupied*
idol means *image* or *object of worship*

>   He did not enjoy having to remain *idle* while he recuperated.
>   Rock musicians are the *idols* of many teenagers.

incidence refers to the *extent or frequency of an occurrence*
incidents refers to *occurrences, events*

>   The *incidence* of rabies has decreased since the beginning of the year.
>   Luckily, the accidents were just minor *incidents*.

lightening means *making less heavy* (from *to lighten*)
lightning means *electric discharge in the atmosphere, flashes of light, moving with great speed*

>   If you remove some books, you will succeed in *lightening* your suitcase.
>   Summer thunderstorms often produce startling *lightning* bolts.

patience means *enduring calmly, with tolerant understanding*
patients means *people under medical treatment*

>   He has very little *patience* with fools.
>   There are twenty *patients* waiting to see the doctor.

precede means *to come before*
proceed means *to go ahead*

>   What events *preceded* the attack?
>   We can *proceed* with our next plan.

prophecy means *prediction* (noun, rhymes with *sea*)
prophesy means *to predict* (verb, rhymes with *sigh*)

>   What is the fortune-teller's *prophecy*?
>   What did the witches *prophesy*?

Drill V: Underline the correct choice. Answers are on page 92.

1. The fact that he nearly had an accident didn't even (faze, phase) him.

2. He earns royalties in (access, excess) of a million dollars a year.

3. Now may we (precede, proceed) with the debate?

4. Her (fort, forte) is writing lyrics for musical comedy.

5. They wondered how they were going to (disburse, disperse) the huge crowd.

6. Everyone was dressed (formally, formerly) for the dinner party.

7. I am not (adverse, averse) to continuing the discussion at another time.

8. Can something be done to retard the (incidence, incidents) of influenza in that area?

9. "Seeing the film in class will serve a (dual, duel) purpose," he explained.

10. I'm not sure I want to (expand, expend) so much energy on that project.

11. Imagine my (discomfit, discomfort) when she showed up at the party too!

12. He was a famous matinee (idle, idol) many years ago.

13. When did they (emigrate, immigrate) from New York to Paris?

14. I think she is part of a (click, clique) of snobs and creeps.

15. She paid little attention to the fortune-teller's (prophecy, prophesy).

Drill VI: Check [✔] the space provided if the sentence is correct; if there is an error, write the correct form. Answers are on page 92.

1. The ring contains several one-carat stones. _____

2. The lights went out when the lightening hit the house. _____

3. I'll provide whatever assistance you require. _____

4. I prefer a nylon tent to one made of canvass. _____

5. I admire the patients with which he is able to treat her lateness. _____

6. We are in eminent danger of losing our reservations. _____

7. Will she be able to adopt to our way of performing the operation? _____

8. The questions served to illicit the necessary information. _____

9. She called in her confidant for a private discussion. _____

10. It is too bad that their expectations accede the possibilities. _____

11. Do you think that the agreement is fare? _____

12. He was in considerable discomfit, so the nurse gave him the medication. _____

13. As we went through the old cemetery, we were fascinated by some of the epitaphs. _____

14. It is remarkable that he was able to prophecy the exact date of the earthquake. _____

15. I'm extremely confidant that the project will succeed. _____

Glossary of Usage—Group I

abbreviate means *to shorten by omitting*
abridge means *to shorten by condensing*

New York is *abbreviated* to NY.
In order to save time in the reading, the report was *abridged.*

ad is used informally, but in formal usage *advertisement* is correct; similarly: exam (examination), auto (automobile), phone (telephone), gym (gymnasium)

advantage means a *superior position*
benefit means a *favor conferred or earned* (as a profit)

> He had an *advantage* in experience over his opponent.
> The rules were changed for his *benefit*.

aggravate means *to make worse*
annoy means *to bother* or *to irritate*

> Your nasty comments *aggravated* a bad situation.
> Your nasty comments *annoyed* him. (Not: Your nasty comments *aggravated* him.)

ain't is an unacceptable contraction for *am not, are not,* or *is not,* although *ain't* is sometimes heard in very informal speech

alibi is an *explanation on the basis of being in another place*
excuse is an *explanation on any basis*

> The accused man's *alibi* was that he was in another town when the robbery occurred.
> Whenever he is late, he makes up a new *excuse*.

all ways means *in every possible way*
always means *at all times*

> He was in *all ways* acceptable to the voters.
> He was *always* ready to help.

almost means *nearly, not quite*
most refers to the *greatest amount or number* or to the *largest part,* a *majority*

> We are *almost* finished writing the book.
> *Most* of the credit should be given to his uncle.

alongside of means *side by side with*
alongside means *parallel to the side*

> He stood *alongside of* her at the corner.
> Park the car *alongside* the curb.

allot means *to give* or *apportion*

> I will *allot* three hours for painting the table.

alot is a misspelling of *a lot*

> He earned *a lot* of money. (better: He earned *a great deal* of money.)

alright is now often employed in common usage to mean *all right* (In formal usage *all right* is still preferred by most authorities.)
all right means *satisfactory, very well, uninjured,* or *without doubt*

> I'm *alright,* thank you.
> It was his responsibility, *all right.*

alternate, as a noun, means a *substitute or second choice*
alternate, as a verb, means *to perform by turns*
alternative means a *choice between two things, only one of which may be accepted*

>   She served as an *alternate* delegate to the convention.
>   The cook *alternated* green beans and cauliflower on the menu.
>   Is there an *alternative* to the proposition? (In less formal usage, *alternative* is
>   not always limited to a choice between *two*.)

alumna means *a female graduate* (plural: alumnae; *ae* rhymes with key)
alumnus means *a male graduate* (plural: almuni; *ni* rhymes with high)

>   She is an *alumna* of Mrs. Brown's School for Young Women.
>   He is an *alumnus* of City College.

among is used to discuss *more than two* items
between is used to discuss *two* items only

>   The work was divided *among* the four brothers.
>   She divided the pie *between* Joe and Marie.

amount is used to refer to a *quantity not individually countable*
number is used to refer to *items that can be counted individually*

>   A tremendous *amount* of work had piled up on my desk.
>   We ate a great *number* of cookies at the party.

annual means *yearly*
biannual means *twice a year* (also *semiannual*)
biennial means *once in two years* or *every two years*

>   Are you going to the *annual* holiday party?
>   I receive *biannual* statements concerning my automobile insurance in April and
>   in October.
>   He gets a new car *biennially*.

anxious means *worried*
eager means *keenly desirous*

>   We were *anxious* about our first airplane flight.
>   I am *eager* to see you again.

anyways is an incorrect form for *anyway*
anywheres is an incorrect form for *anywhere*

>   I didn't want to go *anyway*.
>   I couldn't locate her *anywhere*.

aren't I is used informally, but in formal usage *am I not* is correct

>   *Am I not* entitled to an explanation?

around should not be used in formal writing as a substitute for *about* or *near*

>   I'll be there *about* (not *around*) 2 P.M.

as is not always as clear as *because, for,* or *since* (also see *like*)

>   She wants to cry *because* she is very sad.

as used as a *conjunction,* is followed by a verb
like used as a *preposition,* is *not* followed by a verb

> Do *as* I do, not *as* I say.
> Try not to behave *like* a child.

as . . . as is used in an *affirmative* statement
so . . . as is used in a *negative* statement

> She is *as* talented *as* any other actress in the show.
> He is *not so* reliable *as* his older brother.

as good as is used for *comparisons,* not to mean *practically*

> This bicycle is *as good as* the other one.
> They *practically* promised us a place in the hall. (not They *as good as* promised
> us a place in the hall.)

astonish means *to strike with sudden wonder*
surprise means *to catch unaware*

> The extreme violence of the hurricane *astonished* everybody.
> A heat wave in April would *surprise* us.

at should be avoided when it does not contribute to the meaning of an idea

> *Where do you live at?* may be heard in informal usage, but *Where do you live?* is
> the correct form.
> The group will arrive *about* noon. (not *at about* noon)

awfully is sometimes heard in informal usage. In formal usage, *very* is correct.

> This pie is very good. (not *awfully* good)

a while is used after a preposition (noun)
awhile is used in other cases (adverb)

> I coached the team for *a while*.
> I coached the team *awhile*.

backward, as an adjective, means *slow in learning*
backward and *backwards* both may be used as adverbs

> The *backward* pupil received special tutoring.
> We tried to skate *backward. (or We tried to skate backwards.)*

bad is used after verbs that refer to the senses, such as *look, feel* (adjective)
badly means *greatly, in a bad manner* (adverb)

> He felt *bad* that he could not attend the meeting.
> The young man needs a part-time job very *badly*.

been is the past participle of *to be,* used after helping verbs *have, has,* or *had*
being is the *ing* form of *to be,* usually used after helping verbs *is, am, are, was were*

> I have *been* living here for six years.
> He was *being* a troublemaker, so we told him to stay away from us.

being as and *being that* should not be used in standard English. *Because* and *since* are
preferable.

> *Since* it was dark, we turned on the lights.
> *Because* he is my friend, I gave him a gift.

Drill VII: Check [✔] the space provided if the sentence is correct; if there is an error in usage, write the correct form. Answers are on page 92.

1. He shared the riches between Laura, Millie and Ernestine. _____

2. We are all ways available to baby-sit for you during the week. _____

3. The housing law was rewritten for his advantage. _____

4. Alot of the time, he falls asleep at nine o'clock. _____

5. The colorful advertisement caught my attention as I skimmed through the magazine. _____

6. It was hard to keep track of the amount of people who visited him last week. _____

7. He claims that he ain't going to vote in the next election. _____

8. I see him in the park most every day. _____

9. The coach sent in the alternate quarterback. _____

10. Are you certain that he is alright now? _____

11. She is just beginning to aggravate her mother. _____

12. He is the school's oldest living alumnus. _____

13. I read an abridged version of the novel. _____

14. He invents a new alibi whenever he forgets his keys. _____

15. He guided the canoe alongside of the riverbank. _____

Drill VIII: Answers are on page 92.

1. Being as it is Wednesday, we are going to a Broadway matinee. _____

2. He is anxious to be finished with the dental treatment. _____

3. Let's surprise him with a party tomorrow. _____

4. I been looking for a good used car, but I haven't located one yet. _____

5. The club will hold its luncheon anywheres you decide. _____

6. Where do you want to meet at? _____

7. I feel very badly that I drank all the coffee. _____

8. His manners are terrible; he is eating just as a child. _____

9. I gave you as much as I can afford. _____

10. He is an awfully good instructor. _____

11. He responded in a loud voice: "Am I not capable of deciding for myself?" _____

12. My aunt just went inside to rest a while. _____

13. The backwards student was advised to remain in that class. _____

14. It was around noon when we met for lunch. _____

15. The old edition of the encyclopedia is as good as the new version. _____

Glossary of Usage—Group II

beside means *at the side of*
besides means *in addition to*

> In our tennis game, he played *beside* me at the net.
> We entertained Jim, Sue, and Louise, *besides* the members of the chorus.

better means *recovering*
well means *completely recovered*
better is used with the verb *had* to show desirability

> He is *better* now than he was a week ago.
> In a few more weeks, he will be *well*.
> He *had better* (not *he better*) follow instructions or pay the penalty.

between you and I is incorrect form, since the object of the preposition *between* should be the objective case *me*, not the subjective case *I*

> *Between you and me*, he has not been very helpful this week.

both means *two considered together*
each means *one of two or more*

> *Both* of the applicants qualified for the position.
> *Each* applicant was given a good reference.

bring means *to carry toward the speaker*
take means *to carry away from the speaker*

> *Bring* the coat to me.
> *Take* money for carfare when you leave.

bunch is used informally to describe a group of people, but in formal usage *group* is preferred

> When he returned to his office, he learned that a *group* of students was waiting
> for him.

burst is used in present and past tenses to mean *to explode* (or *to break*)
bust and *busted* are incorrect forms of *burst*

> I do hope the balloon will not *burst*.
> He cried when the balloon *burst*. (not *busted*)

but that is sometimes heard in informal usage, but in formal usage *that* is correct

> He never doubted *that* she would visit him.

can means *able*
may implies *permission* or *possibility*

> I *can* eat both desserts.
> *May* I eat both desserts?
> It *may* snow tonight.

cannot seem is sometimes used informally, but in formal usage *seems unable* is correct

> My elderly uncle *seems unable* to remember his own phone number.

complected should not be used for *complexioned*

> At the beach, the fair-*complexioned* boy stayed under an umbrella.

consistently means *in harmony*
constantly means *regularly, steadily*

> If you give me advice, you should act *consistently* with that advice.
> I *constantly* warned him about leaving the door unlocked.

continual means *happening again and again at short intervals*
continuous means *without interruption*

> The teacher gave the class *continual* warnings.
> Noah experienced *continuous* rain for forty days.

could of is an incorrect form of *could have,* which can be contracted to *could've* in speech or informal writing.

> I wish that I *could've* gone. (better: I wish that I *could have* gone.)

couple refers to *two, several* or *a few* refers to more than two

> Alex and Frieda are the most graceful *couple* on the dance floor.
> A *few* of my cousins—Mary, Margie, Alice, and Barbara—will be at the reunion tonight.

data is the Latin plural of *datum,* meaning *information (data* is preferred with plural verbs and pronouns, but is now acceptable in the singular)

> *These data* were very significant to the study. (or *This data* was very significant to the study.)

did is the past tense of *do*
done is the past participle of *do*

> I *did* whatever was required to complete the job.
> I have *done* what you requested.

different than is often used informally, but in formal usage *different from* is correct

> Jack is *different from* his brother.

disinterested means *impartial*
uninterested means *not interested*

> The judge must be a *disinterested* party in a trial.
> I'm an *uninterested* bystander, so I find the proceedings boring.

doesn't is a contraction of *does not* (third person singular)
don't is a contraction of *do not,* and is not a substitute for *doesn't*

> She *doesn't* go to school.
> They *don't* go to school.

doubt whether is often heard in informal usage, but *doubt that* is the correct form

> I *doubt that* I will be home this evening.

due to is sometimes used informally at the beginning of a sentence, but in formal usage *because of, on account of,* or some similar expression is preferred

> *Because of* (not *due to*) the rain, the game was postponed. (but The postponement was *due to* the rain.)

each other refers to *two persons*
one another refers to *more than two persons*

> Jane and Jessica have known *each other* for many years.
> Several of the girls have known *one another* for many years.

either . . . or is used to refer to *choices*
neither . . . nor is the *negative* form

> *Either* Lou *or* Jim will drive you home.
> *Neither* Alice *nor* Carol will be home tonight.

else than is sometimes heard in informal usage, but in formal usage *other than* is correct

> Shakespeare was rarely regarded by students as anything *other than* the writer of plays.

enthuse or *enthused* should be avoided; use *enthusiastic*

> We were *enthusiastic* when given the chance to travel abroad.

equally as good is an incorrect form; *equally good* or *just as good* is correct

> This bicycle is *just as good* as that one.

etc. is the abbreviation for the Latin term *et cetera,* meaning *and so forth, and other things.* In general, it is better to be specific and not use *etc.*

> I think that oranges, peaches, cherries, *etc.,* are healthful. (*Etc.* is not preceded by *and*)

everyone, written as one word, is a *pronoun*
every one, written as two words, is used to refer to *each individual*

> *Everyone* present voted for the proposal.
> *Every one* of the voters accepted the proposal.

every bit is incorrect usage for *just as*

> You are *just as* (not *every bit as*) clever as she is.

ever so often means *frequently* or *repeatedly*
every so often means *occasionally* or *now and again*

> He sees his brother *ever so often,* practically every day.
> Since tickets are so expensive, we only attend the theater *every so often.*

expect is sometimes used incorrectly to mean *assume* or *presume*

> I *assume* (not *expect*) that he won the race.

Drill IX: Check [✔] the space provided if the sentence is correct; if there is an error in usage, write the correct form. Answers are on page 93.

1. I expect a large bunch of visitors today. _____

2. We wish we could of been with you in Paris. _____

3. She better do what they say. _____

4. The boy got wet when the water balloon busted. _____

5. I brought a couple of books for you; both are historical novels. _____

6. Between you and I, I think that her hat is very unbecoming. _____

7. The continual ticking of the clock was very disconcerting. _____

8. He is standing besides me in the picture. _____

9. We never doubted but that you would make a fine leader. _____

10. Can I have your permission to skip to-night's game? _____

11. Both women were willing to work the night shift. _____

12. Who is your light-complected friend? _____

13. Please take her report card to me at once. _____

14. She cannot seem to get up early enough to eat breakfast with him. _____

15. They are consistently hugging and kissing. _____

Drill X: Answers are on page 93.

1. I expect that you really earned your salary today. _____

2. He said that he done that problem is class. _____

3. They are very enthused about going to the baseball game with you. _____

4. Neither Eleanor or Jan will be dancing in the show tonight, since they are both ill. _____

5. My sister is very different than your sister. _____

6. Because of my heavy work schedule, I can only go fishing every so often. _____

7. I'm truly disinterested in seeing that movie. _____

8. He don't want to cook dinner for us this week. _____

9. You must be every bit as sleepy as I am. _____

10. I doubt whether it will snow today. _____

11. Due to the star's illness, the understudy performed the role. _____

12. My car is equally as good as the one he wants to sell me. _____

13. Sam, Joe, Lou, and Artie have worked with each other before. _____

14. Every one of the soldiers had volunteered for the assignment. _____

15. I like to play racquet sports such as tennis, squash, paddleball, and etc. _____

Glossary of Usage—Group III

fewer is used to refer to items that can be counted
less is used to refer to something viewed as a mass, not as a series of individual items

> I made *fewer* repairs on the new car than on the old one.
> After the scandal, the company enjoyed *less* prestige than it had the previous year.

finalized is used to mean *concluded* or *completed, usually in informal usage; in formal usage, completed* is preferred

> Labor and management *completed* arrangements for a settlement.

flaunt means *to make a display of*
flout means *to show contempt, scorn*

> He *flaunted* his new wealth in an ostentatious manner.
> She *flouted* the policeman's authority.

former means *the first of two*
latter means *the second of two*

> The *former* half of the story was in prose.
> The *latter* half of the story was in poetry.

good is an adjective; *good* is often used informally as an adverb, but the correct word is *well*

> She is a *good* singer.
> She sings *well*.

graduated is followed by the prepositon *from* when it indicates completion of a course of study
graduated also means *divided into categories or marked intervals*

> He *graduated from* high school last year. (or He *was graduated from* high school last year.)
> A *graduated* test tube is one that has markings on it to indicate divisions.

guess is sometimes used informally to mean *think* or *suppose,* but it is incorrect in formal use.

> I *think* (not *guess*) I'll go home now.

habit means an *individual tendency to repeat a thing*
custom means *group habit*

> He had a *habit* of breaking glasses before each recital.
> The *custom* of the country was to betroth girls at an early age.

had ought is an incorrect form for *ought* or *should*
hadn't ought is an incorrect form for *should not* or *ought not*

> The men *ought* (not *had ought*) to go to the game now.
> He *ought not* (not *hadn't ought*) to have spoken.
> He *should not* (not *hadn't ought*) have spoken.

hanged is used in reference to a *person*
hung is used in reference to a *thing*

> The prisoner was *hanged* in the town square.
> The drapes were *hung* unevenly.

have got is incorrect usage; *got* should be omitted

> I *have* an umbrella.

healthful is used to express whatever *gives* health
healthy is used to express whatever *has* health

> He follows a *healthful* diet.
> He is a *healthy* person.

hisself is a misspelling of *himself*

> Let him do it *himself*.

humans is used informally to refer to human beings, but in formal usage *human beings* is correct

> He says that love is a basic need of all *human beings*. (but, used as an adjective: He says that love is a basic *human* need.)

if introduces a *condition*
whether introduces a *choice*

> I shall go to Greece *if* I win the prize.
> He asked me *whether* I intended to go to Greece.

if it was implies that *something might have been true in the past*
if it were implies *doubt* or indicates *something that is contrary to fact*

> If your book *was* there last night, it is there now.
> *If it were* summer now, we would all go swimming.

imply means *to suggest* or *hint* at (the speaker *implies*)
infer means *to deduce* or *conclude* (the listener *infers*)

> Are you *implying* that I have disobeyed orders?
> From your carefree tone, what else are we *to infer*?

in back of means *behind*
in the back of (or *at the back of*) means *in the rear of*

> The shovel is *in back of* (behind) the barn.
> John is sitting *in the back of* the theatre.

in regards to is an incorrect form for *in regard to*

> He called me *in regard to* your letter.

instance where is sometimes used informally, but the correct term is *instance in which*

> Can you tell me of one *instance in which* such a terrible thing occurred?

irregardless is an incorrect form for *regardless*

> I'll be your friend *regardless* of what people say, even if the people are accurate.

is when and *is where* are sometimes used informally, but in formal usage *occurs when* and *is a place where* are correct

> The best scene *occurs when* the audience least expects it.
> My favorite vacation spot *is a place where* there are no telephones.

kind of and *sort of* are informal expressions that should be rephrased in formal writing—for instance, *somewhat* or *rather* are preferable

> I am *rather* sorry he retired.
> He was *somewhat* late for the meeting.

kid is used informally to mean *child* (noun) or *to make fun of* (verb), but is incorrect in formal usage

> My cousin is a very sweet *child*.
> They always laugh when you *make fun of* me.

learn means *to acquire knowledge*
teach means *to give knowledge*

> We can *learn* many things just by observing carefully.
> He is one actor who likes *to teach* his craft to others.

least means the *smallest in degree* or *lowest rank*
less means *the smaller* or *lower of two*

> This is the *least* desirable of all the apartments we have seen.
> This apartment is *less* spacious than the one we saw yesterday.

leave means *to go away from* (a verb is NOT used with *leave*)
let means *to permit* (a verb IS used with *let*)

> *Leave* this house at once.
> *Let* me remain in peace in my own house.

lend is a verb meaning *to give to*
loan is a noun denoting *what is given*
borrow means *to take from*

> The bank was willing to *lend* him $500.
> He was granted a *loan* of $500.
> I'd like *to borrow* your electric drill for an hour.

liable means *responsible according to the law*
likely suggests *probable behavior*

> If he falls down the stairs, we may be *liable* for damages.
> A cat, if annoyed, is *likely* to scratch.

libel is a *written and published statement injurious to a person's character*
slander is a *spoken statement of the same sort*

> The unsubstantiated negative comments about me in your book constitute
> *libel*.
> When you say these vicious things about me, you are committing *slander*.

like is a preposition used to introduce a phrase
as if is used to introduce a clause (a subject and a verb)
as is a conjunction used to introduce a clause
like if is an incorrect form for *like, as,* or *as if*

> It seems *like* a sunny day.
> It seems *as if* it is going to be a sunny day.
> He acted *as* he was expected to act.

many refers to a *number*
much refers to a *quantity* or *amount*

> How *many* inches of rain fell last night?
> *Much* rain fell last night.

may of is an incorrect form for *may have*
might of is an incorrect form for *might have*

> He *may have* been there, but I didn't see him.
> I *might have* gone to the party if I hadn't been ill.

> ▶**Note:** Contractions of these terms are unacceptable in formal
> usage.

Drill XI: Check [✔] the space provided if the sentence is correct; if there is an error in usage, insert the correct form. Answers are on page 93.

1. She asked him if he wanted to have lunch with her or with her sister. _____

2. There are less details to worry about in this project. _____

3. All humans need to take a certain amount of water into their bodies every week. _____

4. I guess he is a good person. _____

5. We hadn't ought to have shouted out the answer. _____

6. We hope to finalize the deal this month. _____

7. She had a custom of wearing the same necklace to every performance. _____

8. He wanted to arrange the flowers hisself, if that is acceptable to you. _____

9. We were upset when she flaunted her mother's orders. _____

10. I hung the heavy picture in the living room. _____

11. The family was extremely proud when she graduated college last week. _____

12. His girlfriend only eats healthy foods. _____

13. Actually, we thought that the latter comment was excellent. _____

14. He runs good. _____

15. I have got your phone number in my book. _____

Drill XII: Answers are on page 93.

1. I'm not certain, but she might of said she was going home. _____

2. Your remark leads me to imply that you are not satisfied. _____

3. He said he can learn you a few things. _____

4. Remember that she is less fortunate than you are. _____

5. How much pounds have you lost so far? _____

6. The swimming pool is in the back of those trees. _____

7. He said such terrible things about her that she is suing him for libel. _____

8. I would like to see you in regards to the apartment you plan to rent. _____

9. "Do you intend to enroll your kid in the nursery school?" _____

10. Please let me be alone. _____

11. She is always late for work, irregardless of how early she wakes up in the morning. _____

12. She treats her stuffed animal like if it were alive. _____

13. He'll loan you money for carfare. _____

14. He's not likely to be ready yet. _____

15. The most exciting part of the film is when he kills the dragon. _____

Glossary of Usage—Group IV

maybe means *perhaps, possibly* (adverb)
may be shows *possibility* (verb)

> *Maybe* he will meet us later.
> He *may be* here later.

mighty means *powerful* or *great;* it should not be used in formal writing to mean *very*

> He was *very* (not *mighty*) sleepy.

media is the Latin plural of *medium;* it refers to a means of mass communication or artistic expression and is used with a plural verb

> Most *media* that report the news realize their responsibility to the public.
> That artist's favorite *medium* is watercolor.

must of is incorrect form for *must have*

> I *must have* been sleeping when you called. (A contraction of this term is unacceptable in formal usage.)

myself is used as an *intensifier* if the subject of the verb is *I*
myself, instead of *I* or *me,* is not correct

> Since I know *myself* better, let me try it my way.
> My daughter and *I* (not *myself*) will play.
> They gave my son and *me* (not *myself*) some food.

nice is used informally to mean *pleasing, good, fine,* but a more exact, less overused word is preferred

> This is *sunny* (or *good* or *fine*) weather (not *nice* weather).
> He is a *good* (or *kind*) person.

nowheres is incorrect usage for *nowhere*

> The dog was *nowhere* to be found.

off of is sometimes used informally, but *off* is correct in formal usage

> Joe was taken *off of* the team. (better: Joe was taken *off* the team.)

okay (O.K.) is used informally but is to be avoided in formal writing

> Informal: His work is *okay.*
> Formal: His work is *acceptable* (or *good*).

on account of is an incorrect form for *because*

> We could not meet you *because* we did not receive your message in time.

oral means *spoken*
verbal means *expressed in words,* either spoken or written

> Instead of writing a note, she gave him an *oral* message.
> Shorthand must usually be transcribed into *verbal* form.

outdoor is an adjective
outdoors is an adverb

> We spent the summer at an *outdoor* music camp.
> We played string quartets *outdoors.*

owing to is used informally, but in formal usage *because* is preferred

> *Because* of a change of management, his company cancelled the takeover attempt.

people comprise a *united or collective group of individuals*
persons are *individuals that are separate and unrelated*

> The *people* of our city will vote for a new bond issue next week.
> Only ten *persons* remained in the theater after the first act.

per is a Latin term used mainly in business: *per diem* (by the day), *per hour* (by the hour). In formal writing, *according to* or *by the* is preferred

> As *per* your instructions . . . (better: *According to* your instructions . . .)

plan on is used informally, but in formal usage *plan to* is correct

> Do you *plan to go* (not *plan on going*) to the lecture?

plenty means *abundance* (noun)
plenty is incorrect as an adverb or adjective

> There is *plenty* of room in that compact car.
> That compact car is *very* large (not *plenty* large).

prefer that than is incorrect form for *prefer that to*

> I should *prefer that to* anything else you might suggest.

put in is incorrect for *to spend*, *make* or *devote*

> Every good student should *spend* (not *put in*) several hours a day doing homework.
> Be sure *to make* (not *put in*) an appearance at the meeting.

quit is sometimes used informally to mean *stop*, but in formal usage *stop* is preferred

> Please *stop* your complaining.

quite is used to mean *very* in informal usage, but in formal usage *very* is preferred

> Your comment was *very* (not *quite*) intelligent.

quite a few is used to mean *many* in informal usage, but in formal usage *many* is preferred

> My car has *many* (not *quite a few*) dents.

read where is heard in informal usage, but in formal usage *read that* is correct

> I *read that* the troops were being reviewed today.

real is sometimes used informally instead of *really* or *very*, but in formal usage *really* is correct

> He's a *real* good ballplayer. (preferred: He's a *very* good ballplayer.)
> He plays *real* well with the band. (preferred: He plays *really* well with the band.)

reason is because is used informally in speech, but in formal usage *the reason is that* is correct

> The *reason* she calls *is that* (not *because)* she is lonely. (or She calls *because* she is lonely.)

refer back/report back: since *re* means *back* or *again,* the word *back* is redundant and should be omitted

> Please *refer* to your notes.
> Please *report* to the supervisor.

repeat again is redundant; *again* should be omitted

> Please *repeat* the instructions.

respectfully means *with respect and decency*
respectively means *as relating to each, in the order given*

> The students listened *respectfully* to the principal.
> Jane and Lena are the daughters *respectively* of Mrs. Smith and Mrs. Jones.

run is used informally to mean *conduct, manage,* but in formal usage *conduct* or a similar word is preferred

> He wants *to conduct* (not *run*) the operation on a profitable basis.

said is sometimes used in business or law to mean *the* or *this;* in formal usage, *the* or *this* is correct
said is also used incorrectly to mean *told someone*

> When *the* (not *said*) coat was returned, it was badly torn.
> The professor *told us* (not *said*) to study for the examination.

same as is an incorrect form for *in the same way as* or *just as*

> The owner's son was treated *in the same way as* any other worker.

says is present tense of *say*
said is past tense of *say*

> He *says* what he means.
> He *said* what he meant. (*Goes* or *went* should not be used instead of *says* or *said*.)

Drill XIII: Check [✔] the space provided if the sentence is correct; if there is an error in usage, write the correct form. Answers are on page 94.

1. We had a very nice time at the museum. _____

2. She maybe one of the finalists in the contest. _____

3. He stayed indoors on account of the bad weather. _____

4. They are two of my favorite persons. _____

5. That was a mighty foolish thing to do. _____

6. My wife and myself wrote the cookbook together. _____

7. The children are playing outdoors. _____

8. The media is doing the job correctly. _____

9. Their oral presentation was excellent. _____

10. Owing to the high interest rates, she decided not to borrow from the bank. _____

11. There is nowhere for us to sit. _____

12. She may be able to bake fresh bread every week. _____

13. It must of been a beautiful house when it was first built. _____

14. The supervisor wrote that his assistant was doing an okay job so far. _____

15. The art director was taken off of the most profitable account. _____

Drill XIV: Answers are on page 94.

1. He got quite bruised in a motorcycle accident.

2. I hope you'll be able to repeat your marvelous performance again. _____

3. I plan on going to college again next year. _____

4. He went, "Let's go to a movie together." _____

5. I hope that she will quit sending us the job applications. _____

6. The policeman waited his turn same as any other citizen. _____

7. His car is plenty expensive. _____

8. He treats his parents respectfully. _____

9. She's a real intelligent woman. _____

10. The reason the baby is crying is because she is hungry. _____

11. He claims to prefer that to any other idea. _____

12. In rehearsal, she never even referred back to the script. _____

13. He put in several months doing public relations work so that the business proposal would be accepted. _____

14. Does he run the department efficiently? _____

15. We read where your favorite program is being discontinued. _____

Glossary of Usage—Group V

saw is the past tense of *see*
seen is the past participle of *see*

> We *saw* a play yesterday.
> I have never *seen* a Broadway show.

seem is used in informal speech and writing in the expressions *I couldn't seem to* and *I don't seem to,* but in formal usage:

> We *can't find* the address. (not We *can't seem to find* the address.)

seldom ever is used informally, but in formal usage *ever* is redundant and should be omitted, or *if* should be inserted

> I *seldom* swim in January.
> I *seldom if ever* swim in January.

shall is used with *I* and *we* in formal usage; informally, I *will (would)* may be used
will is used with *you, he, she, it, they;* when an emphatic statement is intended, the rule is reversed

> I *shall* be there today.
> We *shall* pay the rent tomorrow.
> I certainly *will* be there.
> They *shall* not pass.

shape is incorrect when used to mean *state* or *condition*

> The refugees were in a *serious condition* (not *shape*) when they arrived here.

should of is an incorrect form for *should have,* which can be contracted to *should've* in speech or informal writing

> You *should've* returned that sweater. (better: You *should have* returned that sweater.)

sink down is sometimes heard in informal usage, but *down* is redundant and should be omitted

> You can *sink* into the mud if you are not careful.

some time means a *segment of time*
sometime means *at an indefinite time in the future*
sometimes means *occasionally*

> I'll need *some time* to make a decision.
> Let's meet *sometime* next week.
> *Sometimes* I have an urge to watch a late movie on television.

stayed means *remained*
stood means *took or remained in an upright position* or *erect*

> He *stayed* in bed for three days.
> The scouts *stood* at attention while the flag was lowered.

still more yet is redundant; *yet* should be omitted

> There is *still more* to be said.

sure is used informally to mean *surely* or *certainly,* but in formal usage *surely* or *certainly* are preferred

> She *sure* is pretty! (Better: She *certainly* is pretty!)
> We will *surely* be in trouble unless we get home soon.

testimony means *information given orally*
evidence means *information given orally or in writing;* an *object* which is presented as proof

> He gave *testimony* to the grand jury.
> He presented written *evidence* to the judge.

than any is used informally in a comparison, but in formal usage *than any other* is preferred

> He is smarter *than any other* boy in the class.

the both is used informally, but in formal usage *the* should be omitted

> I intend to treat *both* of you to lunch.

their, in informal usage, often appears in the construction "Anyone can lose their card," but since *anyone* takes a singular personal pronoun, *his* is the correct form
theirselves is an incorrect form for *themselves*

> They are able to care for *themselves* while their parents are at work.

them is the objective case of *they;* it is not used instead of those (the plural of *that*) before a noun

> Give me *those* (not *them*) books!

try and is sometimes used informally instead of *try to,* but in formal usage *try to* is correct

> My acting teacher is going *to try to* attend the opening of my play.

unbeknownst to is unacceptable for *without the knowledge of*

> The young couple decided to get married *without the knowledge of* (not *unbeknownst to*) their parents.

upwards of is an incorrect form for *more than*

> There are *more than* (not *upwards of*) sixty thousand people at the football game.

valuable means *of great worth*
valued means *held in high regard*
invaluable means *priceless*

> This is a *valuable* manuscript.
> You are a *valued friend.*
> A good name is an *invaluable* possession.

wait on is sometimes used informally, but in formal usage *wait for* is correct

> We *waited for* (not *on*) him for over an hour.

which is sometimes used incorrectly to refer to people; it refers to things
who is used to refer to people
that is used to refer to people or things

> He finally returned the books *which* he had borrowed.
> I am looking for the girl *who* made the call.
> He finally returned the books *that* he had borrowed.
> I am looking for the girl *that* made the call.

while is unacceptable for *and, but, whereas,* or *though*

> The library is situated on the south side, *whereas* (not *while*) the laboratory is on the north side.
> *Though* (not *while*) I disagree with you, I shall not interfere with your right to express your opinion.

who is, who am—Note these constructions:

> It is *I* who *am* the most experienced.
> It is *he* who *is . . .*
> It is *he or I* who *am . . .*
> It is *I or he* who *is . . .*
> It is *he and I* who *are . . .*

who, whom—To determine whether to use *who* or *whom* (without grammar rules):

(Who, Whom) do you think should represent our company?

▶**Step One:**   Change the *who—whom* part of the sentence to its natural order:

Do you think *(who, whom)* should represent our company?

▶**Step Two:**   Substitute *he* for *who,* and *him* for *whom:*

Do you think *(he, him)* should represent our company?

▶**Step Three:**   Since *he* would be used in this case, the correct form is:

Who do you think should represent our company?

whoever, whomever (see *who, whom* above)

Give the chair to *whoever* wants it (subject of verb *wants*).
Speak to *whomever* you see (object of preposition *to*).

win—you *win* a game
beat—you *beat* another player

We *won* the contest.
We *beat* (not *won*) the other team.
(*Beat* is incorrect usage for swindle: The hustler *swindled* the gambler out of twenty dollars.)

without is incorrect usage for *unless*

You will not receive the tickets *unless* (not *without*) you pay for them in advance.

worst kind and **worst way** are incorrect usages for terms such as *very badly* or *extremely*

The school is *greatly in need* of more teachers (not *needs teachers in the worst way*).

would of is an incorrect form for *would have,* which can be contracted to *would've* in informal usage

He *would've* treated you to the movies. (Better: He *would have* treated you to the movies.)

Would have is *not* used instead of *had* in an *if* clause: If I *had* (not *would have*) gone, I would have helped him.

Drill XV: Check [✔] the space provided if the sentence is correct; if there is an error in usage, write the correct form: Answers are on page 94.

1. He sure did a good job repairing his car. _____

2. Since he had not exercised in three months, he was in very poor shape. _____

3. I seen that movie a long time ago. _____

4. He always takes sometime to concentrate before he shoots the foul shot. _____

5. Anyone who wants to have their conference with me today is invited to meet in my office at ten o'clock. _____

6. She can't seem to learn how to dance the tango. _____

7. There is still more ice cream yet to be eaten. _____

8. The truck rolled into the lake and began to sink to the bottom. _____

9. We should of purchased our tickets in advance. _____

10. The both of them will receive commendations for meritorious service. _____

11. He seldom eats breakfast. _____

12. She scored more points than any player on the team. _____

13. My sister shall pay the bill later. _____

14. Sometime when I am upset, I eat an entire box of cookies. _____

15. He presented his testimony in a soft voice. _____

Drill XVI: Answers are on page 94.

1. His room is very neat while hers is very messy. _____

2. Joe's friends built the house by theirselves from a set of plans they had drawn up by an architect. _____

3. Of course, I would of taken you with me to California. _____

4. We're tired of seeing them dogs run through our garden. _____

5. Who will stay here with us? _____

6. He will try and be more pleasant to his sister. _____

7. I want to go to the concert in the worst way. _____

8. She wants to meet the boy which scored the winning goal. _____

9. That watch is extremely valuable. _____

10. Unbeknownst to the manager, the men in the shipping department decided to have a party today. _____

11. Upwards of one hundred students attended the lecture this morning. _____

12. "I can't go without you pick me up at home," she said. _____

13. I shall give it to whoever arrives first. _____

14. Mike won Josh in the one-on-one basketball game. _____

15. This time, we will not wait on you for more than ten minutes. _____

Keys to More Effective Expression

Effective expression involves more than just using words correctly. It also means avoiding clichés, using the right idioms, creating images that are both logical and appropriate, and eliminating all unnecessary words.

Avoid Clichés

A cliché is an expression that seems tired and worn out because of its frequent use. As a result, the effectiveness and originality that it once possessed are no longer present and all its freshness is gone. Perhaps the first time someone wrote "busy as a bee" or "blushing bride" the expressions were clever and well tuned, but by now we are so used to hearing these phrases that all the sparkle is gone and they have become clichés. The careful writer will try his best to avoid using trite phrases such as these:

abreast of the times	conspicuous by its absence
acid test	cool as a cucumber
after all is said and done	covers a multitude of sins
agony of suspense	deadly earnest
all in all	deep, dark secret
all work and no play	die laughing
along these lines	doomed to disappointment
as luck would have it	drastic action
at a loss for words	easier said than done
at one fell swoop	equal to the occasion
at the tender age of	eyes like stars
bathed in tears	fair sex
beat a hasty retreat	favor with a selection
beauties of nature	few and far between
better half (wife)	fiber of his (my) being
better late than never	filthy lucre
bitter end	footprints on the sands of time
blood is thicker than water	force of circumstances
blushing bride	generous to a fault
bolt from the blue	goes without saying
brave as a lion	goodly number
bright and early	good points
brown as a berry	green with envy
budding genius	hanging in the balance
burning the midnight oil	heartfelt thanks
busy as a bee	heated argument
by and large	heavy as lead
by leaps and bounds	herculean efforts
center of attention	hungry as bears
checkered career	ignorance is bliss
clear as crystal	in great profusion
clinging vine	in the final analysis
cold as ice	institution of higher learning

it stands to reason
last but not least
last straw
life's little ironies
lion's share
mantle of snow
meets the eye
method to his madness
motley throng
neat as a pin
needs no introduction
never got to first base
nipped in the bud
none the worse for wear
on the ball
paramount issue
partake of refreshment
poor but honest
powers that be
promising future
pure and simple
quick as a flash
rear its ugly head
reigns supreme
riot of color
rotten to the core
sad to relate
sadder but wiser
sea of faces
self-made man
short but sweet
sigh of relief
simple life
skeleton in the closet

slow but sure
snow-capped mountains
soul of honor
steady as a rock
straight from the shoulder
strong, silent type
strong as a lion
struggle for existence
sturdy as an oak
sweat of his brow
take my word for it
thereby hangs a tale
the time of my life
the weaker sex
the worse for wear
this day and age
thunderous applause
time marches on
tiny tots
tired but happy
too funny for words
untiring efforts
veritable mine of information
view with alarm
walk of life
wee, small hours
wend his way
wheel of fortune
white as a sheet
white as snow
with bated breath
words fail me
work like a dog
wreathed in smiles

Using Idioms Correctly

Each language has phrases or expressions peculiar to itself, its own way of expressing an idea. Sometimes these *idioms* do not follow rules of logic or conform to standard grammatical principles. Custom and local usage often dictate the construction of the idiomatic phrase. Special care must be taken to use the correct *preposition* in the idiomatic phrase.

Idioms to Know:

abound in (or *with*) This letter *abounds in* mistakes.

accompanied by (a person) The salesman was *accompanied by* the buyer.

accompanied with (a present) He *accompanied* the closing of the contract *with* a gift.

acquiesce in The executives were compelled to *acquiesce in* the director's policy.

acquit of The manager was *acquitted of* the charges against him.

adept in (or *at*) He is *adept in* typing.

agree to (an offer) The firm *agrees to* your payment in settlement of the claim.

agree upon (or *on*) (a plan) We must *agree upon* the best method.

agree with (a person) I *agree with* the doctor.

angry about (an event, situation) I am very *angry about* the high unemployment rate.

angry at (a thing, an animal) The child is *angry at* his stuffed animals.

angry with (a person) We were *angry with* the careless attendant. (*Mad* is used informally to mean *angry*, but, more properly, it means *insane*.)

appropriate for (meaning *suitable to*) The gown is also *appropriate for* a dinner dance.

available for (a purpose) The specialist is *available for* a consultation now.

available to (a person) What course of action is *available to* you at this time?

averse to The President is *averse to* increasing his staff.

cognizant of He was not *cognizant of* dissension among the workers.

coincide with Your wishes *coincide with* mine in this situation.

commensurate with What you earn will be *commensurate with* the amount of effort you apply to your task.

compare to (shows similarity between things that have different forms) In one sonnet, Shakespeare *compares* a woman's hair *to* wire.

compare with (shows similarity or difference between things of like form) The assignment was to *compare* Thoreau's essays *with* Emerson's.

compatible with The ideas of the section manager should be *compatible with* those of the buyer.

comply with If you do not wish to *comply with* his request, please notify him at once.

conducive to The employer's kindness is *conducive to* good work.

conform to (or *with*) The average person *conforms to* the vote of the majority.

conversant with We need a salesman who is fully *conversant with* what he is selling.

desirous of We are not *desirous of* a price increase.

different from This new machine is *different from* the old one.

differ from (a thing in appearance) A coat *differs from* a cape.

differ with (an opinion) I *differ with* your views on public affairs.

dissuade from She will *dissuade* him *from* making that investment.

employed at (a definite salary) The student aide is *employed at* the minimum wage.

employed in (certain work) His brother is *employed in* reading blueprints.

envious of Some of the employees are *envious of* his good fortune.

identical to (or *with*) These stockings are *identical to* those I showed you last week.

in accordance with Act *in accordance with* the regulations.

infer from I *infer from* his remarks that he is dissatisfied.

in search of He set out *in search of* fame and fortune.

necessary to Your help is *necessary to* the success of the project.

oblivious of (or *to*) The typist is *oblivious of* the construction noise outside.

opposite to (or *from*) (meaning *contrary*) Your viewpoint is *opposite to* mine.

pertinent to Your comment is not really *pertinent to* the discussion.

plan to Do you *plan to* go to the play tonight?

prefer to She *prefers* silk *to* polyester.

prior to You will receive a deposit *prior to* the final settlement.

required of The letter states what is *required of* you.

stay at He wants to *stay at* home this evening.

vie with The salesmen are *vying with* one another for this week's prize.

Watch Out for Mixed Metaphors

A *metaphor* is a figure of speech that makes an implied comparison. Unlike a *simile,* which is a comparison using *like* or *as* as indicators, the metaphor does not make use of indicators. If used correctly, metaphors and similes may add vividness and color to writing, but if used incorrectly, the opposite effect may result and the writing can become trite and even silly. The writer should be careful to use metaphors that are appropriate to the style of the essay and logical in construction. If the logic is faulty, a *mixed metaphor* may result.

> *Good:* James Joyce once wrote, "My body was like a harp and her words and gestures like fingers running upon wires."
>
> *Poor:* The lovely ocean beat against the shore with its strident voice clawing at the sands.
>
> *Good:* The ballet dancer floated through space, her feet tracing graceful circles in the air.
>
> *Poor:* The ballet dancer's feet moved with hushed grace, flapping their wings with flowery movements.

Eliminate Wordiness

Wordiness involves needless repetition of words or phrases which do not add meaning or give called-for emphasis to the sentence. Very often a sentence can be made more effective by eliminating needless repetitions or *redundancies* and expressing the thought in a more compact way.

Repeating Meaning:

Instead of:	*Say:*
the honest truth	the truth
blue in color	blue
same exact	same
the month of June	June
new innovation	innovation
consensus of opinion	consensus
repeat again	repeat

Repeating Words:

Instead of:	*Say:*
In which pool did he swim *in?*	In which pool did he swim?
From what school did you graduate *from?*	From what school did you graduate?
At which position are you working *at?*	At which position are you working?

Unnecessary Use of Pronouns After a Noun:

Instead of:	*Say:*
My aunt *she* is a social worker.	My aunt is a social worker.
The boy and girl *they* will both be here.	The boy and girl will both be here.
The teacher *he* gave a difficult assignment.	The teach gave a difficult assignment.

Unnecessary Expressions:

Instead of:	Say:
In my opinion, I believe that	I believe that
In the event of an emergency	In an emergency
On the possibility that it may	Since it may

Wordy Phrases:

Instead of:	Say:
close to the point of	close to
have need for	need
with a view to	to
in view of the fact that	because
give consideration to	consider
mean to imply	imply
disappear from view	disappear
in this day and age	today
the issue in question	issue
come in contact with	meet

Drill XVII: In the space provided, indicate:

(A) If the sentence contains language that is not idiomatic.

(B) If the sentence contains wordy or repetitious elements.

(C) If the sentence contains a cliché or mixed metaphor.

(D) If the sentence is correct.

Answers are on page 95.

1. He prepared very thoroughly for the interview, because his job was hanging in the balance. _____

2. He is the kindest, happiest person I have ever met. _____

3. Please try not to be too mad at your sister, since your parents are very worried about her health. _____

4. It is amazing and incredible how doctors and physicians are able to replace various and sundry elements of the human body with synthetic plastic parts. _____

5. She wanted to arrive early, but, as luck would have it, the car broke down on the highway almost immediately. _____

6. He launched the program like a rocket but then couldn't keep its momentum above water. _____

7. We need a campaign that is different than the one our adversary is employing in this election year. _____

8. The newly elected member of the forum who was just given membership status was not eager to meet with and be presented to the governing body. _____

9. I am afraid that he was deadly earnest when he told you that story yesterday. _____

10. Did the board of trustees agree with your offer to negotiate the contract after the first of the month? _____

11. They are envious at our family's many close friends and associates. _____

12. Please stop making such a nuisance of yourself. _____

13. When she ran around the corner and collided with the postman, all the wind was taken from her sails and her speed disintegrated. _____

14. I try to see every film that is shown in the movie theater across the street from my office. _____

15. Neither Sue or/nor Mary is going to start to proceed with the test experiment until and unless we are all together in a group again. _____

16. I sent him out in search for a good pastrami sandwich on rye bread. _____

17. My brother Ben, my sibling, is incapable of and unable to accept the position he was offered last night. _____

18. The director stated that the final round of auditions would be held on Monday. _____

19. I may be allowed to attend the concert, perhaps, but yet I shall need to get permission obtained from my mother. _____

20. She was a brilliant child who entered college at the tender age of 15. _____

Answer Key to Usage and Diction Drills

Drill I

1. principal
2. accept
3. weather
4. into
5. advise
6. than

7. all ready
8. stationery
9. effect
10. sit
11. lie
12. altogether
13. passed
14. dessert
15. lose

Drill II

1. affect
2. you're
3. ✔
4. ✔
5. used
6. an

7. rise
8. through
9. Whose
10. quiet
11. supposed
12. ✔
13. its
14. ✔
15. there

Drill III

1. conscious
2. seem
3. allusions
4. complement
5. later
6. build
7. knew

8. personal
9. course
10. cloth
11. elude
12. no
13. ante
14. morale
15. capital

Drill IV

1. ✔
2. angle
3. find
4. sight
5. ✔
6. breath
7. chose
8. ✔
9. decent
10. farther
11. ✔
12. seize
13. seen
14. clothe
15. ✔

Drill V

1. faze
2. excess
3. proceed
4. forte
5. disperse
6. formally
7. averse
8. incidence
9. dual
10. expend
11. discomfort
12. idol
13. emigrate
14. clique
15. prophecy

Drill VI

1. ✔
2. lightning
3. ✔
4. canvas
5. patience
6. imminent
7. adapt
8. elicit
9. ✔
10. exceed
11. fair
12. discomfort
13. ✔
14. prophesy
15. confident

Drill VII

1. among
2. always
3. benefit
4. A lot
5. ✔
6. number
7. is not
8. almost
9. ✔
10. all right
11. annoy
12. ✔
13. ✔
14. excuse
15. alongside (delete *of*)

Drill VIII

1. Since
2. eager
3. ✔
4. have been
5. anywhere
6. delete *at*
7. bad
8. like
9. ✔
10. a very
11. ✔
12. awhile
13. backward
14. about
15. ✔

Drill IX

1. group
2. could have
3. had better
4. burst
5. ✔
6. you and me

7. continuous
8. beside
9. delete *but*
10. May
11. ✔
12. light-complexioned
13. bring
14. seems unable
15. constantly

Drill X

1. assume
2. did
3. enthusiastic
4. nor
5. from
6. ✔

7. uninterested
8. doesn't
9. just as
10. that
11. Because of
12. just as good
13. one another
14. ✔
15. delete *and*

Drill XI

1. whether
2. fewer
3. human beings
4. suppose
5. should not have
6. conclude

7. habit
8. himself
9. flouted
10. ✔
11. graduated from
12. healthful
13. ✔
14. well
15. delete *got*

Drill XII

1. might have
2. infer
3. teach
4. ✔
5. many
6. in back of
7. slander

8. in regard to
9. child
10. ✔
11. regardless
12. as if
13. lend
14. ✔
15. occurs when

Drill XIII

1. a very good (or *enjoyable,* or a similar word) time
2. may be
3. because of
4. people
5. very
6. I

7. ✔
8. are
9. ✔
10. Because of
11. ✔
12. ✔
13. must have
14. an acceptable (or a similar word) job
15. delete *of*

Drill XIV

1. very
2. delete *again*
3. plan to go
4. said
5. stop sending
6. in the same way as
7. very

8. ✔
9. really
10. The reason the baby is crying is *that . . . ,* or: The baby is crying because she is hungry.
11. ✔
12. delete *back*
13. spent
14. manage
15. read *that*

Drill XV

1. certainly, surely
2. condition
3. saw
4. some time
5. his
6. delete *seem to*

7. delete *yet*
8. ✔
9. should have
10. delete *The*
11. ✔
12. than any *other* player
13. will
14. Sometimes
15. ✔

Drill XVI

1. but, not *while* (or add a *semicolon* and delete *while*)
2. themselves
3. would have
4. *those* dogs
5. ✔
6. try to
7. delete *in the worst way;* add *very badly*

8. who
9. ✔
10. Without the knowledge of
11. More than
12. *unless,* not *without*
13. ✔
14. beat
15. wait *for* you

Drill XVII

1. **(C)** The cliché "was hanging in the balance" should be eliminated. Better: "because his job depended on it."

2. **(D)**

3. **(A)** *Mad at* should be changed to *angry with*.

4. **(B)** The sentence contains wordy and repetitious elements *(amazing and incredible, doctors and physicians, various and sundry, synthetic plastic)* that should be condensed.

5. **(C)** The cliché "as luck would have it" should be eliminated.

6. **(C)** Since *rockets* don't operate in *water*, the sentence contains a mixed metaphor.

7. **(A)** *Different than* should be changed to *different from*.

8. **(B)** The sentence contains wordy and repetitious elements *(who was just given membership status, and be presented to)* that should be eliminated.

9. **(C)** The cliché "deadly earnest" should be eliminated. Better: "he was serious."

10. **(A)** *Agree with* should be changed to *agree to*.

11. **(A)** *Envious at* should be changed to *envious of*.

12. **(D)**

13. **(C)** The combination of *she ran, wind was taken from her sails,* and *speed disintegrated* results in a mixed metaphor in the sentence.

14. **(D)**

15. **(B)** The sentence contains wordy and repetitious elements *(or/nor, start to proceed, test experiment, until and unless)* that should be revised or eliminated.

16. **(A)** *In search for* should be changed to *in search of*.

17. **(B)** The sentence contains wordy and repetitious elements *(my sibling, incapable of and)* that should be eliminated.

18. **(D)**

19. **(B)** The sentence contains wordy or repetitous elements *(perhaps, yet; obtained)* that should be eliminated.

20. **(C)** The cliché "the tender age of" should be eliminated. Better: ". . . when she was only 15 years of age."

Spelling

Recently a survey was taken in a college Freshman English class. Students were asked to list their greatest problems in writing. When the results were tabulated, the biggest problem that they had indicated was *spelling*.

Yet when their professor was asked to cite what he considered to be the area of greatest weakness among his students, spelling was not on the list.

Obviously the students and the instructor had different perceptions. Follow-up discussions indicated that student writers are worried about their ability to spell correctly—perhaps more than they need to be. As a result, they avoid using certain words and even "freeze" on certain phrases. This hurts the entire writing process and interrupts the smooth flow of ideas.

Five Spelling Pitfalls

Pitfall One

When does *i* come before *e* and when does the *e* come before the *i?*

▶**Rule:** *I* before *e*
Except after *c,*
Or when sounded like *ay,*
As in *neighbor* and *weigh.*

Exceptions: 1. Words in which both vowels are pronounced use *ie* after *c* as in *society.*
2. Words with a *shen* sound use *ie* after *c* as in *sufficient.*
3. Other exceptions: *either* or *neither, foreign, height, seize, their, weird.*

Pitfall Two

When adding suffixes such as *-ing* and *-ed,* when do I double final consonants?

▶**Rule:** When a word of *one* syllable ends in *one* consonant preceded by *one* vowel, then double the consonant before:

-ing
-ed
-er or -ar

Examples: bar   barred
beg   beggar
stop   stopping

Note: *This applies only if the suffix added begins with a vowel.*

97

▶**Rule:** In a word of more than one syllable, listen very carefully. Pronounce the word aloud. If the accent is on the final syllable, and that syllable ends in one consonant preceded by one vowel, the final consonant is doubled. If the accent is not on the final syllable, do not double the consonant. *This only applies if the suffix begins with a vowel.*

Examples: begin   beginning
              prefer   preferred
But: worship   worshiping
              color   coloring

When the suffix begins with a consonant, do not double the last letter of the word.

Examples: commit   commitment
              prefer   preferment

Pitfall Three

When is the silent *e* at the end of a word dropped?

▶**Rule:** Drop the silent *e* at the end of a word before a suffix beginning with a vowel. Keep the silent *e* before adding a suffix beginning with a consonant.

Examples: shine   shining
              hope   hopeful

Exceptions: Words ending in *c* or *g* maintain the *e* before endings beginning with a vowel. This is done to maintain the original sound of the *c* or the *g*. Verbs ending in *ie* often drop the *e* and change the *i* to *y* before joining with *i*.

Examples: changeable
              peaceable
              dying

Exceptions: Keep the *e* to keep the meaning clear

shoe	+	ing	=	shoeing
toe	+	ing	=	toeing

Exceptions: Before *able*, sometimes the *e* is retained

love	+	able	=	loveable
move	+	able	=	moveable

Exceptions: There are always exceptions!

true	+	ly	=	truly
due	+	ly	=	duly
argue	+	ment	=	argument
whole	+	ly	=	wholly

Pitfall Four

What do I do with a word ending in *y* before I add an ending?

▶**Rule:** Change the *y* to *i* if the letter *before* the *y* is a consonant. Keep the final *y* if the letter before the final *y* is a vowel.

Examples: busy   busily
cloudy   cloudiness
donkey   donkeys
stay   staying

Exceptions: Keep the *y* in words like the following:

babyish
carrying
studying

Pitfall Five

How can I spell suffixes correctly when they all sound alike?

▶**Rule:** *-able* or *-ible?*

If you can form a word ending in *-ation* or *-ance*, choose *-able.*

irritable (irritation)
durable (duration)
variable (variance or variation)

If you can form a related word that ends in *-tion* or *-sion,* choose *-ible.*

admissible (admission)
digestible (digestion)

▶**Rule:** *-ceed, -cede,* or *-sede?*

1. Only one word ends in *-sede—supersede*
2. Only three words end in *-ceed—exceed, proceed, succeed*
3. All other words end in *-cede*

▶**Rule:** *-ful* or *full?*

The only word that ends in full is *full.* All other words end in *ful.*

Ten Special Spelling Hints

1. Keep a record of words that you misspell. Be certain that you spell the words correctly on your list. Review the list periodically.

2. Always proofread your essays to discover careless or inadvertent misspellings. Sometimes these misspellings are simply slips of the pen.

3. Consult a dictionary if you are not certain about a correct spelling.

4. Do not allow mispronunciation to cause you to misspell. Often your ear is an excellent guide for good spelling, but there are times that you may be pronouncing a word incorrectly and either adding extra sounds or omitting sounds.

Examples

February	*not*	Febuary
athlete	*not*	athelete
government	*not*	goverment
modern	*not*	modren
gratitude	*not*	graditude

5. Study the list of words that confuse you. Distinguish between words of similar sound.

Examples

affect	effect
were	where
forth	fourth
sole	soul
wholly	holy

6. Do not drop a final *l* when you add *-ly*.

Examples

real	+	ly	=	really
formal	+	ly	=	formally

7. Be careful when you add a prefix to the stem of the word that you do not omit a letter or add a letter.

Examples

ir	+	rational	=	irrational
mis	+	spell	=	misspell
dis	+	agree	=	disagree
mis	+	spent	=	misspent
dis	+	appear	=	disappear

8. Use the apostrophe correctly when forming contractions.

Examples

do not	=	don't
could not	=	couldn't
they are	=	they're
it is	=	it's

9. Be careful not to use the apostrophe when you form the ordinary plural of pronouns.

Examples

	The boys are here.
not:	The boys' are here.
not:	The boy's are here.

10. Use capital letters only when required. It is just as incorrect to spell a word with a capital letter when it is not needed as it is to omit a needed capital letter.

Spelling Exercises

Exercise I: Fill in the missing letters (ie or ei).

1. f____ld
2. conc____t
3. sl____gh
4. v____ll
5. c____ling

6. n____ce
7. sc____ntific
8. s____zure
9. consc____ntious
10. anc____nt

Exercise II: Add the endings to the following words:

1. fib + ing   = _____
2. beg + ing   = _____
3. control + able = _____
4. commit + ment = _____
5. color + ful   = _____
6. stop + ing   = _____
7. big + est   = _____
8. quit + ing   = _____
9. rob + ing   = _____
10. glad + ly   = _____

Exercise III: Add the suffix indicated to the following words:

1. bride + al   = _____
2. force + ible   = _____
3. force + ful   = _____
4. imagine + ary   = _____
5. hope + less   = _____
6. true + ly   = _____
7. remove + ing   = _____
8. life + like   = _____
9. like + ly   = _____
10. service + able = _____

Exercise IV: Add endings to the following words:

1. fly + er   = _____
2. rely + able   = _____
3. noisy + ly   = _____
4. worry + some   = _____
5. betray + ing   = _____
6. healthy + est = _____
7. mercy + ful   = _____
8. study + ing   = _____
9. easy + est   = _____
10. study + ed   = _____

Exercise V: If a word is misspelled, correct it. If it is spelled correctly, make a [✔] in the space provided.

1. beautiful   _____
2. collectable   _____
3. convertable   _____
4. irritible   _____
5. bountiful   _____
6. commendible   _____
7. preceed   _____
8. procede   _____
9. sucede   _____
10. intersede   _____

Exercise VI: The following three spelling drills are based on words drawn from several lists of "spelling demons" as well as a study of words most frequently misspelled by college freshmen. The words in *Level One* are words constantly used by the average person; the words in *Level Two* are words often used but certainly of greater difficulty; the words in *Level Three* are words occasionally used by students and of greatest difficulty.

In each group of three words, there is one misspelling. Find the misspelled word and spell it correctly on the line provided.

Level One

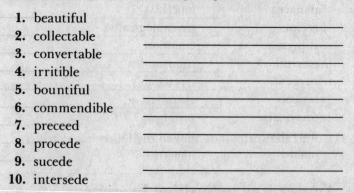

1. carriage   consceince   association   _____
2. achievement   chief   aviater   _____
3. alltogether   almost   already   _____
4. annual   desireable   despair   _____
5. independance ninety   nevertheless _____
6. billian   weather   rhyme   _____
7. quiet   lying   naturaly   _____
8. speach   straight   valleys   _____
9. transfered   tragedy   reference   _____
10. received   reciept   reception   _____

Level Two

1. calender	appropriately	casualties
2. affidavid	colossal	development
3. diptheria	competent	bigoted
4. prevelent	precipice	nauseous
5. fundamentally	obedience	bookeeper
6. tenant	repetetious	serviceable
7. cloudiness	donkies	babyish
8. wholly	wirey	strenuous
9. successfully	renowned	propagander
10. recuperate	vacuum	specificaly

Level Three

1. innoculate	aeronautics	saboteur
2. prejudice	panacea	amethist
3. laringytis	recipe	psychological
4. scissors	supremacy	cinamon
5. rarify	rescind	thousandth
6. superstitious	surgeon	irresistably
7. sophomore	brocoli	synonym
8. questionnaire	mayonaise	prophecy
9. jeoperdy	narrative	monotonous
10. primitive	obedience	mocassin

Answer Key to Spelling Exercises

Exercise I

1. ie
2. ei
3. ei
4. ei
5. ie
6. ie
7. ie
8. ei
9. ie
10. ie

Exercise II

1. fibbing
2. begging
3. controllable
4. commitment
5. colorful
6. stopping
7. biggest
8. quitting
9. robbing
10. gladly

Exercise III

1. bridal
2. forcible
3. forceful
4. imaginary
5. hopeless
6. truly
7. removing
8. lifelike
9. likely
10. serviceable

Exercise IV

1. flyer
2. reliable
3. noisily
4. worrisome

5. betraying
6. healthiest
7. merciful
8. studying
9. easiest
10. studied

Exercise V

1. correct
2. collectible
3. convertible
4. irritable

5. correct
6. commendable
7. precede
8. proceed
9. succeed
10. intercede

Exercise VI—Level One

1. conscience
2. aviator
3. altogether
4. desirable

5. independence
6. billion
7. naturally
8. speech
9. transferred
10. received

Exercise VI—Level Two

1. calendar
2. affidavit
3. diphtheria
4. prevalent

5. bookkeeper
6. repetitious
7. donkeys
8. wiry
9. propaganda
10. specifically

Exercise VI—Level Three

1. inoculate
2. amethyst
3. laryngitis
4. cinnamon
5. rarefy

6. irresistibly
7. broccoli
8. mayonnaise
9. jeopardy
10. moccasin

How to Take an Essay Test

Pre-Writing

Before you begin to write your essay, read the question several times so that you are familiar with the material. You might wish to underline key words or phrases. Do not spend too much time—only two or three minutes—on this planning. What you hope to accomplish during this pre-writing stage is:

1. To gain familiarity with the essay question
2. To develop a point of view, deciding, for instance, whether you are in agreement or disagreement with the statement given
3. To develop a thesis statement that is the essential idea of your essay

Developing a Thesis

The first step in planning an essay is to decide on a *thesis*, the point you intend to make in your essay. It is often of great value to try to state the thesis of your composition in a single sentence during the pre-writing time. When developing a thesis, keep in mind the following ideas.

1. The thesis must be neither too broad nor too narrow.
2. The thesis must be clear to you and to the reader of your essay.
3. Everything in the essay must support the thesis. To introduce material that "drifts away" might well result in a confusing essay and a low score.
4. Use specific details rather than vague generalizations to support your thesis.

Limiting the Subject

A youngster once wanted to learn a little bit about penguins. A librarian suggested a book of well over 500 pages called *Penguins*. When he returned the book, the librarian asked him if he had enjoyed reading the volume. "Well," he replied, "I really didn't need to know so much about penguins."

Most essay tests require compositions of 250 to 500 words. Therefore, you cannot write five hundred pages on a given topic; you must learn to limit your topic in order to discuss it fully in the time allowed. In fact, the more you limit your topic, the more successful your essay is likely to be, since you will be better able to supply the specific details that give an essay interest and life.

Organizing the Essay

Decide how many paragraphs you are going to write. Unless specifically indicated, there is no set rule concerning length. We are often told that "length is not a valid substitute for strength." Therefore, do not write furiously to fill up several pages, so that it will appear that you have many ideas. Actually, this can result in needless repetition, rambling, lack of organization, and muddled thinking. By the same token, you don't want your essay to appear to be skimpy. Obviously, if you write only four or five sentences, the examiner may not be able to get an adequate picture of your writing ability and may penalize you as a result.

Many high school teachers and college instructors indicate that a three or four paragraph development is usually desirable for a 20-minute essay test. This is not to say that some students may not wish to attempt an additional paragraph in the designated time. Here is where practice before the examination can be of great help to you. But remember to time yourself during the practice sessions. If you can only write one paragraph in 20 minutes, then you must continue to write—and perhaps a bit more rapidly—to develop the three-paragraph organization.

The Introduction

There are students who get bogged down before they begin to write. They stare at the blank paper and "choke up," unable to get going. The secret to beginning to write is *to write!*

Start right in. You have analyzed the question in your pre-planning. Now, in your introduction, you want to set down in clear sentences the topic you are going to write about, indicating to the reader perhaps why the topic has value or is cause for concern, giving if you can some background to the situation, and pointing the reader in the general direction that your essay is going to move.

Since you have only four or five minutes for this introduction, it is often sufficient to accomplish one or two of these tasks in three to six sentences.

Five Items to Bear in Mind

1. In writing your introduction, keep in mind the key words of the question.

2. Avoid being "cute" or funny, ironic or satiric, overly emotional or too dramatic. Set the tone or attitude in your first sentence. You may well wish to appear sincere, clear, and straightforward.

3. Don't bother repeating the question word for word. A paraphrase in your own words is far better than just copying the words of the exam question.

4. Try in your first paragraph to let the reader know what your essay is going to deal with and what your controlling idea is. This can be accomplished in a clear topic sentence.

5. Each sentence should advance your topic and be interesting to your reader.

Test Yourself: Here are four sentences. Which one do you feel is the best topic sentence for an opening paragraph?

1. I have an aunt who is quite old, past eighty, and she lives alone in a very run-down neighborhood.

2. Old age can be a real problem.

3. I am going to do my best in the next twenty minutes to try to let you know what I really and truly believe about this problem that was stated in the essay question assigned to us.

4. Since people are living to a more advanced age, we might do well to examine how we can utilize the wisdom and experience that our senior citizens have to offer instead of just disregarding them.

Answer:

Sentence four is the best opening sentence since it states the topic clearly, limits the scope of the essay, and even presents the attitude of the writer.

Recognizing Effective Introductions

An *effective* introduction often refers to the subject of the essay, explains the value of the topic, or attracts the attention of the reader by giving a pertinent illustration. Ineffective beginnings often contain unrelated material, ramble, and lack clarity.

Test Yourself: Examine the following five introductory paragraphs and decide whether each is effective or ineffective. Be able to defend your decision.

1. I agree that older people have many problems just as young people do. Adolescents often say that it's tough being young and I guess I agree.

2. Today more than ever before child abuse is coming under careful scrutiny. Although it is true that children have been abused in the past, the focus has never been clearer and that is all for the better.

3. It's really very important to think about and discuss such things. I know many people are very concerned about it.

4. Corruption in government must be everyone's concern. We can no longer hide behind the old saying, "You can't fight City Hall." Actually we can and we must.

5. I'm tired of hearing about dirty politics. It was always there just like sickness and other problems only now we read more about it. Sometimes I get disgusted because with all my schoolwork I can't pay attention to taking care of other matters. And then I'm criticized.

Answers:

1. *Ineffective.* The conclusion is not clear. The writer confuses the reader by discussing young people, older people, and adolescents.

2. *Effective.* The writer presents a strong statement on the need for writing the essay and addressing the topic.

3. *Ineffective.* The paragraph is not clear. The use of the phrase "such things" and the pronoun "it" without an appropriate antecedent tend to confuse the reader.

4. *Effective.* The initial sentence contains a strong and valid thesis. The use of a quotation tends to reinforce the subject under discussion. The paragraph is clear and the tone is strong.

5. *Ineffective.* The paragraph is rambling and muddled. The writer never presents a clear thesis statement.

The Development

The heart of the essay is the development, or the middle paragraph or paragraphs. Here the writer must attempt, in one or two paragraphs, to support the main idea of the essay through illustrations, details, and examples. The developmental paragraphs must serve as a link in the chain of ideas and contribute directly to the essay's central thought. All the sentences of the development must explain the essential truth of the thesis or topic sentence without digression.

In the limited time available on most essay tests, you can take only about ten minutes to produce six to ten sentences that will support the main thesis of the essay and prove the reality of your point of view. You may do this through a style that is descriptive, narrative, or expository, using a factual approach or an anecdotal one. Whatever approach you choose and whatever style you adopt, your writing must be coherent, logical, unified, and well ordered.

Caution! Avoid the following pitfalls in the development of your essay:

1. Using sentences that are irrelevant and contain extraneous material
2. Using sentences that have no sequence of thought but seem to jump from one idea to another
3. Using sentences that do not relate to the topic sentence or do not flow from the preceding sentence

The good writer makes use of transitional words or phrases to connect thoughts and to provide for a logical sequence of ideas. Therefore, you would be wise to examine the following list of transitional ideas so that you might select those that you feel are most helpful in developing your middle paragraphs:

therefore	first of all	then
moreover	secondly	indeed
however	for example	in any case
consequently	for instance	on the other hand
of course	finally	nevertheless

Many other good linking expressions can be added to the above list, but if you choose judiciously from these fifteen expressions, you will find that your development will be more coherent and unified.

Test Yourself: In the following three samples, the transition is missing. Supply a transitional word or phrase that will allow the second sentence to follow smoothly or logically from the first.

1. He is an excellent piano player. There are times when his technique seems weak.
2. Generally, I believe doctors are very dedicated to helping people. There are exceptions to this.
3. He arrived late to take the examination. He dropped his pen and book when he finally got to his seat.

Answers:

1. Choose one of the following transitional expressions to indicate a contrast: *and yet, but, however, nevertheless, still, yet*

   He is an excellent piano player; however, there are times when his technique seems weak.

2. Choose an expression from the following list to indicate concession: *although this may be true, at the same time, granted that, no doubt, doubtless*

   Generally, I believe doctors are very dedicated to helping people. No doubt, there are exceptions.

3. Use one of the following expressions to start your second sentence to indicate the idea of "in addition": *furthermore, in addition, also, then.*

> He arrived late to take the examination. Furthermore, he dropped his pen and book when he finally got to his seat.

Effective Writing

There are three important factors that should be considered in writing an essay:

- Unity
- Coherence
- Support

Essays are judged by how well they meet these three basic requirements. To improve an essay you are writing, ask yourself these questions:

Unity

1. Do all the details in the essay support and develop the main thesis?
2. Do all the illustrations relate to the main point and add to the general effectiveness of the essay?
3. Have irrelevant ideas been deleted?

Coherence

1. Does the essay show a sense of organization?
2. Is the material presented logically?
3. Does the essay include transitional words or phrases that allow the reader to move easily from one idea to the next?

Support

1. Does the essay use details that make it interesting and vivid?
2. Is the main idea supported with concrete and specific illustrations?
3. Does the essay contain sufficient supporting details to clarify and persuade?

The Conclusion

Lewis Carroll once gave some very good advice. He said, "When you come to the end, stop!" The successful writer, like the wise guest, knows that he must not prolong his stay; when he comes to the end of his essay, he must draw his comments together in a strong, clear concluding paragraph.

A good concluding paragraph should give the reader the feeling that the essay has made its point, that the thesis has been explained, or that a point of view has been established. This can be accomplished in about three to six sentences in one of the following ways:

1. Through a *restatement* of the main idea
2. Through a *summary* of the material covered in the essay
3. Through a *clear statement of the writer's opinion* of the issue(s) involved

Of course, if you had a good deal of time, there would be many additional techniques that you could employ to conclude your composition. But on an essay test, your time is limited, and you will have only five minutes or so to write a conclusion that will leave the reader feeling that you are a competent writer.

Caution! Just as there are good techniques, there are also some very ineffective methods that students are tempted to use in drawing a composition to a close. Try to avoid falling into the following traps:

1. Apologizing for your inability to discuss all the issues in the allotted time
2. Complaining that the topics did not interest you or that you don't think it was fair to be asked to write on so broad a topic
3. Introducing material that you will not develop, rambling on about non-pertinent matters, or using material that is trite or unrelated

Keep in mind that a good conclusion is related to the thesis of the essay and is an integral part of the essay. It may be a review or a restatement, or it may lead the reader to do thinking on his or her own, but the conclusion must be strong, clear, and effective.

Recognizing Effective Conclusions

Remember that an *effective* concluding paragraph may restate the thesis statement, summarize the main idea of the essay, draw a logical conclusion, or offer a strong opinion of what the future holds. An *ineffective* final paragraph often introduces new material in a scanty fashion, apologizes for the ineffectiveness of the material presented, or is illogical or unclear.

Exercise 1

Why are the following sentences ineffective in a concluding paragraph?

1. I wish I had more time to write a more convincing paper, but I find that in the allotted time this is all that I could do.
2. Although I have not mentioned this before, many senior citizens centers are being set up all over the country.
3. Now that I have explained my point of view, perhaps you would care to share you ideas with me on this topic.

Answers:

1. Avoid using a complaining or apologetic tone in your conclusion. This detracts from the strength of your conclusion and serves to point out your inability to communicate ideas.
2. Do not add an idea that is completely new in your conclusion unless you are prepared to justify its inclusion and to develop it before you end your essay.
3. This kind of sentence is unrealistic and trite. The reader is not going to be able to share his or her ideas nor is he or she required to do so in this examination. This sentence seems to indicate that the writer was unable to find a satisfactory conclusion and resorted to a shop-worn comment.

Exercise 2

Examine the following five conclusions and decide whether each is effective or ineffective.

1. That's all I have to say about the topic. I know I'm not an expert, but at least this is my opinion and what I believe.

2. Certainly we can conclude that we are affected by the media. The advertisers are beginning to control our thinking and our decision making. The alert consumer must recognize this and act accordingly.

3. We must find other solutions to this problem. I know in England they have developed hospices to handle the terminally ill. But we can't discuss that here because of lack of time.

4. From all evidence we have, smoking presents a clear and present danger to the young person. The best cure for the habit appears to be to stop before beginning.

5. So be careful not to skip school. You must realize that a good education is important for you and so you should take advantage of your teachers when you are young. You won't be sorry.

Answers:

1. *Ineffective.* This statement is a repetitious apology.

2. *Effective.* The paragraph is strong and clear. The conclusion is logical and the writer's opinion is well stated.

3. *Ineffective.* New material is presented but not developed.

4. *Effective.* The conclusion drawn appears to be logical. The phrasing is concise and to the point.

5. *Ineffective.* The tone is preachy; it is preferable to avoid addressing the reader directly or giving commands. It would be better to use the third person.

Proofreading

Proofreading is an essential part of the writing experience. At least five minutes of an essay test should be reserved for proofreading your work and making any needed corrections. There are certain "errors" that you may discover during the proofreading period:

1. Omission of words—especially *the, a, an*

2. Omission of final letters on words

3. Careless spelling errors

4. Incorrect use of capital letters

5. Faulty punctuation

In addition, as you proofread you may change a word or adjust a phrase to make your essay more effective. However, remember that you will not have time to revise your entire essay or rewrite a paragraph.

Proofreading Exercises

The following drills will help you recognize and correct common errors. The first six drills each focus on one error such as the fragment, comma-splice or run-on, homonym confusion, omission of final letters, etc., and the seventh drill presents a paragraph with a combination of errors. Rewrite each paragraph, correcting all the errors you find. You can check your response with the corrected paragraphs following the drills.

Exercise 1

Perhaps the most important person in his life was his mother. A beautiful woman who devoted her life to her family. She had married his father when she was quite young. Not quite eighteen. And hardly out of high school. As a result, her plans to enter college had to be deferred for a while. "It's all a matter of priorities," she said. Feeling that she was in love and wanted to start a family. "I'll get back to my schooling one day," she told her friends. She did. Although it took over fifty years.

Exercise 2

Everybody seems to be on a diet nowadays perhaps it's because we all want to be youthful. All you have to do is pick up a newspaper or magazine, the pictures of slim, athletic men and women look back at you, challenging you to lose weight the easy way. Actually there is no easy way, I discovered after going on diets for over five years. First I'd stare, and then I'd stuff, the result was that I lost thirty pounds, and I gained thirty-five pounds, as a consequence, I'm now five pounds heavier than I was last year.

Exercise 3

There are some people who cant seem to concentrate in a quiet room. "Its too quiet," they complain. They seem to thrive on some low level of noise, and so while theyre studying, they turn on the radio or the television set. Their parents, not understanding the situation, may ask, "Whats going on here? Youre never going to be able to do your assignment with all that noise!" Yet its precisely the "noise" that helps them to do the homework. A radios music provides the accompaniment to start the days work. As my friends brother once said, "Everyone has the right to choose his own place to work. Whats important is that the professors assignment gets completed."

Exercise 4

I much prefer city life to country life. I remember I once spent my vacation in a sleepy town in Tennessee where my uncle live. It was so quiet! Perhaps some people will think I could have relax there but actually I was bore because I was not interest in any of the things or activities that took place there. When I arrive at my uncle's home, I thought that I would enjoy the change. But my enjoyment last only one day. Then I start to feel restless and I count the days until I would return to the "big city" with its excitement and bustle.

Exercise 5

Their are many reasons for students to go too college. First of all, college has a definite effect on our lives, since its a place were we are exposed to people of diverse backgrounds and also to many different branches of learning. Then too, at college students have a choice of extracurricular activities that they can choose to attend and to farther they're interests and abilities. All considered, people should follow the advise of those who advocate a college education.

Exercise 6

We have been told that there has always been a generation gap between the old and the young. As a result, communication between children and parent is at best difficult. My own mother often tell me that when she was young she could not discuss many important subject with her parents and so she relied on her few close friend for these discussion. Yet today she does not fully understand why it so difficult for me to bridge this gap and communicate openly. She feel that now it different, and she is more understanding than either of her parent was. Oh well, let see what happen when I have children.

Exercise 7

Everyone should have a hobby. A special interest to cultivate during spare time. For some individual Sports and Athletic are good way to keep themself amuse and occupy, other people prefer the theater more and attending various Culture Event. In my opinion a hobby should be a way to develop your personality. And also to make you a more interesting person. Someone who is well round and who will be appreciate by others, therefore, I urge each and everyone to make good use of there leisure time and spend free hour widely.

Answers to Proofreading Exercises

Exercise 1

Perhaps the most important person in his life was his mother, ~~A~~ [mother, a] beautiful woman who devoted her life to her family. She had married his father when she was quite ~~young. Not~~ [young, not] quite eighteen, ~~And~~ [eighteen, and] hardly out of high school. As a result, her plans to enter college had to be deferred for a while. "It's all a matter of priorities," she ~~said. Feeling~~ [said, feeling] that she was in love and wanted to start a family. "I'll get back to my schooling one day," she told her friends. She ~~did. Although~~ [did, although] it took over fifty years.

Exercise 2

Everybody seems to be on a diet ~~nowadays perhaps~~ [nowadays. Perhaps] it's because we all want to be youthful. All you have to do is pick up a newspaper or magazine; the pictures of slim, athletic men and women look back at you, challenging you to lose weight the easy way. Actually there is no easy way, I discovered after going on diets for over five years. First I'd ~~stare,~~ [starve,] and then I'd ~~stuff, the~~ [stuff. The] result was that I lost thirty pounds, and I gained thirty-five ~~pounds, as~~ [pounds. As] a consequence, I'm now five pounds heavier than I was last year.

Exercise 3

There are some people who ~~cant~~ [can't] seem to concentrate in a quiet room. "~~Its~~ ["It's] too quiet," they complain. They seem to thrive on some low level of noise, and so while ~~theyre~~ [they're] studying, they turn on the radio or the television set. Their parents, not understanding the situation, may ask, "~~Whats~~ ["What's] going on here? ~~Youre~~ [You're] never going to be able to do your assignment with all that noise!" Yet ~~its~~ [it's] precisely the "noise" that helps them to do the homework. A ~~radios~~ [radio's] music provides the accompaniment to start the ~~days~~ [day's] work. As my ~~friends~~ [friend's] brother once said, "Everyone has the right to choose his own place to work. ~~Whats~~ [What's] important is that the ~~professors~~ [professor's] assignment gets completed."

Exercise 4

I much prefer city life to country life. I remember I once spent my vacation in a sleepy town in Tennessee where my uncle ~~live.~~ [lived.] It was so quiet! Perhaps some

people will think I could have relax [relaxed] there but actually I was ~~bore~~ [bored] because I was
not ~~interest~~ [interested] in any of the things or activities that took place there. When I ~~arrive~~ [arrived]
at my uncle's home, I thought that I would enjoy the change. But my enjoyment
~~last~~ [lasted] only one day. Then I ~~start~~ [started] to feel restless and I ~~count~~ [counted] the days until I would
return to the "big city" with its excitement and bustle.

Exercise 5

~~Their~~ [There] are many reasons for students to go ~~too~~ [to] college. First of all, college has
a definite effect on our lives, since ~~its~~ [it's] a place ~~were~~ [where] we are exposed to people of
diverse backgrounds and also to many different branches of learning. Then too,
at ~~college~~ [college,] students have a choice of extracurricular activities that they can
choose to attend and to ~~farther~~ ~~they're~~ [further their] interests and abilities. All considered,
people should follow the ~~advise~~ [advice] of those who advocate a college education.

Exercise 6

We have been told that there has always been a generation gap between the
old and the young. As a result, communication between children and ~~parent~~ [parents] is
at best difficult. My own mother often ~~tell~~ [tells] me that when she was young she could
not discuss many important ~~subject~~ [subjects] with her parents and so she relied on her few
close ~~friend~~ [friends] for these ~~discussion.~~ [discussions,] Yet today she does not fully understand why it [is]
so difficult for me to bridge this gap and communicate openly. She ~~feel~~ [feels] that now
it [is] different, and she is more understanding than either of her ~~parent~~ [parents] was. Oh
well, ~~let~~ [let's] see what ~~happen~~ [happens] when I have children.

Exercise 7

Everyone should have a hobby, [a] ~~A~~ special interest to cultivate during spare
time. For some ~~individual~~ [individuals,] ~~Sports and Athletic are~~ [participating in sports is a] good way to keep ~~themself~~ [themselves]
~~amuse~~ [amused] and occupy, [ied. Other] ~~other~~ people prefer, the theater, [to attend] ~~more and attending various~~ [or other cultural events.]
~~Culture Event.~~ In my opinion, a hobby ~~should~~ [can] be a way to develop ~~your~~ [the] personal-
ity, [a] And ~~also to~~ make ~~you~~ a more interesting, [people] ~~person. Someone who is~~ well-round~~ed~~ [ed]
and ~~who will be~~ appreciate~~d~~ [d] by others, [people should] ~~therefore, I urge each and everyone to~~
make ~~good~~ use of ~~there~~ [their] leisure time, ~~and spend free-hour widely~~

Sample Essay Questions

Three essay questions follow. For each one, you should first write your own 20-minute response. Next, you should examine the sample responses and come to a conclusion as to how successfully the writer has satisfied the assignment. Then you should compare your view with the analysis of each sample response.

Sample Essay Question 1

Topic: In a recent article, a major university asked several faculty members to discuss what they considered the most important problem plaguing our country and the world. The professors spoke of the widespread hunger confronting half of the people on earth, the extinction of hundreds and even thousands of species because of the destruction of tropical forests, and the overwhelming poverty in many countries. There are other concerns that might be mentioned: the prejudice and lack of understanding among people and nations, the inadequate distribution of wealth, and the threat of nuclear annihilation.

Assignment: Choose at least one problem that you feel should be the prime concern of mankind and discuss how it should be addressed in the remaining years of the twentieth century.

Sample Response 1A

As we near the turn of the century there are so many major problems plaguing humanity that it is hard to know where to begin to solve them. It is terribly sad to see so much hunger and poverty throughout the world—in our country and elsewhere. But perhaps the most frightening problem we face is what to do to avoid nuclear annihilation.

Destruction will not come with a "whimper" but with a "bang" I'm afraid. So many countries possess nuclear weapons—superpowers and smaller countries as well—that the likelihood of a catastrophe, accidental or otherwise is great. Events in the United States and in Russia have proven that nuclear reactors are not all that safe. Then there are the threats made by smaller nations at war against other small nations. The prospect is possible and terrible.

Many people do not even bother to have children or get married nowadays. They say it's better to just enjoy the little time they have left before the world is blown up. It's a very depressing situation and not easy to explain to youngsters. Also, some people say that they can't trust politicians to do the right thing.

Therefore, this is a very serious problem that must be addressed before the end of the century—as soon as possible in fact. But intelligent answers to this very difficult problem do not seem to be at hand.

Analysis of Sample Response 1A

Strengths

1. The essay is well organized, keeping to the subject and developing its arguments in a logical progression.

2. The introduction is well developed as it moves from the general to the specific—from "many major problems" to the problem of avoidance of nuclear annihilation.

3. The second paragraph begins with an *allusion*, the technique of making indirect reference to an author or work of literature. In this case, the writer alludes to T. S. Eliot's famous line "This is how the world ends, not with a bang but a whimper"—a most appropriate way to suggest a point of view.

4. The concluding paragraph is signaled by a transition ("Therefore") that prepares the reader for a summation of the preceding arguments and uses some of the language of the topic that the writer has chosen to discuss.

Suggestions for Improvement

1. The essay might be revised to address or elaborate on certain ideas. First, the writer should suggest how the problems noted might be addressed, since that is what the question required. Second, the discussion of the breakdown of social values and family life needs specific development and details so that it will be more germane to the central issue.

2. In the second paragraph, specific examples of conflicts between nations might have provided illustration of the thesis.

3. Revisions are needed to make the tone more consistent. In the third paragraph, the tone becomes informal and the argument wanders.

4. In the opening sentence of the concluding paragraph, the word "this" is vague and its antecedent is not clear. If the author means "the possibility of nuclear annihilation," it should be stated.

5. Several commas might be added for appropriate pauses:

Paragraph 1: "As we near the turn of the century,"

Paragraph 2: "but with a 'bang,' I'm afraid."

Paragraph 4: "as soon as possible, in fact."

Sample Response 1B

Over the past years there has been an area of concern that people have forgotten, and yet I feel that this should be our cheif concern. The area is that of pollution. Our entire world is suffering from various forms of pollution and I feel that if we do not open our eyes to this problem we will soon see the general breakdown of our universe.

Because of the increasing number of cars on our streets and the various forms of mass transportation, our air is becoming polluted. All sorts of harmful gasses are being given off into the air, and we are breathing in fumes that will surely cause us many kinds of diseases. We pollute our bodies with cigarete smoke and drugs but we also pollute our bodies with gasoline fumes and taken together we are shortening our lives.

Garbage and poisons are polluting our soil and our streams. Newspaper articles always point out that all the chemicals that we use to grow bigger and more delicious fruits and vegetables and to destroy the bugs are going to destroy us as well. The chemicals get into our foods and then we eat them, and soon we will suffer the affects. Garbage is thrown into the waters and rivers and our fish become contaminated.

Of course, poverty, nuclear war, and hunger are problems, but so is pollution, and pollution is a problem that people overlook; that is why it is so dangerous. I think that over the next few years laws should be passed to regulate air pollution, to solve the problem of garbage disposal, and to deal with the use of chemicals and agriculture. In my opinion, this should be our major concern.

Analysis of Sample Response 1B

Strengths

1. The writer shows an intelligent handling of the topic. Choosing pollution, an area not mentioned in the question, the writer provides a thoughtful alternative approach.

2. The four paragraphs are well organized and well developed. Specific examples are provided in the body of the essay.

3. The essay is clear, generally well written, and consistent with the writer's thesis statement. The reader feels that the author strongly believes in the point of view presented.

Suggestions for Improvement

1. The author's suggestions for addressing the problem should be stated clearly and developed specifically earlier in the essay, not merely in a brief concluding comment.

2. The author appears to overstate the case in writing in the introduction that "people have forgotten" pollution, and in the conclusion that "people overlook" this problem.

3. More careful proofreading might result in the correction of usage and spelling errors: in paragraph one, *cheif* should be *chief;* in paragraph two, *cigarete* should be *cigarette;* in paragraph three, *affects* should be *effects.*

4. In paragraph three, the concluding sentence might well be eliminated, since it adds no new ideas and simply repeats what has been stated earlier in the paragraph.

Sample Essay Question 2

Topic: Were the good old days actually that good? We must remember that our grandparents did not have all the modern conveniences to make life easier. There were no airplanes or cars, no washing machines, no television, no computers. Therefore, it is better to live today in the modern world than to look back to the last century.

Assignment: Agree or disagree with this statement, drawing upon your personal experiences, your observations of others, or your reading.

Sample Response 2A

I prefer to be living today rather than when my grandparents were born in the last century or before that even. Today young people can really enjoy themselves they have TV and discos and movies and all sorts of entertainment. Not like long ago when all you did all day was work and then at night you were to tired to do anything accept sleep.

Today we have greater opportunities to do things and to get ahead. There is less prejudism against people because of there race or color or religion. You can go to more kinds of colleges like a two year school or a four year school and there are even many programs to help you if you are financially unable to pay the tuition costs and payments.

I don't believe that the good old days were really that good. I'm very happy to be living today in today world. These are the good days.

Analysis of Sample Response 2A

Strengths

1. There is a sense of organization. The essay is divided into three paragraphs—an introduction, a development, and a conclusion.

2. The author attempts to stick to the topic and provide examples.

3. Although there are technical errors in the third paragraph, the conclusion provides an interesting summary.

Suggestions for Improvement

1. The essay lacks clarity and is wordy. The opening sentence could have been concluded after "born." In the second paragraph, the first sentence is vague; "to do things" and "to get ahead" should be explained and clarified. The third sentence of the second paragraph needs to be tightened: "There are two- and four-year colleges with various programs to assist those in financial need."

2. There are sentence structure problems. The second sentence of the first paragraph is a run-on sentence. A period should follow "them selves." The sentence that follows is a fragment. "Not like long ago" could be changed to add clarity and also to provide a subject for the sentence: "This is different from times past when all people did. . . ."

3. There are several errors in word choice. In the last sentence of the first paragraph, *to tired* should be changed to *too tired*, and *accept* should be *except*. In the second sentence of the second paragraph, *prejudism* should be *prejudice* and *there* should be *their*.

4. There is an error in the use of the possessive form. In the second sentence of the third paragraph, *today world* should be *today's world*.

Sample Response 2B

Someone once said that for everything you gain you have to give up something. I agree. We gained the subway, but we have to put up with being crowded like sardines and herded like cattle, being pushed and shoved. We gained large buildings and big cities, but we lost our privacy and we are forced to live in little cubby holes. We gained airplanes and automobiles and with it comes all the dirty air and pollution.

Our grandparents worked hard and didn't have time to relax but maybe they got real pleasure from their work. At least they ate the food that they grew and weren't concerned about all the chemicals and sprays and sickness that came from the fruit and vegetables. Maybe they developed a real feeling of accomplishment too. They didn't have TV or radios but they had good neighbors and they would enjoy visiting with friends and family. We gained television but we lost the ability to have a good conversation and to enjoy the company of other people.

Every century has its good points and its problems. I don't want to go back to living a hundred years ago but I do feel that we could learn from the way they lived. Maybe we could adopt some of their customs and bring some of the good old days into today's world.

Analysis of Sample Response 2B

Strengths

1. There is an excellent three-paragraph organization. The introduction is fully developed with several pertinent illustrations. The body provides several additional points that support the writer's contention. The conclusion is a thought-provoking summary of the essay.

2. The use of contrast between past and present provides a fine frame for the essay. The theme of "gain and loss" is carried through with appropriate illustrations and a mature vocabulary.

3. There are no errors in sentence structure and the writer reveals that he can use both simple and complex sentences effectively.

Suggestions for Improvements

1. The second sentence of the opening paragraph seems ineffective in the context of so many mature comments. It could be rewritten: "This is especially true in comparing our world with the world of our grandparents."

2. There is a problem with pronouns and antecedents; this results in a lack of clarity. In the last sentence of the first paragraph, the singular pronoun "it" is incorrect since it does not agree with the plural "airplanes and automobiles." It would be better to write: "We gained airplanes and automobiles, but with modern means of travel we must suffer dirty air and pollution." So too, the second sentence of the concluding paragraph could be rewritten to clarify the pronoun "they": ". . . but I do feel that we could learn from the way our grandparents lived." This change clarifies the use of the pronoun "their" in the subsequent sentence.

Sample Essay Question 3

Topic: Our government is spending millions of dollars in the area of space exploration. This expenditure represents a misdirection of funds. It would be far better to use these funds to improve our own society and to upgrade our living conditions.

Assignment: Are these statements justified? Using your observations, reading, and study, explain and support your answer.

Sample Response 3A

I can see the point of those who say that "this expenditure represents a misdirecting of funds." However, I feel it is necessary for mankind to explore the stars and outer space in order to acquire more knowledge of the universe. Humans have always tried to learn more, even when it gets them in trouble. Wouldn't it be terrible if we bother some aliens and get destroyed by strange creatures who don't want us bothering them?

Anyhow, it is still important to send up rockets and space capsules to explore. The pictures we got to see and rock samples that come back are also fascinating. Someday maybe people will travel to far off countries and set up new civilizations. This would be a good chance to eliminate some of the overcrowded life on earth. We could also learn alot about what kind of gas or air, or surface other places have. This might help us back on earth too. The space program is also good for people's egos. It makes them feel good, and better than the Russians, to get to foreign places first. It also may take their minds off of problems in our own world, which is not so bad.

We are spending far too much money on space travel and space exploration. As the question points out it would be far better to use these funds to help improve our own society and better our living conditions here on earth.

Analysis of Sample Response 3A

There are several weaknesses in the essay. First, the writer does not take a clear stand. Does this student support or reject the thesis that space travel is of value and should be funded by the government? The first paragraph presents both views. The second paragraph basically supports the need for space exploration. The third paragraph, the concluding one, rejects this view, pointing out that too much money is needlessly spent on "space travel and space exploration." The essay tends to be confusing and disorganized.

The essay also contains many weaknesses in technical English. Problems in spelling and diction appear throughout (*humans* instead of *human beings* in the third sentence of the first paragraph; *alot* instead of *a lot* in the fifth sentence of the second paragraph; *off of* instead of *off* in the eighth sentence of the second paragraph). There are several awkward and ill-phrased sentences. In the second paragraph, the first sentence ends with the infinitive "to explore," but lacks an object of the infinitive. The second sentence of the second paragraph has a poorly ended verb clause. A better sentence would be, "The pictures and rock samples that came back to us. . . ." The word *good* is used three times in the second paragraph and should be replaced by more specific words, such as *valuable* or *important*.

The writer appears to understand the basic elements of essay organization, and the essay contains an introduction referring to the question, a development of supporting details, and a summarizing conclusion. Unfortunately, the lack of coherence strongly detracts from the value of the piece.

Sample Response 3B

In our own country we have so many people who are unemployed and without jobs. Their families are without proper shelter and often don't have the money to buy the necessary food and clothing. If we took a portion of this money and provided employment for the jobless and homes for the homeless we would be doing our citizens a service. We could also use this money to develop research in medicine and find the cures for fatal diseases like cancer and now herpes. Then we would be using our money correctly. What good is it to read about a flight to the moon when you are hungry or out of work.

I know that many people say that we must keep up with the Russians and the Soviet Union and that if they spend millions of dollars so should we so that we will be proud of the achievements of our scientists. Also we would learn so many things about our vast universe and the world in which we live in.

Does this make good sense. I think that Charity begins at home. Lets not worry about what's happening on the moon. Let's be more concerned about what's happening here on the earth.

Analysis of Sample Response 3B

Unlike the author of Essay 3A, this writer presents a point of view that is clear and consistent. This student feels that the funds being spent on space exploration are misdirected and could be better utilized to help improve living conditions in our own society. The concluding statements provide a summary and reinforce this point of view.

Unfortunately, the many errors in punctuation, grammar, and usage seriously reduce the effectiveness of the essay and would doubtless lower the grade considerably. The writer should try to eliminate redundancies such as "unemployed and without jobs," and "Russians and the Soviet Union." The essay also contains a factual error; herpes might be unpleasant, but it is certainly not fatal. End-stop punctuation is weak. The author uses periods instead of question marks to conclude the interrogative sentence in the last sentence of the first paragraph and the first sentence of the concluding paragraph. There is no reason to capitalize "Charity" (in the second sentence of the third paragraph), and although "Let's" is spelled correctly in the fourth sentence of the third paragraph, the necessary apostrophe is omitted in the same word in the preceding sentence. A careful proofreading of the essay might have helped the writer to locate and correct many of these errors.

Essay Topics for Additional Practice

Since many essay topics that are assigned are based on a short quotation or familiar saying, a good way to practice for the examination is to select a short statement and to react to it in a composition of three or more paragraphs. Following is a list of comments. For each, write a theme in which you agree or disagree with the statement. Use your knowledge of history, the arts, literature, current affairs, or the media to add validity to your position. Do not take more than 15 or 20 minutes to write your theme, and then allow three to five minutes to proofread what you have written.

1. "I'm in favor of the death penalty; it saves lives."
2. "To be able to fill leisure intelligently is the last product of civilization."
3. "Life is not a spectacle or a feast; it is a predicament."
4. "There is only one thing age can give you, and that is wisdom."
5. "Not to know is bad; not to wish to know is worse."

For each of the topics below, you should take a stand concerning the major idea presented. Then, drawing from your experiences or from your readings, you should support your opinion, supplying details to justify your position. Allow yourself 20 minutes to write the essay. Remember to proofread carefully.

1. The media present a slanted or unfair view in reporting news stories.
2. Public employees should not have the right to strike.
3. Both women and men have a responsibility to serve in the armed forces.
4. Euthanasia (mercy killing) is never justified.
5. Insanity cannot be considered a legitimate defense for those who commit murder.

Part II

Practice SAT II Writing Tests

The six practice tests that follow have been modeled after the actual SAT II Writing Test. Each test consists of a 20-minute essay and 60 multiple-choice questions. Allow yourself 40 minutes to answer all 60 multiple-choice questions.

Guidelines for Taking the Practice Tests

1. Do not guess wildly, since there is a penalty for choosing the wrong answer. If, however, you can make an "educated guess" by narrowing your possible choices, you should do so.

2. Do not spend too much time on any one question. You have a better chance of scoring high if you go back and answer the more difficult questions only after you have answered all the questions you know.

3. Do not choose answers that contain colloquial phrases, slang expressions, or informal usage. Remember, this is a test of your command of standard written English.

4. Use the specially constructed answer sheets to record your answers just as you will do on the actual test.

5. After taking each test, check your answers against the answers and explanations that follow. Analyze your errors and consult the appropriate sections of the Guide to Good Writing to eliminate weaknesses.

Answer Sheet for Practice Test 1
Part A: Essay Section

Use this space for your essay response.

Part B: Multiple-Choice Section

1 (A)(B)(C)(D)(E)   13 (A)(B)(C)(D)(E)   25 (A)(B)(C)(D)(E)   37 (A)(B)(C)(D)(E)   49 (A)(B)(C)(D)(E)

2 (A)(B)(C)(D)(E)   14 (A)(B)(C)(D)(E)   26 (A)(B)(C)(D)(E)   38 (A)(B)(C)(D)(E)   50 (A)(B)(C)(D)(E)

3 (A)(B)(C)(D)(E)   15 (A)(B)(C)(D)(E)   27 (A)(B)(C)(D)(E)   39 (A)(B)(C)(D)(E)   51 (A)(B)(C)(D)(E)

4 (A)(B)(C)(D)(E)   16 (A)(B)(C)(D)(E)   28 (A)(B)(C)(D)(E)   40 (A)(B)(C)(D)(E)   52 (A)(B)(C)(D)(E)

5 (A)(B)(C)(D)(E)   17 (A)(B)(C)(D)(E)   29 (A)(B)(C)(D)(E)   41 (A)(B)(C)(D)(E)   53 (A)(B)(C)(D)(E)

6 (A)(B)(C)(D)(E)   18 (A)(B)(C)(D)(E)   30 (A)(B)(C)(D)(E)   42 (A)(B)(C)(D)(E)   54 (A)(B)(C)(D)(E)

7 (A)(B)(C)(D)(E)   19 (A)(B)(C)(D)(E)   31 (A)(B)(C)(D)(E)   43 (A)(B)(C)(D)(E)   55 (A)(B)(C)(D)(E)

8 (A)(B)(C)(D)(E)   20 (A)(B)(C)(D)(E)   32 (A)(B)(C)(D)(E)   44 (A)(B)(C)(D)(E)   56 (A)(B)(C)(D)(E)

9 (A)(B)(C)(D)(E)   21 (A)(B)(C)(D)(E)   33 (A)(B)(C)(D)(E)   45 (A)(B)(C)(D)(E)   57 (A)(B)(C)(D)(E)

10 (A)(B)(C)(D)(E)   22 (A)(B)(C)(D)(E)   34 (A)(B)(C)(D)(E)   46 (A)(B)(C)(D)(E)   58 (A)(B)(C)(D)(E)

11 (A)(B)(C)(D)(E)   23 (A)(B)(C)(D)(E)   35 (A)(B)(C)(D)(E)   47 (A)(B)(C)(D)(E)   59 (A)(B)(C)(D)(E)

12 (A)(B)(C)(D)(E)   24 (A)(B)(C)(D)(E)   36 (A)(B)(C)(D)(E)   48 (A)(B)(C)(D)(E)   60 (A)(B)(C)(D)(E)

TEAR HERE

Practice Test 1

Part A: Essay Section
(20 Minutes)

Directions: You have 20 minutes in which to plan and write the essay assigned below. Make certain that you do not stray from the topic, that you give specific details as supporting evidence, and that you organize your ideas logically. Remember to proofread carefully to be certain that you have expressed your ideas in standard written English.

Topic: "The ends justify the means."

Assignment: Write an essay in which you agree or disagree with this statement. Support your opinions with specific examples from your personal experiences, your observations of others, or your reading.

YOU MAY USE THE SPACE BELOW FOR NOTES. BEGIN YOUR ESSAY ON THE ANSWER SHEET PROVIDED.

Part B: Multiple-Choice Section

(40 Minutes)

Directions: Some of the sentences below contain an error in grammar, usage, word choice, or idiom. Other sentences are correct. Parts of each sentence are underlined and lettered. The error, if there is one, is contained in one of the underlined parts of the sentence. Assume that all other parts of the sentence are correct and cannot be changed. For each sentence, select the one underlined part that must be changed to make the sentence correct and mark its letter on your answer sheet. If there is no error in a sentence, mark answer space E. No sentence contains more than one error.

	Example	**Sample Answer**

<u>Being that</u> <u>it's</u> such a lovely day, we
   A   B

<u>are having</u> a difficult time
   C

<u>concentrating</u> on our assignment.
   D

<u>No error</u>
  E

Sample Answer
●ⒷⒸⒹⒺ

---

1. Trouble developed at the power plant when <u>a number</u> of fuses blew<u>;</u> I <u>don't</u>
        A   B   C
know how it happened but it certainly didn't seem <u>to phase</u> the workers.
            D
<u>No error</u>
  E

2. The <u>amount</u> of people who
    A
<u>have registered</u> for this course <u>is</u> so high
   B   C
<u>that</u> two sections will be created.
 D
<u>No error</u>
  E

3. I thought the books <u>were</u> <u>their's</u>, <u>but</u> I
             A   B   C
see now <u>that</u> I was mistaken. <u>No error</u>
    D   E

4. <u>In order to</u> protect themselves <u>when</u>
   A   B
writing a research paper, students <u>should be</u> certain they know the meaning
                C
of the work <u>"plagiarism."</u> <u>No error</u>
        D   E

5. The police officer <u>claims</u> that you <u>drunk</u>
           A   B
<u>too much</u> liquor before you <u>drove home</u>
  C   D
last night. <u>No error</u>
        E

6. I would <u>much rather</u> be outside playing
       A
football <u>then</u> inside studying for the
      B
math <u>test, but</u> I know I will never pass the
     C
course <u>unless</u> I learn the material thor-
     D
oughly. <u>No error</u>
     E

7. This evening <u>when</u> I <u>went</u> outside to
         A   B
feed my cat, the animal <u>was</u> <u>nowheres</u> to
               C   D
be found. <u>No error</u>
      E

8. The most <u>exciting</u> part of the novel
            A

  <u>was when</u> Matilda rejected <u>Count</u>
     B   C

  Vladimir and accepted the proposal of the

  <u>peasant, Hugo.</u> <u>No error</u>
      D   E

9. We were <u>constantly</u> arguing <u>with</u> John
           A   B

  and <u>her</u> concerning their support of our
      C

  <u>government's</u> policies. <u>No error</u>
     D   E

10. I <u>can hardly</u> believe that you <u>drank</u> all
     A   B

  the coffee and <u>didn't leave none</u> for the
              C

  <u>other workers.</u> <u>No error</u>
     D   E

11. You are <u>liable</u> <u>to be selected</u> to be the next
       A   B

  <u>chairperson</u> of the <u>department</u> since you
     C   D

  possess the necessary skills. <u>No error</u>
                      E

12. We are not pleased with <u>him</u> being
                   A

  <u>chosen</u> as our new <u>president</u>, but
    B   C

  we know that we have to become

  <u>reconciled to</u> the decision made by our
     D

  peers. <u>No error</u>
        E

13. All the reviews <u>claimed</u> that the novel
              A

  <u>was</u> very well written, I hoped
   B

  <u>to have read</u> <u>it.</u> <u>No error</u>
     C   D   E

14. <u>Whatever</u> problem the players face,
     A

  <u>the coach</u> is the one person <u>who</u> <u>they</u>
     B   C D

  always consult. <u>No error</u>
            E

15. <u>The mayor</u> is a woman <u>with great integrity</u>
    A   B

  and <u>who</u> should <u>receive</u> our financial sup-
     C   D

  port. <u>No error</u>
       E

16. <u>Having won</u> the divisional final, our high
    A

  school team <u>are</u> <u>getting</u> ready <u>to play</u>
          B   C   D

  for the state championship next week.

  <u>No error</u>
    E

17. The early morning delivery <u>did not</u> add to
                      A

  traffic <u>congestion, he</u> was pleased <u>to note.</u>
        B   C   D

  <u>No error</u>
   E

18. Isolated on a remote island, with

  <u>little work</u> to <u>occupy them</u>, the soldiers
     A   B

  <u>suffered from</u> boredom and <u>low moral.</u>
     C   D

  <u>No error</u>
   E

19. The child's <u>forthrightness</u> <u>could not but</u>
         A   B

  <u>disconcert</u> the old man, who expected
    C

  children to be <u>cowed</u> by authority.
            D

  <u>No error</u>
   E

20. The <u>only</u> ones <u>who</u> oppose <u>the merger</u>
     A   B   C

  are Mr. Rasmussen and <u>him</u>. <u>No error</u>
                  D   E

GO ON TO THE NEXT PAGE

Directions: The sentences below may contain problems in grammar, usage, word choice, sentence construction, or punctuation. Part or all of each sentence is underlined. Following each sentence you will find five ways of expressing the underlined part. Answer choice (A) always repeats the original underlined section. The other four answer choices are all different. You are to select the lettered answer that produces the most effective sentence. If you think the original sentence is best, choose (A) as your answer. If one of the other choices makes a better sentence, mark your answer sheet for the letter of that choice. Do not choose an answer that changes the meaning of the original sentence.

Example

I have always enjoyed <u>singing as well as to dance</u>.
(A) singing as well as to dance
(B) singing as well as dancing
(C) to sing as well as dancing
(D) singing in addition to dance
(E) to sing in addition to dancing

Sample Answer
Ⓐ ● Ⓒ Ⓓ Ⓔ

---

21. <u>Neither the boys nor their teacher are</u> responsible for causing the situation.
    (A) Neither the boys nor their teacher are
    (B) Neither the boys nor their teacher is
    (C) Neither the boys or their teacher are
    (D) Neither the boys or their teacher is
    (E) Neither the boys nor there teacher is

22. Over the loudspeaker, <u>the principle announced that the school was going to change its attendance policy</u>.
    (A) the principle announced that the school was going to change its attendance policy
    (B) the principle announced that the school was going to change their attendance policy
    (C) the principal announced that the school was going to change it's attendance policy
    (D) the principal announcing that the school was going to change its attendance policy
    (E) the principal announced that the school was going to change its attendance policy

23. If we had left the house earlier, we <u>might of been on time</u> for the plane.
    (A) might of been on time
    (B) could of been on time

    (C) should of been in time
    (D) might have been on time
    (E) might of made it in time

24. They <u>arrived on time and were able</u> to witness the entire graduation ceremony.
    (A) arrived on time and were able
    (B) have arrived on time and were able
    (C) were arriving on time in order
    (D) arrived in time
    (E) arrived on time being able

25. He was <u>more aggravated than us</u> by the boy's behavior.
    (A) more aggravated than us
    (B) more aggravated than we
    (C) more annoyed then us
    (D) more annoyed than we
    (E) more annoyed than us

26. Playing ball, swimming in the pool, and a <u>diet without starchy foods help</u> keep his weight down.
    (A) a diet without starchy foods help
    (B) avoiding starchy foods help
    (C) dieting without starchy foods helps
    (D) avoiding starchy foods helps
    (E) a diet without starchy foods helped

27. According to the *Farmer's Almanac,* it looks like this will be the coldest winter in many years.
    (A) it looks like this will be the coldest winter in many years
    (B) it looks like this winter will be colder than many other years
    (C) it looks like a cold winter is coming this year
    (D) this may be the coldest winter in many years.
    (E) this year will be a cold winter

28. To decipher the instructions for assembling this tuner it demands the clairvoyance of genius.
    (A) it demands the clairvoyance of genius
    (B) the clairvoyance of genius are demanded
    (C) the clairvoyance of genius is demanded
    (D) it demands genius clairvoyance
    (E) demands the clairvoyance of genius

29. If the stage sets were to be designed by him, I would have more confidence in the production.
    (A) the stage sets were to be designed by him
    (B) he were designing the stage sets
    (C) he were to be designing the stage sets
    (D) the stage sets are designed by him
    (E) the stage sets by him were to be designed

30. Jennifer lined the walls of her room with shelves, making them straight by means of using a level.
    (A) making them straight by means of using a level
    (B) straightening them up by means of using a level
    (C) using a level to make them straight
    (D) making them, by means of a level, straight
    (E) using the means of a level to make them straight

31. Because the drug had been proved to cause cancer in mice, the FDA banned its use as a food additive.
    (A) Because the drug had been proved to cause
    (B) Since the drug had been proved to cause
    (C) Seeing as how the drug was proved to cause
    (D) Because the drug had been proven to be a cause of
    (E) Because the drug, as it proved, was a cause of

32. Some gardeners put dead leaves or straw between the rows of seedlings so that the ground doesn't dry out and you don't have to weed as much.
    (A) you don't have to weed as much
    (B) they don't have to weed as much
    (C) they don't have weeding as much as before
    (D) your weeding is less
    (E) you don't have as much weeding to do

33. If all of this bickering were to be stopped by you children, we might be able to reach an equitable solution.
    (A) all of this bickering were to be stopped by you children
    (B) all this bickering were stopped by you children
    (C) all of you children had stopped this bickering
    (D) all of this bickering stopped you children
    (E) you children stopped all of this bickering

34. Perched on the roof like a fantastic mechanical bird, electricity is generated by the windmill to light the classroom building.
    (A) electricity is generated by the windmill to light the classroom building
    (B) the classroom building is lit by electricity generated by the windmill
    (C) the windmill's electricity is generated to light the classroom building
    (D) the windmill generates electricity and lights the classroom building
    (E) the windmill generates electricity to light the classroom building

35. I am in the market for <u>a comfortable for long trips and inexpensive to operate car</u>.
    (A) a comfortable for long trips and inexpensive to operate car
    (B) a car that will be comfortable for long trips and inexpensive to operate
    (C) a car that will be comfortable and inexpensive for long trips and to operate
    (D) an inexpensively comfortable for long trips car
    (E) a car to operate inexpensively and comfortably on long trips

36. <u>After starting to attend the art class</u>, Edward's sketches were more lifelike.
    (A) After starting to attend the art class
    (B) Since starting to attend the art class
    (C) After the art class began to be attended
    (D) After he started attending the art class
    (E) After starting and attending the art class

37. The world seems to grow smaller as <u>they devise faster means of communication</u>.
    (A) they devise faster means of communication
    (B) they device faster means of communication
    (C) means of communication are devised faster
    (D) they devise faster communication means
    (E) faster means of communication are devised

38. The April weather was so invigorating that we did not realize until we came to the signpost <u>how far it was that we had walked</u>.
    (A) how far it was that we had walked
    (B) how far we had walked
    (C) how far we walked
    (D) how far it was that we walked
    (E) how far we walked to

GO ON TO THE NEXT PAGE

Directions: Questions 39–44 are based on a passage that might be an early draft of a student's essay. Some sentences in this draft need to be revised or rewritten to make them both clear and correct. Read the passage carefully; then answer the questions that follow it. Some questions require decisions about diction, usage, tone, or sentence structure in particular sentences or parts of sentences. Other questions require decisions about organization, development, or appropriateness of language in the essay as a whole. For each question, choose the answer that makes the intended meaning clearer and more precise and that follows the conventions of standard written English.

(1) At one time, New Yorkers pointed with pride to the fact that the United Nations had as its headquarters their home city and this gave them a sense of being a special place. (2) One reason for this sense of pride was that our city was the mecca for people of all backgrounds, from all countries and from all diverse cultures to come together to work in our backyard. (3) Another is because we felt that the United Nations had a lofty purpose: to foster peace and to be above the petty political squabbles of people and nations.

(4) But now this is not the case. (5) I, for one, have become terribly disillusioned. (6) For example, I see foreign diplomats literally getting away with murder. (7) They park cars illegally and commit petty crimes. (8) They violate laws that the rest of us must obey. (9) They claim that they have diplomatic immunity.

(10) In addition, the diplomats use the United Nations as a forum to vent their anger and to ridicule their host country, taking their money and their hospitality and showing only disrespect to us. (11) And when we try to solve the problems of other nations, they accuse us of trying to be the policemen of the world.

(12) Perhaps it is about time for us to step back and take a long hard look at the United Nations. (13) As long as you are paying the bill, perhaps you should call the tune as well. (14) Unless the diplomats of the U.N. begin to show respect for the city which houses them, they might consider that one day, they will no longer be welcome guests in our house. (15) Perhaps that will be an unpleasant day for us. (16) But it will be a sad and costly one for those diplomats who felt that they were being given a free ride.

39. Which of the following is the best revision of the underlined portion of sentence (1) below?

At one time, New Yorkers pointed with pride to the fact that the United Nations had as its headquarters their home <u>city and this gave them a sense of being a special place.</u>

(A) city, this gave them a sense of being a special place.
(B) city, giving it a sense of being a special place.
(C) city, and giving them a sense of being a special place.
(D) city; giving it a sense of being special.
(E) city and this gives them a feeling of being a special place.

40. Which of the following is the best revision of the underlined portion of sentence (3) below?

Another <u>is because we felt</u> that the United Nations had a lofty purpose: to foster peace and to be above the petty political squabbles of people and nations.

(A) is that we feel
(B) is due to the fact
(C) reason is that we felt
(D) results in our feeling
(E) is caused by feeling

41. Which of the following is the best way to combine sentences (8) and (9)?

(A) They violate laws and they claim that they have diplomatic immunity, laws that we have to obey.

(B) They violate laws that the rest of us must obey having diplomatic immunity.

(C) They violate laws that the rest of us must obey, they claim that they have diplomatic immunity.

(D) They violate laws that the rest of us must obey and claiming that they have diplomatic immunity.

(E) Claiming that they have diplomatic immunity, they violate laws that the rest of us must obey.

42. In relation to the passage as a whole, which of the following best describes the writer's intention in the second paragraph?

(A) To convince the reader that the position set forth in the introductory paragraph is no longer valid

(B) To propose a possible solution

(C) To indicate that the problem may be insoluble

(D) To provide examples to substantiate the position set forth in the previous paragraph

(E) To show the dilemma faced by the writer

43. Which of the following is the best revision of the underlined portion of sentence (10) below?

In addition, the diplomats use the United Nations as a forum to vent their anger and to ridicule their host country, <u>taking their money and their hospitality and showing only disrespect to us</u>.

(A) taking their money and hospitality, showing disrespect

(B) by taking their money and hospitality as well as showing disrespect to us

(C) taking their money and their hospitality and showing us their disrespect

(D) having taken their money and hospitality and then showing disrespect to us

(E) taking its money and hospitality and showing us disrespect

44. In the context of the sentences preceding and following sentence (13), which of the following is the best revision of sentence (13)?

(A) As long as we are paying the bill perhaps we should also call the tune.

(B) As long as the bill is being paid, perhaps the tune should be called.

(C) If you pay the bill, you should call the tune.

(D) Since you are paying the bill, you can also call the tune.

(E) Those who call the tune, should also pay the bill.

GO ON TO THE NEXT PAGE

Directions: Questions 45–50 are based on a passage that might be an early draft of a student's essay. Some sentences in this draft need to be revised or rewritten to make them both clear and correct. Read the passage carefully; then answer the questions that follow it. Some questions require decisions about diction, usage, tone, or sentence structure in particular sentences or parts of sentences. Other questions require decisions about organization, development, or appropriateness of language in the essay as a whole. For each question, choose the answer that makes the intended meaning clearer and more precise and that follows the conventions of standard written English.

(1) Sex education should be the province of the parent and not left to the school. (2) I don't believe that it should be left to the professionals. (3) The argument that the highly trained professional is best able to handle such a delicate matter of instruction, and teaching young children about matters relating to sex, is not valid. (4) Parents know their children and know best how to teach them about moral and personal issues.

(5) There are people who will say that if we put the responsibility of sex education in the hands of parents, many of them will not take it or will not do it well. (6) Perhaps we could offer parent workshops led by professionals who could help parents and teach them how to deal with this sensitive matter. (7) Perhaps then parents could be trained so that they would know how to instruct their children. (8) A parent could be given the appropriate knowledge and skills so that they could help their children.

(9) Parents are really role models. (10) Ethics and morals begin in the home. (11) A strong sense of family is needed today. (12) Parents could be helped to become positive role models and they must assume the responsibility of sex instruction in accordance with their religious and personal beliefs.

45. Which of the following is the best way to revise the underlined portion of sentence (2) below?

I don't believe <u>that it should be left to the professionals.</u>

(A) leaving it to the professionals works.
(B) that we should leave it to those who are teachers.
(C) that sex education is best placed in the hands of educators.
(D) that it should be left in the province of those who educate our children.
(E) leaving it with those who are professionally trained.

46. Which of the following is the best revision of the underlined portion of sentence (3)?

The argument that the highly trained professional is best able to handle such a delicate matter of <u>instruction, and teaching young children</u> about matters relating to sex, is not valid.

(A) instruction and having taught young children
(B) instruction, and they teach young children
(C) instructing the teaching of young children
(D) instruction, teaching young children
(E) instruction, and young children being taught

47. Which of the following best describes the writer's purpose in the first paragraph?

(A) To present a solution to a problem
(B) To state the topic and to give the writer's position
(C) To indicate that the writer has no definite opinion since there are two sides to the issue
(D) To provide a good back-up argument by way of examples
(E) To indicate that the problem presented has no clear-cut solutions

48. Which of the following is the best revision of the underlined portion of sentence (5) below?

There are people who will say that if we put the responsibility of sex education in the hands of parents, many of them <u>will not take it or will not do it well.</u>

(A) will neither take nor do it well.
(B) will not take it well and not do it.
(C) will not take it or will not perform the job well.
(D) will not be able to take it or do it.
(E) will not do or take the responsibility correctly.

49. Which of the following choices below is the best way to revise the underlined portion of sentence (8) below?

A parent could be given the appropriate knowledge and skills <u>so that they could help their children.</u>

(A) to provide help for the children.
(B) in order that their children could be helped.
(C) to provide assistance for their children.
(D) so that they could have their children be helped.
(E) in order for their children to receive proper instruction.

50. Which of the following is the most effective way to combine sentences (9), (10), and (11)?

(A) Parents are really role models and ethics and morals begin in the home, therefore a strong sense of family is needed today.
(B) A strong sense of family with ethics and morals is needed for parents.
(C) Since a strong sense of family is needed today, ethics and morals begin in the home and parents will see them as role models.
(D) A strong sense of family, with ethics and morals starting in the home, and parents serving as role models.
(E) A strong sense of family is needed today, since ethics and morals start in the home with parents serving as role models.

GO ON TO THE NEXT PAGE

Directions: Some of the sentences below contain an error in grammar, usage, word choice, or idiom. Other sentences are correct. Parts of each sentence are underlined and lettered. The error, if there is one, is contained in one of the underlined parts of the sentence. Assume that all other parts of the sentence are correct and cannot be changed. For each sentence, select the one underlined part that must be changed to make the sentence correct and mark its letter on your answer sheet. If there is no error in a sentence, mark answer space E. No sentence contains more than one error.

Example

Being that it's such a lovely day, we
  A   B

are having a difficult time
    C

concentrating on our assignment.
    D

No error
  E

Sample Answer
● Ⓑ Ⓒ Ⓓ Ⓔ

---

51. For him to be re-elected, it is not essential
    A
that his policies work, only that the public
                   B
believe that they will. No error
  C   D   E

52. The film is an excoriating comment on
            A
what happens to apparently normal people
  B
when all social restraints on their behavior
                   C
is removed. No error
  D   E

53. The government admitted the presence of
              A
the troops, claiming their being there
             B
solely as advisors. No error
  C   D   E

54. I resented the bystander interfering in
   A   B
what was none of his business. No error
  C   D   E

55. The professor whom she mentioned
        A   B
is known to all we social science stu-
  C   D
dents. No error
    E

56. A *roman à clef* is a novel in which the
              A
fictional characters and plot based
  B   C
closely on actual persons and events.
  D
No error
  E

57. The interview went well, so I believe I
          A B
have a reasonable good chance
      C
of being accepted. No error
    D   E

58. The nation must now act quickly,
      A
generously, and with imagination.
  B   C   D
No error
  E

59. They are both exciting adventure stories,
  A
but the second has the more coherent
    B   C   D
plot. No error
    E

60. His letters protesting the newspaper's
sensationalist editorials on street crime
  A   B
failed to illicit any response. No error
    C   D   E

End of Practice Test 1

Sample Essay Responses

Essay A

Some people really believe that "the end justifies the means." They say it doesn't matter what you do or who you hurt along the way as long as you get what you desire in the end.

I couldn't disagree more with this idea. No one should be so anxious to obtain something that he will do anything just to achieve that thing. Like lying or stealing or acting immorally.

Just think if someone wanted to become the mayor or the governor or even our president and felt that he would do almost anything to achieve that goal. He would hurt people, tell lies about his opponents, say things he didn't really believe just to get votes. And then, just think of how horrible it would be if he did get elected. What kind of a president or governor or mayor would he make? He would be power hungry and probably just continue lying and cheating to keep himself in office. The people would be the ones who would suffer.

We once read a play about Faust. He sold his soul to the devil in order to get what he wanted. But once he got what he thought would make himself happy, it really didn't. And in the end he had to give up everything.

It is more important to do the right thing and to behave in the correct way in order to achieve your goal. If you do everything right and you do not get what you are striving for at least you will be able to live with yourself. If you do get your heart's desire then you will be even happier because you will know that you earned your reward.

Essay B

In a popular movie about the world of finance, a wall street tycoon insists that whatever he does in order to make more and more money is correct and acceptable. In another recent work, about finance and "yuppies," a character makes the same point. That it is okay to do whatever is necessary in order to be successful in business and make as much money as possible. These two works are typical of the prevailing philosophy that, "The ends justify the means." You can do anything you want as long as it gets you what you want.

You can throw a spitball if it will result in a strikeout. You can cheat on a test if it will result in a higher score. You can use an inferior part in a piece of equipment if it will result in a greater margin of profit.

What a terrible philosophy! How sad it is to think of all the people who are influenced by films, books, t.v., and unscrupulous people in the news to believe in selfish, illegal ways in order to acquire possessions or make money or become famous for a brief time. The journalist who makes up sources for a story, the doctor who prepares phony medicare bills, the lawyer who charges for more time than he spends on a case, the businessman who fixes up his home and charges stockholders for the work. All these are common examples of too many people today.

Nobody wants to be a good guy who finishes last. And society seems to condone this attitude. What ever happened to the old-fashioned view of morality and ethics?

Analysis of Essay Responses

Essay A

The writer of this essay develops the thesis in an organized essay that stays on the topic and presents a clear point of view. The examples from politics are appropriate and serve as effective supporting material. The conclusion provides a summary.

The essay could be improved by eliminating some technical flaws and strengthening word choice and clarity. In paragraph two, the last sentence is a fragment (it might be joined to the sentence that precedes it), and *like* should be changed to *such as*. To improve clarity and diction, a number of words should be changed. In paragraph one, *who* should be changed to *whom*. In paragraph two, *will* should be changed to *would*, and *thing* should be changed to *goal*. In paragraph three, "the mayor," "the governor," "our president" would be better phrased as "a mayor," "a governor," "the president"; "felt that" should be deleted; and in the hypothetical examples "would hurt people" and "would be power hungry," *might* should replace *would*. In paragraph four, the pronoun *We* is not clear and should be *I*, and *himself* is awkward and should be *him*. And in paragraph five, since the writer starts out with the third person *people*, it would be preferable not to change to the second person *your*, *you*, and *yourself*. Removing the inconsistency would improve the tone. Also, the first sentence of the second paragraph is better phrased as "I strongly disagree with this idea."

Essay B

There are several serious errors in technical English that detract from the rather good content of this essay. In the first paragraph, the third sentence (beginning with "That it is . . .") is a fragment, as is the third sentence of paragraph three (beginning with "The journalist . . ."). An error in capitalization appears in the first sentence of the essay; *Wall Street* should be capitalized.

The style is rather informal, and this is certainly acceptable. However, certain devices should be avoided; it is better to use a third-person approach (*people*) rather than a second-person approach (*you*). The last sentence of the first paragraph would be stylistically improved in this way, as would the second paragraph. Also, words such as *okay* should be changed to *acceptable* or *permissible*.

The content is clear and the writer addresses the central issue throughout the essay. Good examples are provided in the third paragraph. The first sentence of the third paragraph captures the attention of the reader, as does the final sentence of the essay.

Answer Key to Practice Test 1

1.	D	13.	C	25.	D	37.	E	49.	A
2.	A	14.	C	26.	B	38.	B	50.	E
3.	B	15.	B	27.	D	39.	B	51.	E
4.	E	16.	B	28.	E	40.	C	52.	D
5.	B	17.	E	29.	B	41.	E	53.	B
6.	B	18.	D	30.	C	42.	A	54.	B
7.	D	19.	B	31.	A	43.	E	55.	D
8.	B	20.	D	32.	B	44.	A	56.	C
9.	E	21.	B	33.	E	45.	C	57.	C
10.	C	22.	E	34.	E	46.	D	58.	D
11.	A	23.	D	35.	B	47.	B	59.	E
12.	A	24.	A	36.	D	48.	C	60.	C

Explanatory Answers to Practice Test 1

1. **(D)** *Phase,* meaning "an aspect," is incorrect; substitute *faze,* meaning "to disturb."

2. **(A)** The correct word for countable items is *number.*

3. **(B)** The correct word is *theirs.*

4. **(E)** The sentence is correct.

5. **(B)** The correct word is *drank.*

6. **(B)** The correct word to indicate a comparison is *than.*

7. **(D)** The standard form is *nowhere.*

8. **(B)** The correct phrase is *occurred when.*

9. **(E)** The sentence is correct.

10. **(C)** The correct phrase is *didn't leave any* since the double negative must be eliminated.

11. **(A)** The correct word is *likely,* suggesting "probable behavior"; *liable* means "responsible according to law."

12. **(A)** The participle *being* should be preceded by the possessive *his.*

13. **(C)** The correct verb is *hoped to read* since the action has not yet occurred.

14. **(C)** The objective form *whom* is required.

15. **(B)** For parallel structure, the sentence should be rephrased: a woman *who has great integrity.*

16. **(B)** The singular verb form *is* is required since *team* is a collective noun that should be considered singular.

17. **(E)** The sentence is correct.

18. **(D)** Substitute *morale,* a noun denoting the state of the spirits of a person or group, for *moral,* an adjective meaning ethical.

19. **(B)** The expression *not but* is a double negative. Use *could but* or *could only.*

20. **(D)** *Are* is a linking verb. It simply links or equates the subject, *ones,* with its complement, *Mr. Rasmussen and he.* The linked terms must be in the nominative case on both sides of the equation.

21. **(B)** In a neither-nor construction, the verb agrees with the closest subject. In this example, the singular *is* should agree with *teacher*.

22. **(E)** The correct word for the head of a school is *principal;* therefore, (A) and (B) are wrong. (C) uses the contraction for *it is* instead of the possessive *its*. (D) has no verb in the main clause.

23. **(D)** *Might of, could of,* and *should of* are nonstandard English. The correct form is might *have* (or, informally, might've).

24. **(A)** The sentence is correct. Both verbs should be in the past tense.

25. **(D)** The correct word is *annoyed*, meaning made angry; *aggravated* means made worse. The completed comparison is *than we (were)*. Only (D) meets both of these requirements.

26. **(B)** To maintain parallel structure, the participle *avoiding* is required. The verb must be the plural *help* to agree with the compound subject.

27. **(D)** The original sentence uses *like* where *as if* is required. (B) and (C) have the same problem. (E) is not idiomatic. (D) is both correct and concise.

28. **(E)** The use of *it* in the original sentence is awkward and unnecessary.

29. **(B)** Avoid the awkward use of the passive.

30. **(C)** *By means of* means the same as *using;* the use of the two together is redundant.

31. **(A)** The sentence is correct.

32. **(B)** Do not switch from the third person (*gardeners*) to the second person (*you*) in the middle of a sentence.

33. **(E)** Avoid the awkward use of the passive as in (A) and (B) and unnecessary shifts in tense as in (C).

34. **(E)** The original sentence contains a dangling phrase. Since *perched* must refer to *windmill*, *windmill* should be made the subject of the sentence.

35. **(B)** Avoid placing too many modifiers in front of a noun.

36. **(D)** Since *starting* cannot refer to *Edward's sketches*, the original phrase must be rewritten as a clause containing its own subject.

37. **(E)** Avoid using *they* without a clear antecedent.

38. **(B)** The original version is wordy.

39. **(B)** Choice (B) is best since it corrects the awkward use of *them*. People are not a special place; a city is special. Therefore, *them* should be replaced by *it*. Choice (D) is not correct because the semi-colon is used incorrectly.

40. **(C)** *Reason* should be followed by *that*, as in choice (C). The other choices are awkward.

41. **(E)** The best way to combine the two sentences is to subordinate sentence (9) by making it a participle phrase modifying *they*.

42. **(A)** The introductory paragraph presents the position that New Yorkers formerly were happy that their city housed the United Nations. The second paragraph shows why New Yorkers no longer feel this way.

43. **(E)** In the underlined portion, the antecedent of *their* is not clear. The sense of the sentence indicates that it should be *host country*, a singular noun, making *their*, a plural, incorrect. The pronoun *its* is better; therefore, choice (E) is correct.

44. **(A)** Sentences (12), (14), and (15) use the first person plural pronouns *us* and *our*. Sentence (13) changes to *you*. Choice (A) is correct since the pronoun used is consistent with the one in the previous and following sentences.

45. **(C)** In the second sentence, the antecedent of the pronoun *it* is vague. Grammatically the antecedent appears to be *school*, but this does not make sense. Only choice (C) addresses this error and corrects it.

46. **(D)** A subordinating idea, a phrase that would modify *instruction*, is necessary. The participle phrase supplied in choice (D) meets this need. The other choices are awkward or inappropriate.

47. **(B)** In the first paragraph, the writer indicates that the topic of the essay is sex instruction and states the belief that this area of education should be the province of parents, not professionals.

48. **(C)** The antecedent of *it*, which appears twice in the underlined portion, is apparently *responsibility*. Although it is correct to *take responsibility*, it is not correct to *do responsibility*. Therefore, choices (A), (B), (D), and (E) do not correct the error. Choice (C) corrects the error by substituting the phrase *perform the job*.

49. **(A)** The problem presented is that the antecedent of the plural pronoun *they* is the singular noun *parent*. Only choice (A) addresses this error and corrects it.

50. **(E)** Choice (A) contains a comma splice error and choice (D) is a fragment. Choice (B) omits the sense of sentence (9) and choice (C) changes the meaning of the three original sentences. Choice (E) is best.

51. **(E)** The sentence is correct.

52. **(D)** The plural verb form *are removed* is required to agree with the plural subject *restraints*.

53. **(B)** Substitute *they were* for the awkward, unidiomatic term *their being*.

54. **(B)** What is resented is not the *bystander* but *his* interfering, that is, the *bystander's interfering*.

55. **(D)** The preposition *to* takes the objective case: *to all us . . . students*.

56. **(C)** The verb form is incomplete; it should be *are based*. Without the auxiliary *are*, the statement is a sentence fragment.

57. **(C)** The adverb *reasonably* is needed to modify the adjective *good*.

58. **(D)** Substitute *imaginatively* for *with imagination* to complete the parallel structure begun with *quickly* and *generously*.

59. **(E)** The sentence is correct.

60. **(C)** *Illicit*, an adjective meaning "not sanctioned by custom or by law," is incorrect. Substitute *elicit*, a verb meaning "to evoke, to draw forth."

Answer Sheet for Practice Test 2
Part A: Essay Section
Use this space for your essay response.

Part B: Multiple-Choice Section

1 Ⓐ Ⓑ Ⓒ Ⓓ Ⓔ 13 Ⓐ Ⓑ Ⓒ Ⓓ Ⓔ 25 Ⓐ Ⓑ Ⓒ Ⓓ Ⓔ 37 Ⓐ Ⓑ Ⓒ Ⓓ Ⓔ 49 Ⓐ Ⓑ Ⓒ Ⓓ Ⓔ
2 Ⓐ Ⓑ Ⓒ Ⓓ Ⓔ 14 Ⓐ Ⓑ Ⓒ Ⓓ Ⓔ 26 Ⓐ Ⓑ Ⓒ Ⓓ Ⓔ 38 Ⓐ Ⓑ Ⓒ Ⓓ Ⓔ 50 Ⓐ Ⓑ Ⓒ Ⓓ Ⓔ
3 Ⓐ Ⓑ Ⓒ Ⓓ Ⓔ 15 Ⓐ Ⓑ Ⓒ Ⓓ Ⓔ 27 Ⓐ Ⓑ Ⓒ Ⓓ Ⓔ 39 Ⓐ Ⓑ Ⓒ Ⓓ Ⓔ 51 Ⓐ Ⓑ Ⓒ Ⓓ Ⓔ
4 Ⓐ Ⓑ Ⓒ Ⓓ Ⓔ 16 Ⓐ Ⓑ Ⓒ Ⓓ Ⓔ 28 Ⓐ Ⓑ Ⓒ Ⓓ Ⓔ 40 Ⓐ Ⓑ Ⓒ Ⓓ Ⓔ 52 Ⓐ Ⓑ Ⓒ Ⓓ Ⓔ
5 Ⓐ Ⓑ Ⓒ Ⓓ Ⓔ 17 Ⓐ Ⓑ Ⓒ Ⓓ Ⓔ 29 Ⓐ Ⓑ Ⓒ Ⓓ Ⓔ 41 Ⓐ Ⓑ Ⓒ Ⓓ Ⓔ 53 Ⓐ Ⓑ Ⓒ Ⓓ Ⓔ
6 Ⓐ Ⓑ Ⓒ Ⓓ Ⓔ 18 Ⓐ Ⓑ Ⓒ Ⓓ Ⓔ 30 Ⓐ Ⓑ Ⓒ Ⓓ Ⓔ 42 Ⓐ Ⓑ Ⓒ Ⓓ Ⓔ 54 Ⓐ Ⓑ Ⓒ Ⓓ Ⓔ
7 Ⓐ Ⓑ Ⓒ Ⓓ Ⓔ 19 Ⓐ Ⓑ Ⓒ Ⓓ Ⓔ 31 Ⓐ Ⓑ Ⓒ Ⓓ Ⓔ 43 Ⓐ Ⓑ Ⓒ Ⓓ Ⓔ 55 Ⓐ Ⓑ Ⓒ Ⓓ Ⓔ
8 Ⓐ Ⓑ Ⓒ Ⓓ Ⓔ 20 Ⓐ Ⓑ Ⓒ Ⓓ Ⓔ 32 Ⓐ Ⓑ Ⓒ Ⓓ Ⓔ 44 Ⓐ Ⓑ Ⓒ Ⓓ Ⓔ 56 Ⓐ Ⓑ Ⓒ Ⓓ Ⓔ
9 Ⓐ Ⓑ Ⓒ Ⓓ Ⓔ 21 Ⓐ Ⓑ Ⓒ Ⓓ Ⓔ 33 Ⓐ Ⓑ Ⓒ Ⓓ Ⓔ 45 Ⓐ Ⓑ Ⓒ Ⓓ Ⓔ 57 Ⓐ Ⓑ Ⓒ Ⓓ Ⓔ
10 Ⓐ Ⓑ Ⓒ Ⓓ Ⓔ 22 Ⓐ Ⓑ Ⓒ Ⓓ Ⓔ 34 Ⓐ Ⓑ Ⓒ Ⓓ Ⓔ 46 Ⓐ Ⓑ Ⓒ Ⓓ Ⓔ 58 Ⓐ Ⓑ Ⓒ Ⓓ Ⓔ
11 Ⓐ Ⓑ Ⓒ Ⓓ Ⓔ 23 Ⓐ Ⓑ Ⓒ Ⓓ Ⓔ 35 Ⓐ Ⓑ Ⓒ Ⓓ Ⓔ 47 Ⓐ Ⓑ Ⓒ Ⓓ Ⓔ 59 Ⓐ Ⓑ Ⓒ Ⓓ Ⓔ
12 Ⓐ Ⓑ Ⓒ Ⓓ Ⓔ 24 Ⓐ Ⓑ Ⓒ Ⓓ Ⓔ 36 Ⓐ Ⓑ Ⓒ Ⓓ Ⓔ 48 Ⓐ Ⓑ Ⓒ Ⓓ Ⓔ 60 Ⓐ Ⓑ Ⓒ Ⓓ Ⓔ

TEAR HERE

Practice Test 2

Part A: Essay Section
(20 Minutes)

Directions: You have 20 minutes in which to plan and write the essay assigned below. Make certain that you do not stray from the topic, that you give specific details as supporting evidence, and that you organize your ideas logically. Remember to proofread carefully to be certain that you have expressed your ideas in standard written English.

Topic: "The squeaky hinge gets the grease."

Assignment: Write an essay in which you agree or disagree with this statement. Support your opinions with specific examples from your personal experiences, your observations of others, or your reading.

YOU MAY USE THE SPACE BELOW FOR NOTES. BEGIN YOUR ESSAY ON THE ANSWER SHEET PROVIDED.

Part B: Multiple-Choice Section
(40 Minutes)

Directions: Some of the sentences below contain an error in grammar, usage, word choice, or idiom. Other sentences are correct. Parts of each sentence are underlined and lettered. The error, if there is one, is contained in one of the underlined parts of the sentence. Assume that all other parts of the sentence are correct and cannot be changed. For each sentence, select the one underlined part that must be changed to make the sentence correct and mark its letter on your answer sheet. If there is no error in a sentence, mark answer space E. No sentence contains more than one error.

Example

Being that it's such a lovely day, we
  A   B

are having a difficult time
    C

concentrating on our assignment.
      D

No error
  E

Sample Answer
●BCDE

---

1. My brother's mother-in-law always flouts
    A   B   C

   her newly acquired possessions in a

   most boastful manner. No error
    D   E

2. If the letter was placed on the table an
           A

   hour ago, it is certain to be there now.
  B   C   D

   No error
  E

3. If you exceed to their unreasonable
      A   B

   demands this time, they will not hesitate
                    C

   to impose on you again. No error
  D   E

4. In the four years since the course

   was instituted, no more than ten students
  A   B

   has signed up for it in any one semester.
    C   D

   No error
  E

5. It is to be hoped that the reward will be
      A

   commensurate to all the effort that
      B   C

   we expended. No error
    D   E

6. Although Dolores is in this country since
    A   B

   she was a little girl, she still thinks of
            C

   Colombia as home. No error
  D   E

7. There were at least three new innovations
  A   B

   that the chairman suggested at the first
     C

   meeting over which he presided. No error
      D   E

8. The singer was oblivious of
          A

   the orchestra leader's agitation
         B

   immediately before the last aria. No error
    C   D   E

9. There chartered flight to Amsterdam was
      A   B
   delayed for several hours because of a
                              C
   strike by airline employees. No error
           D   E

10. To impress a prospective employer, one
      A   B
    should dress neatly, be prompt, and
                      C
    displaying interest in the job. No error
      D   E

11. Each successive appeal for donations have
         A   B   C
    elicited a wider and more enthusiastic
                      D
    response. No error
           E

12. Neither her parents nor her grandmother
            A   B
    is going to be available on Friday night.
     C   D
    No error
     E

13. My older brother and myself will both
        A   B
    play percussion instruments, but my sister
              C
    will sing a solo. No error
        D   E

14. If the costume is not your's, then please
                  A
    ascertain if it is Mary's or Jane's. No error
       B   C   D   E

15. The consensus of opinion was that the
            A
    time was not ripe for the election of such
                 B
    a liberal candidate; therefore, we
             C
    decided to wait until next year to

    nominate Mr. Jones. No error
        D   E

16. Fewer then a hundred people were
      A   B
    in attendance and the performers
          C
    were quite disappointed. No error
      D   E

17. I will award the prize to whoever com-
      A   B
    pletes his work with the greatest
           C
    amount of accuracy. No error
        D   E

18. Andrew, my father's younger brother,
      A   B
    will not be at the picnic, much to the
         C
    families disappointment. No error
          D   E

19. His parents' graduation gift cannot be
         A
    compared with any present that
         B   C
    was given to him at the time. No error
      D   E

20. In order to correct the problem,
               A
    a steady regimen of exercise, proper food,
        B   C
    and rest were prescribed. No error
          D   E

GO ON TO THE NEXT PAGE

Directions: The sentences below may contain problems in grammar, usage, word choice, sentence construction, or punctuation. Part or all of each sentence is underlined. Following each sentence you will find five ways of expressing the underlined part. Answer choice (A) always repeats the original underlined section. The other four answer choices are all different. You are to select the lettered answer that produces the most effective sentence. If you think the original sentence is best, choose (A) as your answer. If one of the other choices makes a better sentence, mark your answer sheet for the letter of that choice. Do not choose an answer that changes the meaning of the original sentence.

Example

I have always enjoyed <u>singing as well as to dance</u>.
(A) singing as well as to dance
(B) singing as well as dancing
(C) to sing as well as dancing
(D) singing in addition to dance
(E) to sing in addition to dancing

Sample Answer
Ⓐ ● Ⓒ Ⓓ Ⓔ

---

21. Having been financially independent for the past three years, <u>his parents no longer pay for his tuition</u>.
    (A) his parents no longer pay for his tuition
    (B) his tuition is no longer paid by his parents
    (C) he no longer relies on his parents to pay his tuition
    (D) he does not need his parents any longer
    (E) his parents do not pay his tuition any more

22. The silent movie star was unable to make the transition to "talkies" <u>because she spoke in a stilted manner and affectedly</u>.
    (A) because she spoke in a stilted manner and affectedly
    (B) because she spoke in a stilted and affected manner
    (C) because of speaking in a stilted manner and affectedly
    (D) since she speaks in a stilted and affected manner
    (E) since her speech is stilted and affected

23. <u>When the department was expanded it was clearly a wise move.</u>
    (A) When the department was expanded it was clearly a wise move.
    (B) Expanding the department it was clearly a wise move.

(C) Expanding the department was clearly a wise move.
(D) Clearly, it was a wise move for the department to be expanded.
(E) When the department was expanded, clearly, the move was wise.

24. <u>Except for the fact that</u> you are missing three pages of work, your portfolio appears to be of extremely high caliber.
    (A) Except for the fact that
    (B) Besides that
    (C) Due to the fact that
    (D) Excepting that
    (E) Excepting

25. The ribbon on this machine is <u>like my typewriter</u>.
    (A) like my typewriter
    (B) like my typewriter's
    (C) similar to my typewriter
    (D) like to my typewriter
    (E) likely my typewriter's

26. Everyone in the family <u>except I and Tracy</u> had gone to the drive-in.
    (A) except I and Tracy
    (B) except Tracy and me
    (C) but Tracy and I
    (D) accept me and Tracy
    (E) with the exception of I and Tracy

27. At first it seemed an impossible <u>feat, and with careful planning</u> and great expense it became a reality.
    (A) feat, and with careful planning
    (B) feat; and with careful planning
    (C) feat, but with careful planning
    (D) fete, but by planning carefully
    (E) feets, and by planning carefully

28. Beginning in World War II, objective tests were <u>put into use widely</u> by the Army to measure intelligence and ability.
    (A) put into use widely
    (B) use widely
    (C) used widely
    (D) used far and wide
    (E) being put into use widely

29. The applicant expressed an avid interest in astronomy, photography, and <u>he's an opera fan</u>.
    (A) he's an opera fan
    (B) he's a fan of opera
    (C) he loves opera
    (D) in opera
    (E) opera

30. A heap of broken glass and twisted metal, <u>the wreck, he thought, was</u> an eyesore.
    (A) the wreck, he thought, was
    (B) the wreckage, he thought, was
    (C) the wreck to his thought was
    (D) he considered the wreck to be
    (E) he thought the wreck was

31. Although her parents, naturally, were worried, they <u>did not try and dissuade</u> her.
    (A) did not try and dissuade
    (B) didn't try and dissuade
    (C) tried not dissuading
    (D) did not try to dissuade
    (E) do not try and dissuade

32. <u>Critics agree that Keats poetry</u> is among the most beautiful in the English language.
    (A) Critics agree that Keats poetry
    (B) Critic's agree that Keats poetry
    (C) Critics agree that Keat's poetry
    (D) Critics agree that Keats' poetry
    (E) Critics' agree that Keats' poetry

33. She was the singer, I was told, <u>whom won the grand prize</u> at the talent show.
    (A) whom won the grand prize
    (B) which won the grand prize
    (C) of whom won the grand prize
    (D) whosoever won the grand prize
    (E) who won the grand prize

34. <u>The data are not sufficient to require</u> an investigation.
    (A) The data are not sufficient to require
    (B) The data is not sufficient to require
    (C) The data is not sufficient for requiring
    (D) The data are not, sufficient for the requiring of
    (E) The data is not enough to require

35. The material <u>was highly inflammable, we were advised</u> to use extreme caution.
    (A) was highly inflammable, we were advised
    (B) was not highly inflammable and so we were advised
    (C) was highly flammable, advising us
    (D) was greatly flammable, we were advised
    (E) was highly inflammable, and so we were advised

36. The instructor entered the auditorium, glanced angrily about the room, <u>and then strides up to</u> the podium.
    (A) and then strides up to
    (B) striding up to
    (C) and then strode up to
    (D) afterwards he strode on
    (E) in which he strode up to

37. <u>If a person wants to be well educated, they</u> must be prepared to devote many hours to reading and studying.
    (A) If a person wants to be well educated, they
    (B) If a person wants to be well educated, one
    (C) When a person wants an education, they
    (D) A person who wants to be well educated
    (E) A person who wants to be well educated, he

38. The meeting degenerated into a heated argument about <u>economical conditions throughout the world.</u>
    (A) economical conditions throughout the world
    (B) world-wide economic conditions
    (C) economics conditions of the world
    (D) economy condition throughout the world
    (E) economical conditions world-wide

Directions: Questions 39–44 are based on a passage that might be an early draft of a student's essay. Some sentences in this draft need to be revised or rewritten to make them both clear and correct. Read the passage carefully; then answer the questions that follow it. Some questions require decisions about diction, usage, tone, or sentence structure in particular sentences or parts of sentences. Other questions require decisions about organization, development, or appropriateness of language in the essay as a whole. For each question, choose the answer that makes the intended meaning clearer and more precise and that follows the conventions of standard written English.

(1) Today more and more people are losing their respect for authority. (2) A reason for this may be because there is corruption in high places. (3) Those whom we have put our trust in and who should have faith in our society have not earned it. (4) As a result, our society is in a turmoil.

(5) In many cities, riots have broken out and there has been looting and vandalism. (6) What has precipitated this you may ask. (7) Sometimes this has resulted from an unpopular decision in the courts. (8) Groups then complain that they are being disen- *franchised and that justice is not equal for all. (9) They, then, in their anger and frustration, seek to break the fabric of our society apart. (10) Because they feel that they have nothing to lose, they seek to destroy.*

(11) We may agree or disagree with the methods being used by those who feel neglected and shut out. (12) Whatever our opinion, we must agree that there is a real problem. (13) Young people are taking matters into their own hands. (14) They feel that they cannot trust their elders and so they lash out against society.

---

39. Which of the following is the best revision of the underlined portion of sentence (2) below?

    A reason for this <u>may be because there is</u> corruption in high places.

    (A) may be that there is
    (B) is because there may be
    (C) may be possibly there is
    (D) may possibly be there is
    (E) may be because possibly there is

40. Which of the following is the best revision of the underlined portion of sentence (3) below?

    Those whom we have put our trust in and who should have faith in our society <u>have not earned it.</u>

    (A) are not and have not deserved it.
    (B) are losing it.
    (C) have not earned our trust.
    (D) do not have it.
    (E) are not and have not earned our trust.

41. Which is the best way to combine sentences (6) and (7)?
    (A) Has this been precipitated by an unpopular court decision?
    (B) Sometimes an unpopular court decision has precipitated this.
    (C) You may well ask if an unpopular court decision precipitated this.
    (D) Have court decisions precipitated this?
    (E) You may ask if court decisions that precipitated this were unpopular.

42. Which of the following is the best revision of the underlined portion of sentence (9) below?

    They, then, in their anger and frustration, <u>seek to break the fabric of our society apart.</u>

    (A) seek to break the fabric of our society apart.
    (B) seek the breaking of the fabric of our society.
    (C) seek to destroy the fabric of our society apart.
    (D) seek to break apart the fabric of our society.
    (E) seek to rend the fabric of our society.

43. In relation to the passage as a whole, which of the following is the best description of the writer's intention in the third paragraph?
(A) To change the position of the reader
(B) To indicate that a problem exists and should be addressed
(C) To present contradictory viewpoints
(D) To provide additional examples or illustrations
(E) To suggest a solution to a serious situation

44. Which is the best way to combine sentences (13) and (14)?
(A) Young people are taking matters into their own hands, they lash out against society, feeling they cannot trust their elders.
(B) They take matters into their own hands when they lash out against society, feeling they can put no trust in their elders.
(C) Because they feel that they cannot trust their elders, they take matters into their own hands and lash out against society.
(D) Feeling that they cannot trust their elders, young people take matters into their own hands and lash out against society.
(E) When they feel that they cannot trust their elders or society and take matters into their own hands.

GO ON TO THE NEXT PAGE

Directions: Questions 45–50 are based on a passage that might be an early draft of a student's essay. Some sentences in this draft need to be revised or rewritten to make them both clear and correct. Read the passage carefully; then answer the questions that follow it. Some questions require decisions about diction, usage, tone, or sentence structure in particular sentences or parts of sentences. Other questions require decisions about organization, development, or appropriateness of language in the essay as a whole. For each question, choose the answer that makes the intended meaning clearer and more precise and that follows the conventions of standard written English.

(1) Jazz is still my favorite! (2) I spent my vacation studying rock and roll, folk, classical, rhythm and blues, and reggae, even a few minutes of punk and heavy metal, and I enjoyed nearly everything I heard, but when all was said and done, the winner was jazz, which I have listened to for many years now, ever since I was a youngster. (3) Rolling Stones, Beatles, Dylan, Baez, Bach, Brahms, B.B. King, Bob Marley, Jimmy Cliff. (4) I love them all! (5) But in the final analysis, truth be told, I'd choose Miles, Brubeck, Coltrane, and Monk over them all. (6) Or maybe Bird and Diz, Wynton, Branford, Modern Jazz Quartet.

(7) Especially late at night, I enjoy turning on the radio to catch a show or two. (8) I also enjoy going downtown to a club to hear live music. (9) Recently I spent a lovely Sunday eating lunch while being entertained by a group of excellent young artists. (10) They were just beginning to make a name for themselves. (11) Their playing was very exciting. (12) College radio stations often program an hour or two of jazz daily, and so does several of the local public radio networks.

(13) I have a number of hobbies—playing sports, traveling, and exercising, for example—but my favorite and most relaxing is listening to music. (14) As I suggested earlier, my taste is eclectic; therefore, I sometimes find it hard to choose between jazz and rock and roll, folk, classical, rhythm and blues, and reggae. (15) But when it comes right down to it, jazz is still my favorite type of music.

45. Which of the following is the best way to improve the structure of sentence (2)?
    (A) I spent my vacation studying rock and roll, folk, classical, rhythm and blues, and reggae; even a few minutes of punk and heavy metal; and I enjoyed nearly everything I heard; but when all was said and done, the winner was jazz; which I have listened to for many years now, ever since I was a youngster.
    (B) I spent my vacation studying rock and roll, folk, classical, rhythm and blues, and reggae, even a few minutes of punk and heavy metal and I enjoyed nearly everything I heard, but when all was said and done, the winner was jazz, which I have listened to for many years now ever since I was a youngster.
    (C) I spent my vacation studying rock and roll, folk, classical, rhythm and blues, and reggae I even listened to a few minutes of punk and heavy metal; and I enjoyed nearly everything I heard; but when all was said and done the winner was jazz; I have listened to it for many years now ever since I was a youngster.
    (D) I spent my vacation studying rock and roll, folk, classical, rhythm and blues and reggae, punk and heavy metal, and I enjoyed nearly everything I heard, but when all was said and done, the winner was jazz, which I have listened to for many years now, since I was a youngster.
    (E) I spent my vacation studying rock and roll, folk, classical, rhythm and blues, reggae and even a few minutes of punk and heavy metal. I enjoyed nearly everything I heard, but when all was said and done, the winner was jazz, which I have listened to for many years now, ever since I was a youngster.

46. Which of the following would be the best way to improve the first paragraph?
    (A) Add and develop one or two examples
    (B) Eliminate one or two examples
    (C) Revise to eliminate cliches and be more concise
    (D) Correct spelling errors
    (E) Add a thesis statement

47. The second paragraph should be revised in order to
    (A) eliminate the inappropriate analogy
    (B) improve the organization
    (C) make the tone more consistent
    (D) make the vocabulary more sophisticated
    (E) discuss the tunes played by the young artists

48. Which of the following is the best way to combine sentences (9) and (10)?
    (A) While being entertained at lunch by a group of young artists who were just beginning to make a name for themselves.
    (B) Recently I spent a lovely Sunday eating lunch while being entertained by a group of excellent young artists who were just beginning to make a name for themselves.
    (C) Recently at Sunday lunch, a group of young artists entertained me, beginning to make a name for themselves.
    (D) A group of young artists entertained me recently at lunch beginning to make a name for themselves.
    (E) While at lunch recently, a group of young artists making a name for themselves entertained me.

49. Which of the following is the best way to revise the underlined portion of sentence (12) below?

    College radio stations often program an hour or two of jazz <u>daily, and so does several of the local public radio networks.</u>

    (A) daily; and so does several of the local public radio networks.
    (B) daily; as well as several of the local public radio networks.
    (C) daily, as well as several of the local public radio networks.
    (D) daily, and so do several of the local public radio networks.
    (E) on a daily basis, and so does several of the local public radio networks.

50. Which of the following is the best revision of the underlined portion of sentence (14) below?

    As I suggested earlier, <u>my taste is eclectic; therefore, I sometimes find it hard to choose between</u> jazz, rock and roll, folk, classical, rhythm and blues, and reggae.

    (A) my taste is eclectic; therefore, I sometimes find it hard to choose among
    (B) my tastes are eclectic; therefore I sometimes find it hard to choose between
    (C) my taste is eclectic, therefore, I sometimes find it hard to choose among
    (D) my taste is eclectic, so I sometimes find it hard to choose between
    (E) since my taste is eclectic, therefore I sometimes find it hard to choose between

GO ON TO THE NEXT PAGE

Directions: Some of the sentences below contain an error in grammar, usage, word choice, or idiom. Other sentences are correct. Parts of each sentence are underlined and lettered. The error, if there is one, is contained in one of the underlined parts of the sentence. Assume that all other parts of the sentence are correct and cannot be changed. For each sentence, select the one underlined part that must be changed to make the sentence correct and mark its letter on your answer sheet. If there is no error in a sentence, mark answer space E. No sentence contains more than one error.

Example

Being that it's such a lovely day,
  A   B

we are having a difficult time
    C

concentrating on our assignment.
  D

No error
 E

Sample Answer
● Ⓑ Ⓒ Ⓓ Ⓔ

51. The door had barely slammed behind
      A   B
me when I began to regret that we
   C
quarreled. No error
  D   E

52. They had not been informed of the length of
    A   B
the program or of how much it would cost.
  C   D
No error
 E

53. Please check her background to see
         A   B
whether she is capable to do whatever is
        C
necessary to assure the success of the
    D
operation. No error
    E

54. The ground is so hot that I can feel the
       A   B
heat coming up through the soles of
          C
my shoes. No error
  D   E

55. If you know how badly they feel, why don't
       A   B
you help them to rectify the situation?
    C   D
No error
 E

56. Your relatives appreciated me giving
  A   B C
them the use of my apartment when they
were in town for the convention. No error
  D   E

57. Both Mr. Blake and his son
  A
had been invited to the opening, but he
   B   C
was unable to attend on such short notice.
    D
No error
 E

58. When the stores were having
a half-price sale, it was nearly impossible
  A   B
to get a parking space in the shopping
  C   D
center lot. No error
    E

59. "Loan them your car so they can go to
  A   B   C
the picnic with us," he ordered. No error
    D   E

60. They would much rather go to the
      A
stadium than watching the game
    B   C
on television. No error
  D   E

End of Practice Test 2

Sample Essay Responses

Essay A

If you want something, you've got to ask for it, the old saying goes. It's not enough to wait quietly for someone to read your mind and satisfy your desires. Rather it is necessary to speak out and take action, to be the "squeaky hinge" that will get "the grease."

This concept is proven by the actions of a number of special interest groups in our country. For instance, if the civil rights activists of the 1950s and 1960s had not made plenty of noise and demanded satisfaction of their legal rights, who knows how much progress would have been made in the area of human rights by the late 1980s. Similarly, organizations that feed the homeless or the needy also must make enough political noise so that they will have access to government funds to continue their good work.

However, making too much noise can have a reverse effect. If the public's perception is that a person or group is complaining too much, or asking for too much, then that group may be acting in a counterproductive manner. So it is important to strike the proper balance.

With all the budgetary cuts on local, state, and federal levels, it is crucial for public interest groups to "squeak" for the "grease." Without attention from media and without money from benefactors or government sources, it is extremely difficult for organizations or agencies to exist and succeed.

Essay B

It just doesn't pay to suffer in silence any more. If you keep still, no one will know you're around or if they do they will not care. If you have a complaint you have to yell or make noise. Then people will hear you and take action.

For example, I remember that my father once told me that he worked in a factory under very poor conditions and everyone felt that their had to be improvement so they went to the boss and gave him a list of there demands. They waited many weeks maybe even months and there was no results. Finally all the men got together and had a sit-in at the plant and they made a lot of noise and then the boss arrange for a meeting and even improved the problems.

Many of us were brought up and told to be polite and not to make trouble. We were told to listen to our parents and obey our teachers. But now we know that there are times when the people in authority can be wrong. We hear of police brutality and we know that they do many things to hurt people. And parents aren't always right either or else why would we have child abuse and dreadful things like that.

I think that the conclusion we have to come to is that if we want to get any action and make changes in the world or in our living conditions then we have to make a fuss and raise our voices. We see from our study of history and current events that it was only when people went out and took action that they were able to change their society and improve their living conditions because then people had to listen and hear what was said and they were force to take action and make changes.

Analysis of Essay Responses

Essay A

This is an excellent essay. It focuses clearly upon the topic and does not stray. The organization into four well-defined paragraphs is well handled. Both the first and last paragraphs cleverly make reference to words in the quotation *(squeaky hinge, squeak, grease)* so that the reader is always aware of the citation which is at the heart of the essay.

The punctuation is accurate. The vocabulary is mature. The content is well developed. The writer makes use of appropriate transitional phrases and words *(For instance, however)*. The essay takes into account both the positive and negative aspects of the issue and then comes to a strong and valid conclusion. This is a well-written paper and deserves high praise.

Essay B

Although the essay shows a sense of organization (there are four paragraphs with a clear introduction and conclusion), there appears to be a lack of specific examples to substantiate arguments. Thus, in the final paragraph, the conclusion reached is that "it was only when people went out and took action that they were able to change their society. . . ." This statement is not followed by a specific example or even an historical allusion. Certainly the illustration of the factory workers in the second paragraph is valid and indicates that the writer is aware of the need for specifics.

There is a problem in tone. The second person "you" is used in the first paragraph and then abandoned. It would be preferable to use a third person construction throughout the essay. Errors in technical English also detract. Omission of the final "d" in the past tense of verbs *(arrange, force)*, errors of agreement *(everyone . . . they)*, and spelling errors *(their* for *there)* also hurt the writing as does the vague phrase concluding the third paragraph *(dreadful things like that)*.

Answer Key to Practice Test 2

1. **C**	13. **B**	25. **B**	37. **D**	49. **D**
2. **E**	14. **A**	26. **B**	38. **B**	50. **A**
3. **A**	15. **A**	27. **C**	39. **A**	51. **D**
4. **C**	16. **B**	28. **C**	40. **C**	52. **D**
5. **B**	17. **E**	29. **E**	41. **B**	53. **C**
6. **B**	18. **D**	30. **A**	42. **E**	54. **E**
7. **B**	19. **C**	31. **D**	43. **B**	55. **A**
8. **E**	20. **D**	32. **D**	44. **D**	56. **B**
9. **A**	21. **C**	33. **E**	45. **E**	57. **C**
10. **D**	22. **B**	34. **A**	46. **C**	58. **E**
11. **C**	23. **C**	35. **E**	47. **B**	59. **A**
12. **E**	24. **A**	36. **C**	48. **B**	60. **C**

Explanatory Answers to Practice Test 2

1. **(C)** *Flouts*, meaning "scorns," is incorrect. The correct word is *flaunts*, meaning "makes a display of."

2. **(E)** The sentence is correct.

3. **(A)** The writer has confused *exceed*, meaning "surpass," with *accede*, meaning "yield."

4. **(C)** *Students* is plural and takes a plural verb; hence, ". . . ten students *have signed up*."

5. **(B)** The correct idiom is *commensurate with*, not *to*.

6. **(B)** The context requires the present perfect for action (or state of being) that began at a point in the past and has continued to the present: "Dolores *has been* in this country since . . . ."

7. **(B)** *New innovations* is redundant since innovations means "new concepts"; therefore, omit *new*.

8. **(E)** The sentence is correct.

9. **(A)** *There*, meaning "in that place," should be *their*, meaning "belonging to them."

10. **(D)** *Displaying* should be *display* to parallel *dress* and *be*.

11. **(C)** The subject is singular: *appeal*. Therefore the verb should be singular: *has elicited*.

12. **(E)** The sentence is correct.

13. **(B)** *Myself* is incorrect since neither an intensive nor a reflexive is required. The correct word is *I*.

14. **(A)** The possessive pronoun is *yours*, without the apostrophe.

15. **(A)** *Consensus of opinion* is redundant; *of opinion* should be deleted.

16. **(B)** *Than*, not *then*, is used in a comparison.

17. **(E)** The sentence is correct.

18. **(D)** The plural *families* is incorrect; the possessive *family's* is required.

19. **(C)** The correct expression is "any *other* present."

20. **(D)** The subject is *regimen*, a singular noun; as a result, the verb should be singular, *was prescribed*.

21. **(C)** The subject of the introductory phrase and the main clause is *he*, not *his parents* or *his tuition*. Both (C) and (D) provide the required subject, but (D) changes the meaning of the original sentence.

22. **(B)** The original is incorrect because the two modifiers of *spoke* are not parallel. (B), (D), and (E) correct the error in parallelism, but (D) and (E) introduce a new error by changing the tense of the dependent clause from the past to the present tense.

23. **(C)** The pronoun *it* is ambiguous and unnecessary in (A) and (B). (C) omits the unnecessary *it* and uses the active rather than the passive voice, thus making a more effective statement than either (D) or (E).

24. **(A)** The sentence is correct.

25. **(B)** Choices (A), (C), and (D) all liken a part to the whole, a ribbon to a typewriter. What is intended is to liken the *ribbon on this machine* with the *ribbon on the writer's machine* as in (B).

26. **(B)** The object of the preposition *except* must be in the objective case: not *I* but *me*. That rules out (A), (C), and (E). (D) confuses *except* with *accept*.

27. **(C)** *But* is the conjunction needed to show contrast between the clauses. (D) confuses *feat* with *fete*.

28. **(C)** *Put into use* takes three words to say what *used* says by itself.

29. **(E)** The original is incorrect because it is not a parallel construction. (B) and (C) have the same problem. (D) contains an incorrect *in*.

30. **(A)** The sentence is correct. The introductory phrase modifies *the wreck*, and so that term must immediately follow *metal*.

31. **(D)** The verb *try* takes the preposition *to*, not the conjunction *and*.

32. **(D)** *Keats* must be possessive: *Keats'*. *Critics* is simply plural. Only (D) solves both problems.

33. **(E)** *Who* is correct as the subject of the verb *won*.

34. **(A)** The sentence is correct, since *data* is a plural subject and requires a plural verb, *are*.

35. **(E)** Choices (A) and (D) are run-ons. (B) reverses the intended meaning and (C) does not make sense. Note that *flammable* and *inflammable* are synonyms; the prefix *in* is an intensive.

36. **(C)** The third verb must be in the same tense as the first two verbs: *entered, glanced,* and *strode*. (D) and (E) fail to maintain the parallel structure of (C).

37. **(D)** *A person* takes the singular pronoun *he* or *she*; therefore, (A), (B), and (C) are incorrect. (E) contains a superfluous *he*.

38. **(B)** *Economics* is a noun meaning the study of the production, distribution, and consumption of wealth. *Economical* is an adjective meaning *thrifty*. The adjective that refers to the science of economics is *economic*.

39. **(A)** Idiomatic construction requires that the word *that*—not *because*—should be used. Therefore, choices (B) and (E) are poor. Choices (C) and (D) are awkward since the word *possibly* following *may* is not necessary. Choice (A) is best.

40. **(C)** As it stands, the sentence is awkward since the antecedent for the pronoun *it* appears to be *society* and not *trust*, as was intended. Choice (A) corrects this error.

41. **(B)** Asking a question is contrived here and providing an answer makes the essay unnecessarily wordy. To add strength to the paragraph, a simple declarative statement as shown in choice (B) is best.

42. **(E)** The metaphor *fabric of our society* should be consistent with its accompanying verb. The verb *break* is not appropriate because one does not *break fabric* as stated in the original sentence as well as in choices (B) and (D). Choice (C) is incorrect because the preposition *apart* at the end of the sentence is wrong. The correct choice is (E).

43. **(B)** Sentence (12) states that a problem exists, and the two sentences that follow present this problem which requires a solution.

44. **(D)** Choice (A) contains a comma splice error. Choices (B) and (C) are poor since the antecedent of *they* is not clear in either sentence. Choice (E) is a fragment and is incorrect. Choice (D) is best.

45. **(E)** The best way to improve sentence (2) is to break it up into two shorter and more manageable sentences as in choice (E). Choice (A) uses semicolons incorrectly. Choices (B), (C), and (D) are all unnecessarily long and complicated. Also, (B) and (C) need a comma between *now* and *ever since I was a youngster.*

46. **(C)** Such phrases as "all was said and done," "in the final analysis," and "truth be told," are clichés and should be eliminated. Choice (C) is correct.

47. **(B)** The organization of the second paragraph is weak. Sentence (12) does not necessarily follow the preceding sentences. The entire paragraph should be strengthened and more tightly organized. Choice (B) is correct.

48. **(B)** Choice (A) is a fragment. Choice (C) is awkward because of the placement of the final phrase. Choices (D) and (E) are also clumsily phrased and garbled. Choice (B) is best.

49. **(D)** There is a problem of subject-verb agreement here. The subject *networks* is plural and requires a plural verb, *do*. Choices (A) and (E) do not correct this error. Choices (B) and (C) are awkward and ungrammatical. Choice (D) is correct.

50. **(A)** The transitional adverb *therefore* should be followed by a comma; therefore, choices (B) and (E) are incorrect. Choices (B), (D), and (E) use the preposition *between* rather than *among*. When three or more objects follow, the preposition should be *among*. Choice (A) is correct.

51. **(D)** The quarrel occurred before the speaker began to regret it; therefore, the past perfect *had quarreled* is needed.

52. **(D)** For parallel structure, the sentence should be rephrased: "or *of the cost.*"

53. **(C)** The correct idiom is "capable *of doing.*"

54. **(E)** The sentence is correct.

55. **(A)** The adjective *bad* should be used to modify a word that describes one of the senses ("feel").

56. **(B)** The possessive *my* is required before the gerund *giving*.

57. **(C)** It is unclear whether the pronoun *he* refers to Mr. Blake or to his son.

58. **(E)** The sentence is correct.

59. **(A)** *Lend* is correct as a verb; *loan* is correct as a noun.

60. **(C)** For parallel structure, *watching* should be *watch*.

Answer Sheet for Practice Test 3
Part A: Essay Section

Use this space for your essay response.

TEAR HERE

Part B: Multiple-Choice Section

1 Ⓐ Ⓑ Ⓒ Ⓓ Ⓔ   13 Ⓐ Ⓑ Ⓒ Ⓓ Ⓔ   25 Ⓐ Ⓑ Ⓒ Ⓓ Ⓔ   37 Ⓐ Ⓑ Ⓒ Ⓓ Ⓔ   49 Ⓐ Ⓑ Ⓒ Ⓓ Ⓔ

2 Ⓐ Ⓑ Ⓒ Ⓓ Ⓔ   14 Ⓐ Ⓑ Ⓒ Ⓓ Ⓔ   26 Ⓐ Ⓑ Ⓒ Ⓓ Ⓔ   38 Ⓐ Ⓑ Ⓒ Ⓓ Ⓔ   50 Ⓐ Ⓑ Ⓒ Ⓓ Ⓔ

3 Ⓐ Ⓑ Ⓒ Ⓓ Ⓔ   15 Ⓐ Ⓑ Ⓒ Ⓓ Ⓔ   27 Ⓐ Ⓑ Ⓒ Ⓓ Ⓔ   39 Ⓐ Ⓑ Ⓒ Ⓓ Ⓔ   51 Ⓐ Ⓑ Ⓒ Ⓓ Ⓔ

4 Ⓐ Ⓑ Ⓒ Ⓓ Ⓔ   16 Ⓐ Ⓑ Ⓒ Ⓓ Ⓔ   28 Ⓐ Ⓑ Ⓒ Ⓓ Ⓔ   40 Ⓐ Ⓑ Ⓒ Ⓓ Ⓔ   52 Ⓐ Ⓑ Ⓒ Ⓓ Ⓔ

5 Ⓐ Ⓑ Ⓒ Ⓓ Ⓔ   17 Ⓐ Ⓑ Ⓒ Ⓓ Ⓔ   29 Ⓐ Ⓑ Ⓒ Ⓓ Ⓔ   41 Ⓐ Ⓑ Ⓒ Ⓓ Ⓔ   53 Ⓐ Ⓑ Ⓒ Ⓓ Ⓔ

6 Ⓐ Ⓑ Ⓒ Ⓓ Ⓔ   18 Ⓐ Ⓑ Ⓒ Ⓓ Ⓔ   30 Ⓐ Ⓑ Ⓒ Ⓓ Ⓔ   42 Ⓐ Ⓑ Ⓒ Ⓓ Ⓔ   54 Ⓐ Ⓑ Ⓒ Ⓓ Ⓔ

7 Ⓐ Ⓑ Ⓒ Ⓓ Ⓔ   19 Ⓐ Ⓑ Ⓒ Ⓓ Ⓔ   31 Ⓐ Ⓑ Ⓒ Ⓓ Ⓔ   43 Ⓐ Ⓑ Ⓒ Ⓓ Ⓔ   55 Ⓐ Ⓑ Ⓒ Ⓓ Ⓔ

8 Ⓐ Ⓑ Ⓒ Ⓓ Ⓔ   20 Ⓐ Ⓑ Ⓒ Ⓓ Ⓔ   32 Ⓐ Ⓑ Ⓒ Ⓓ Ⓔ   44 Ⓐ Ⓑ Ⓒ Ⓓ Ⓔ   56 Ⓐ Ⓑ Ⓒ Ⓓ Ⓔ

9 Ⓐ Ⓑ Ⓒ Ⓓ Ⓔ   21 Ⓐ Ⓑ Ⓒ Ⓓ Ⓔ   33 Ⓐ Ⓑ Ⓒ Ⓓ Ⓔ   45 Ⓐ Ⓑ Ⓒ Ⓓ Ⓔ   57 Ⓐ Ⓑ Ⓒ Ⓓ Ⓔ

10 Ⓐ Ⓑ Ⓒ Ⓓ Ⓔ   22 Ⓐ Ⓑ Ⓒ Ⓓ Ⓔ   34 Ⓐ Ⓑ Ⓒ Ⓓ Ⓔ   46 Ⓐ Ⓑ Ⓒ Ⓓ Ⓔ   58 Ⓐ Ⓑ Ⓒ Ⓓ Ⓔ

11 Ⓐ Ⓑ Ⓒ Ⓓ Ⓔ   23 Ⓐ Ⓑ Ⓒ Ⓓ Ⓔ   35 Ⓐ Ⓑ Ⓒ Ⓓ Ⓔ   47 Ⓐ Ⓑ Ⓒ Ⓓ Ⓔ   59 Ⓐ Ⓑ Ⓒ Ⓓ Ⓔ

12 Ⓐ Ⓑ Ⓒ Ⓓ Ⓔ   24 Ⓐ Ⓑ Ⓒ Ⓓ Ⓔ   36 Ⓐ Ⓑ Ⓒ Ⓓ Ⓔ   48 Ⓐ Ⓑ Ⓒ Ⓓ Ⓔ   60 Ⓐ Ⓑ Ⓒ Ⓓ Ⓔ

TEAR HERE

Practice Test 3

Part A: Essay Section
(20 Minutes)

Directions: You have 20 minutes in which to plan and write the essay assigned below. Make certain that you do not stray from the topic, that you give specific details as supporting evidence, and that you organize your ideas logically. Remember to proofread carefully to be certain that you have expressed your ideas in standard written English.

Topic: The Bible states, "There is nothing new under the sun."

Assignment: Write an essay in which you discuss this quotation. Support your views with specific examples from your personal experiences, your observations of others, or your reading.

YOU MAY USE THE SPACE BELOW FOR NOTES. BEGIN YOUR ESSAY ON THE ANSWER SHEET PROVIDED.

Part B: Multiple-Choice Section

(40 Minutes)

Directions: Some of the sentences below contain an error in grammar, usage, word choice, or idiom. Other sentences are correct. Parts of each sentence are underlined and lettered. The error, if there is one, is contained in one of the underlined parts of the sentence. Assume that all other parts of the sentence are correct and cannot be changed. For each sentence, select the one underlined part that must be changed to make the sentence correct and mark its letter on your answer sheet. If there is no error in a sentence, mark answer space E. No sentence contains more than one error.

Example

Being that it's such a lovely day, we
  A   B

are having a difficult time
  C

concentrating on our assignment.
    D

No error
  E

Sample Answer
● Ⓑ Ⓒ Ⓓ Ⓔ

---

1. The paper attempted to magnify the impor-
          A
tance of Defoe's novel's by belittling the
         B   C
achievements of his predecessors. No error
              D   E

2. If the game went into extra innings, the
         A   B
relief pitcher would have won it for the vis-
   C   D
iting team. No error
        E

3. It is all together too early to
     A
forecast accurately what the rate of
    B   C
inflation will be by year's end. No error
          D   E

4. My girlfriend and myself plan
  A   B
to get married next year, if we are able to
  C   D
finish our education by that time.

No error
  E

5. Even after Richard Cory killed himself
(in the famous poem), many of the
        A
townspeople who had envied him
    B   C
probably still wished they could have
            D
lived in his situation. No error
           E

6. When my mother first learned to knit, she
made a beautiful sweater for my father;
                A
it only didn't fit him too well. No error
  B   C   D   E

7. Hardly no one is able to compete in
    A   B
professional sports after the age of forty.
      C   D
No error
  E

8. He was around three years of age when
      A   B
his father became ill and was taken to the
      C   D
hospital. No error
     E

9. <u>Admirers</u> of American ballet have made
   A
   the claim that <u>its</u> stars can dance <u>as well</u> or
                        B   C
   <u>better than</u> the best of the Russian artists.
   D
   <u>No error</u>
   E

10. <u>During the winter recess,</u> I <u>plan to study</u>
    A   B
    for final examinations in the library

    <u>since it is</u> very quiet <u>there.</u> <u>No error</u>
    C   D   E

11. If he <u>had had</u> the <u>foresight</u> to <u>call first for</u> an
          A   B   C
    appointment, his reception <u>would of been</u>
                                  D
    more friendly. <u>No error</u>
                      E

12. Bill, not to mention his friends, <u>are</u>
                                         A
    <u>to be held</u> <u>accountable</u> for the damage
    B   C
    <u>done</u> to the student lounge. <u>No error</u>
    D   E

13. Everyone was asked, <u>in fact ordered,</u>
                          A
    <u>to take</u> <u>their</u> coat to the locker room
    B   C
    <u>prior to</u> the game. <u>No error</u>
    D   E

14. She <u>could hardly</u> <u>accept</u> the invitation
        A   B
    <u>since</u> it was extended in <u>so half-hearted</u> a
    C   D
    manner. <u>No error</u>
               E

15. <u>In regards to</u> the problem <u>presented</u>, I
    A   B
    feel that all <u>aspects</u> must be considered
                    C
    <u>carefully.</u> <u>No error</u>
    D   E

16. I hope you do not feel <u>too</u> <u>badly</u>, but I
                             A   B
    must <u>inform</u> you that it is quite <u>likely</u> your
         C   D
    application will be rejected. <u>No error</u>
                                     E

17. <u>There is</u> certainly sufficient reasons
    A
    <u>for</u> <u>his being rejected</u> by the
    B   C
    group's membership. <u>No error</u>
                           D   E

18. <u>All the members</u> of the group
    A
    <u>were required</u> to swear that they would tell
    B
    <u>the honest truth</u> even though they disliked
    C
    <u>the concept</u> of an investigation. <u>No error</u>
    D   E

19. A person may study <u>diligently,</u> <u>but without</u>
                          A   B
    adequate sleep <u>you</u> cannot expect to do
                     C
    <u>well.</u> <u>No error</u>
    D   E

20. <u>In order to produce</u> <u>a more effective</u> open-
    A   B
    ing <u>paragraph, sentences</u> three and four
        C
    should be <u>combined together.</u> <u>No error</u>
                D   E

GO ON TO THE NEXT PAGE

Directions: The sentences below may contain problems in grammar, usage, word choice, sentence construction, or punctuation. Part or all of each sentence is underlined. Following each sentence you will find five ways of expressing the underlined part. Answer choice (A) always repeats the original underlined section. The other four answer choices are all different. You are to select the lettered answer that produces the most effective sentence. If you think the original sentence is best, choose (A) as your answer. If one of the other choices makes a better sentence, mark your answer sheet for the letter of that choice. Do not choose an answer that changes the meaning of the original sentence.

Example

I have always enjoyed <u>singing as well as to dance</u>.
(A) singing as well as to dance
(B) singing as well as dancing
(C) to sing as well as dancing
(D) singing in addition to dance
(E) to sing in addition to dancing

Sample Answer
Ⓐ ● Ⓒ Ⓓ Ⓔ

---

21. It is perfectly satisfactory to give the sample test <u>to whomever you think needs it</u>.
    (A) to whomever you think needs it
    (B) to whomsoever has a need for it
    (C) to whosoever you think has a need of it
    (D) to whoever you think needs it
    (E) to who you think has need of it

22. The painting titled "Solitude" is certainly one of the most remarkable studies <u>that was done by Gauguin</u>.
    (A) that was done by Gauguin
    (B) that has been done
    (C) that were done by Gauguin
    (D) which Gauguin done
    (E) that Gauguin done

23. <u>Due to the pressure being placed</u> on the workers to meet the deadline, all leaves had to be cancelled.
    (A) Due to the pressure being placed
    (B) Due to the pressure placed
    (C) Due to the pressure having been placed
    (D) Notwithstanding the pressure being placed
    (E) Because of the pressure being placed

24. He plays the violin with ease and with <u>skill; hardly taking time</u> to glance at the score.
    (A) skill; hardly taking time
    (B) skill, hardly taking time
    (C) skill; scarcely taking time
    (D) skill. Hardly taking time
    (E) skill, he hardly takes time

25. When I was riding on the bus to school, my best friend <u>comes and sits beside me</u>.
    (A) comes and sits beside me
    (B) comes and sits besides me
    (C) came and sat beside me
    (D) came and sat besides me
    (E) comes to sit beside me

26. If the highway is widened, the maple trees <u>that give such beauty to the summer and the fall</u> will have to be cut down.
    (A) that give such beauty to the summer and the fall
    (B) that had given such beauty to the summer and the fall
    (C) that makes the summer and fall so beautiful
    (D) which makes it so beautiful in the summer and the fall
    (E) that makes it so beautiful all summer and fall

27. Lou, a tenor in the men's chorus, sings better <u>than any tenor</u> in the chorus.
    (A) than any tenor
    (B) than any other tenor
    (C) then any tenor
    (D) of all the tenors
    (E) then the tenors

28. When the first quarter ended, the home team <u>were leading by ten points</u>.
    (A) were leading by ten points
    (B) leads by ten points
    (C) is leading by ten points
    (D) was leading by ten points
    (E) has a ten-point lead

29. Avoiding fatty foods, exercising regularly, <u>and visits to the doctor for annual blood tests were recommended</u> as an important regimen.
    (A) and visits to the doctor for annual blood tests were recommended
    (B) and visits to the doctor for annual blood testing was recommended
    (C) and visiting the doctor for annual blood tests were recommended
    (D) and annual visits to the doctor for blood tests were recommended
    (E) and visiting the doctor for annual blood tests was recommended

30. In the second act, <u>it shows very clearly that</u> her motivation is greed.
    (A) it shows very clearly that
    (B) it very clearly shows that
    (C) the author shows very clearly that
    (D) it is showed very clearly how
    (E) the author showed how

31. <u>Between you and me, it is no longer so important as it once was</u> for you to pay cash for your supplies.
    (A) Between you and me, it is no longer so important as it once was
    (B) Between you and me, it is no longer as important as it once was
    (C) Between you and I, it is no longer so important as it once was
    (D) Between you and I, it is no longer as important as it once was
    (E) Between us, it is not as important as it once was

32. In the final act, the climactic scene <u>is when the mother and father</u> are reunited.
    (A) is when the mother and father
    (B) is where the mother and father
    (C) occurs at the point when they
    (D) occurs where the mother and father
    (E) occurs when the mother and father

33. There is really no valid excuse <u>for him refusing to accept</u> the invitation.
    (A) for him refusing to accept
    (B) for his refusing to accept
    (C) for his refusal of accepting
    (D) of his refusal to accept
    (E) for his refusing to except

34. I ordered <u>the sort of a dessert that no one except her could</u> finish.
    (A) the sort of a dessert that no one except her could
    (B) the sort of a dessert that no one except she could
    (C) the type of dessert she only could
    (D) a dessert no one could
    (E) the sort of dessert that no one except her could

35. The examiner told us <u>that the instructions were to be read by us carefully</u>.
    (A) that the instructions were to be read by us carefully
    (B) that the instructions were read by us carefully
    (C) that careful reading of the instructions was required of us
    (D) to read the instructions carefully
    (E) carefully to read the instructions

36. <u>After failing the first examination,</u> the teacher recommended that he come in after school for extra help.
    (A) After failing the first examination,
    (B) After he had failed the first examination,
    (C) Having failed the first examination,
    (D) Failing the first examination,
    (E) He failed the first examination,

37. After years of walk-ons and bit parts, I finally awoke to the realization that <u>I never have and never will be the actor I had dreamed of becoming</u>.

(A) I never have and never will be the actor I had dreamed of becoming

(B) never have I and never will I be the actor of my dreams

(C) I never have been and never will be the actor I had dreamed of becoming

(D) I never had and never will be the actor I dreamed of becoming

(E) never had I been and never would I be an actor like I dreamed of

38. Although some of the writers honored the picket line, many others went to work at the <u>studios, which ended the strike</u> almost as soon as it had begun.

(A) studios, which ended the strike

(B) studios, thus ended the strike

(C) studios, which had ended the strike

(D) studios, ending the strike

(E) studios; ending the strike

GO ON TO THE NEXT PAGE

Directions: Questions 39–44 are based on a passage that might be an early draft of a student's essay. Some sentences in this draft need to be revised or rewritten to make them both clear and correct. Read the passage carefully; then answer the questions that follow it. Some questions require decisions about diction, usage, tone, or sentence structure in particular sentences or parts of sentences. Other questions require decisions about organization, development, or appropriateness of language in the essay as a whole. For each question, choose the answer that makes the intended meaning clearer and more precise and that follows the conventions of standard written English.

(1) Voting is not only a privilege, it is also a responsibility. (2) There are people who say that it doesn't really make any difference whether or not you vote. (3) They say that it is almost predetermined who will win an election. (4) They claim that only those with a good deal of money are chosen to run for office. (5) They further state that poor people are never selected to run for office.

(6) In many countries, a free and open election is unheard of. (7) There is a one party system. (8) As a result, the average citizen's right to vote is nonexistent. (9) To vote in an unchallenged way, to exercise free speech, and enjoy open political debate are all forbidden by the state. (10) How they must envy us when they see what we enjoy in our country. (11) Even if our choice is limited, at least we can vote for whomever we feel has the best qualifications.

(12) And yet, there are those who ignore this situation. (13) They don't realize how fortunate we are, they are like the pessimists who see only the half-empty glass, not the half-full one. (14) For years, women and minorities have struggled for the right to vote. (15) Now that we have it, you shouldn't waste it.

39. Which of the following best describes the writer's intention in sentence (1)?
(A) To present two points of view
(B) To suggest that a solution is needed
(C) To present a "straw man"
(D) To change a reader's opinion
(E) To present the main thesis of the essay

40. Which of the following is the best way to combine sentences (3), (4), and (5)?
(A) Claiming that only the wealthy are chosen to run for office, they say that winning an election is almost predetermined.
(B) They claim that only the rich can afford to run and poor people are never chosen.
(C) Since it requires a good deal of money to run for public office, the choice of candidates is determined in advance.
(D) Election results are predetermined since only the rich are chosen to run and the poor are disenfranchised.
(E) Since it is predetermined who will win an election, they claim only the wealthy, and never the poor, are selected.

41. Which of the following best characterizes sentence (5)?
(A) It provides an alternate viewpoint.
(B) It restates sentence (4), without adding anything new.
(C) It provides a summary to the introductory paragraph.
(D) It provides a bridge between paragraph one and paragraph two.
(E) It adds further proof that the system is not working.

42. Which of the following is the best revision of the underlined portion of sentence (11) below?

Even if our choice is limited, at least we can vote <u>for whomever we feel has the best qualifications.</u>

(A) for whomever we feel is the best qualified.
(B) the candidate whom we feel has the best qualifications.
(C) for whoever we feel has the best qualifications.
(D) for whomever we feel have the best qualifications.
(E) for the candidates whom we feel have the best qualifications.

43. Which of the following is the best revision of the underlined portion of sentence (13) below?

They don't realize how fortunate <u>we are, they are like</u> the pessimists who see only the half-empty glass, not the half-full one.

(A) they are, they are like
(B) they are, they act like
(C) we are, they behave like
(D) we are, like
(E) we are; acting like

44. In light of the sentence that precedes it, which is the best way to revise sentence (15)?
(A) Now that the right to vote has been achieved, it shouldn't be wasted.
(B) You shouldn't waste the vote, if you have it.
(C) Now that this important right has been gained, work for it.
(D) Since other nations are not so lucky, we shouldn't waste our right to vote.
(E) You shouldn't waste the right, once you have the vote.

GO ON TO THE NEXT PAGE

Directions: Questions 45–50 are based on a passage that might be an early draft of a student's essay. Some sentences in this draft need to be revised or rewritten to make them both clear and correct. Read the passage carefully; then answer the questions that follow it. Some questions require decisions about diction, usage, tone, or sentence structure in particular sentences or parts of sentences. Other questions require decisions about organization, development, or appropriateness of language in the essay as a whole. For each question, choose the answer that makes the intended meaning clearer and more precise and that follows the conventions of standard written English.

(1) Almost every time you pick up a newspaper or turn on a radio, you hear a report of child abuse. (2) Personally, I am appalled by this situation. (3) I think there is no excuse for adults to hurt poor, defenseless children, whether they hurt them psychologically, emotionally, or physically.

(4) The story of Paul for example. (5) Paul came to the shelter where I work. (6) Paul was an abused, five-year-old little boy. (7) Paul was abused by his parents both physically and mentally. (8) He was actually abandoned. (9) He had scars and burns all over his body. (10) These were the outward signs of the physi-

cal abuse his parents had used as a means of discipline. (11) But worse than it were the scars he carried that no one could see. (12) Those were the scars that he had on his soul.

(13) I say we must pass stricter laws to punish parents who abuse their children. (14) Before they strike a child, parents must be made to think of all the harm they will be doing. (15) Parents who cannot help themselves must turn to agencies which can help you. (16) Child abuse is an evil that must be eliminated from our society.

45. Which of the following is the best revision of the underlined portion of sentence (3) below?

    I think there is no excuse for adults to hurt poor, defenseless children, <u>whether they hurt them</u> psychologically, emotionally, or physically.

    (A) either they injure them
    (B) injuring them
    (C) no one should hurt them
    (D) even if they hurt them
    (E) they must not be allowed to hurt them

46. Which of the following is the best revision of sentence (4)?
    (A) For example, the story of Paul.
    (B) Paul's story for example.
    (C) An example of Paul's story.
    (D) The story of Paul provides a good example.
    (E) Paul's story, for example, is a good one.

47. Which of the following is the best way to combine sentences (6), (7), and (8)?
    (A) Paul was an abused boy by his parents, who later abandoned him when he was five years old.
    (B) Paul's parents abandoned him and then abused him both physically and mentally, as a five-year-old little boy.
    (C) Paul was abandoned by his parents who left him in the shelter after abusing him.
    (D) His parents abused and abandoned Paul, a five-year-old little boy, both physically and mentally.
    (E) A five-year-old little boy, Paul was abandoned by his parents who had abused him both physically and mentally.

48. In relation to the passage as a whole, which of the following best describes the writer's intention in the second paragraph?
    (A) To provide an illustrative anecdote
    (B) To present the problem
    (C) To provide a summary
    (D) To present contradictory evidence
    (E) To convince the reader to change his or her opinion

49. Which of the following is the best revision of the underlined portion of sentence (11) below?

But worse than it were the scars he carried that no one could see.

(A) But worse than the scars on his body
(B) But worse then these scars
(C) These scars
(D) Scars that are worse than the ones
(E) But the worst of it

50. In the context of the sentences preceding and following sentence (15), which of the following is the best revision of sentence (15)?
(A) If parents cannot be helped, we must turn to agencies that can help.
(B) Parents who cannot help themselves must turn to agencies that can help them.
(C) Agencies can provide help to parents who cannot be helped.
(D) If parents are to be helped, you must turn to agencies that can help.
(E) If you cannot help yourself, then we must seek the help of outside agencies.

GO ON TO THE NEXT PAGE

Directions: Some of the sentences below contain an error in grammar, usage, word choice, or idiom. Other sentences are correct. Parts of each sentence are underlined and lettered. The error, if there is one, is contained in one of the underlined parts of the sentence. Assume that all other parts of the sentence are correct and cannot be changed. For each sentence, select the one underlined part that must be changed to make the sentence correct and mark its letter on your answer sheet. If there is no error in a sentence, mark answer space E. No sentence contains more than one error.

Example	Sample Answer

<u>Being that</u> <u>it's</u> such a lovely day, we
   A   B
 	
<u>are having</u> a difficult time
     C
 	
<u>concentrating</u> on our assignment.
     D
 	
<u>No error</u>
  E
	●ⒷⒸⒹⒺ

---

51. The manufacturers are <u>obliged</u> <u>to contact</u>
             A   B
all <u>those workers</u> <u>whom</u> they think may
      C   D
have been contaminated. <u>No error</u>
                 E

52. Because I <u>use</u> to live with them when I
        A
was very young, there has always been a

strong <u>bond</u> of affection <u>between</u> my
      B   C
cousins and <u>me.</u> <u>No error</u>
         D   E

53. Miguel's looks are very <u>similar to</u> his
                A
<u>brother;</u> the <u>family resemblance</u> is <u>truly</u>
 B   C   D
striking. <u>No error</u>
      E

54. <u>Evaluating</u> <u>others'</u> performances <u>makes</u> one
   A   B   C
more critical of <u>your</u> own efforts. <u>No error</u>
         D   E

55. The advance of the glaciers <u>were</u> gradual
               A
but <u>irresistible;</u> they crushed <u>and buried</u>
    B   C
<u>everything</u> in their paths. <u>No error</u>
   D   E

56. <u>Of</u> the four women in the <u>quartet,</u> Cindy
  A   B
has <u>the lower</u> vocal <u>range.</u> <u>No error</u>
    C   D   E

57. <u>As the result of</u> an <u>intensive</u> campaign to
     A   B
educate the public by the Health Depart-

ment, the incidence <u>of these diseases</u>
                C
among students in city high schools

<u>have fallen</u> dramatically. <u>No error</u>
  D   E

58. <u>Being able</u> to trust <u>his</u> <u>sources, it</u> is
   A   B   C
<u>indispensable for</u> the investigative
        D
reporter. <u>No error</u>
       E

59. The influence of <u>early</u> blues <u>to</u> the devel-
            A   B
opment <u>of jazz</u> <u>has</u> long been recognized.
       C   D
<u>No error</u>
  E

60. The firm is <u>optimistic</u> about the <u>affect</u> of
         A   B
the new <u>regulations</u> <u>on</u> the industry.
       C   D
<u>No error</u>
  E

End of Practice Test 3

Sample Essay Responses

Essay A

In the Bible the writer points out, "There is nothing new under the sun." What he means is that no matter how hard we try to achieve something new, it has been done before, and maybe even better. This is a very pessimistic attitude but I think he is right.

For example, poverty. There have always been poor people. Even Jesus told his followers that the poor are always among us. Today we call them street people or the homeless. We try to help them but it doesn't really matter since no matter how hard we try there will always be poor people. Sometimes I feel that the government isn't doing enough to help the poor but yet I know that it's like throwing money into a bottomless pit. Still I suppose we can't give up, we must keep trying.

There is also the problem of communication. Parents and children and children and parents have a really hard time getting to communicate with each other. We call it the generation gap but no matter what name we give it the problem has always been with us. I remember that my mother was once complaining to my aunt about her children and my aunt said, "So, what else is new?" Meaning that this is nothing that is different and has always been with us.

Human nature doesn't change. People are prejudice today and have always been. Only before they use to hide it away and not call someone prejudice but today we say that there is prejudice against women and minority and old people and we pass laws trying to make it illegal to discriminate. We can make it illegal but we can't change peoples emotions and feeling and what's going inside of them.

So I guess the Bible is right that there really is nothing new. People are people and have always had the same problems and same feelings. Only maybe today we can pass laws and also develop better ways of education so that we can learn to control our feelings so that we will not hurt other people so much as we once did. Then even though there will be "nothing new under the sun" at least what is old will not do too much harm. As it is stated in the Bible, "There is nothing new under the sun."

Essay B

In many ways it is true that "there is nothing new under the sun"; but in many ways the biblical writer is not quite correct. For although people continue to exist and act in much the same way as they have for thousands of years, there have been numerous changes and developments in the twentieth century that the ancient people could never have imagined.

Certainly there is still "a time to live and a time to die." There is still the terrible problem of war, which is at least as prevalent today as it was when the statement was written. Mankind has not yet learned the futility of continuing to wage war, of destroying man-made and natural wonders. This is perhaps the saddest example one can provide to illustrate the statement. Unfortunately, other unpleasant illustrations abound; disease and prejudice remain with us, for instance, and there is little likelihood of their eradication in our time.

On a happier note, there are things that contribute to please people as they have since the beginning of history. There is still "a time to plant and a time to reap what has been planted," still "a time to sing" and "a time to dance."

However, there are many new things under the sun—people exploring outer space, creating new machines to make life easier or better, developing ways to reproduce genetic material even to create new life in test tubes. This would surely shock the author of the statement, "There is nothing new under the sun."

Thus, it is a matter of perspective whether or not the statement is accurate. It might depend on the era in which one is living or on the point of view of the observer.

Analysis of Essay Responses

Essay A

The writer uses five paragraphs to develop the essay. The introduction cites the biblical verse and then the writer returns to this same verse in the concluding paragraph, citing it twice. Perhaps it would be better to eliminate one of the biblical quotations in the last paragraph, or, at least, to paraphrase it. There is good use of specific examples (poverty and the generation gap) in the developmental paragraphs. The writer does well to compare the past with the present to substantiate the thesis.

Unfortunately, the weaknesses in technical English detract from the ideas presented. There are several serious errors in sentence structure; there is a fragment at the beginning of the second paragraph and a fragment concluding the third paragraph. The writer should review the use of the comma after introductory subordinate clauses (sentence five, paragraph two, following *try*) and in long compound sentences. The final "d" is omitted in "prejudice*d*" and "use*d*" (as in the fourth paragraph) and the final "s" in "emotion*s*" and in "feeling*s*" (in the same paragraph). Also, in the same paragraph, the apostrophe is omitted in the possessive "people'*s*." Avoiding repetitious phrases would tighten the essay and strengthen the response.

Essay B

The writer shows a sense of organization. The essay is developed in five paragraphs with a clear introduction, three-paragraph development, and conclusion. Paragraphs two and three, in addition, show that the writer organized material first with negative details and then with positive ones.

The use of quotations shows that the writer is aware of the biblical text from which the quotation is excerpted. The quotations are judiciously placed throughout the essay.

Technical English is exemplary. The writer appears to be well aware of rules governing punctuation and sentence structure. The use of transitional words *however* and *thus* to begin paragraphs four and five is very good.

The composition is excellent and shows that the writer can develop an essay with ease.

Answer Key to Practice Test 3

1.	B	13.	C	25.	C	37.	C	49.	A
2.	A	14.	E	26.	A	38.	D	50.	B
3.	A	15.	A	27.	B	39.	E	51.	D
4.	B	16.	B	28.	D	40.	A	52.	A
5.	E	17.	A	29.	C	41.	B	53.	B
6.	B	18.	C	30.	C	42.	C	54.	D
7.	A	19.	C	31.	A	43.	D	55.	A
8.	A	20.	D	32.	E	44.	A	56.	C
9.	C	21.	D	33.	B	45.	B	57.	D
10.	E	22.	C	34.	E	46.	D	58.	C
11.	D	23.	E	35.	D	47.	E	59.	B
12.	A	24.	B	36.	B	48.	A	60.	B

Explanatory Answers to Practice Test 3

1. **(B)** The sentence requires novels (plural), not *novel's* (possessive).

2. **(A)** The past subjunctive *had gone* is needed in the first clause to coordinate with the past conditional in the second clause (*would have won*).

3. **(A)** *All together*, which means "everybody or everything together," should be *altogether*, which means "entirely or completely."

4. **(B)** As part of the compound subject, the correct pronoun is *I*, not *myself.*

5. **(E)** The sentence is correct.

6. **(B)** *Only* should precede *it.*

7. **(A)** *Hardly no one* is a double negative and is incorrect. The correct phrase is *Hardly any one.*

8. **(A)** The correct word is *about.*

9. **(C)** The phrase *as well as* is needed for a complete comparison: *its stars can dance as well as the best.*

10. **(E)** The sentence is correct.

11. **(D)** The correct form is *would have been.*

12. **(A)** The singular subject *Bill* requires the singular verb *is.*

13. **(C)** The singular pronoun *his* (or *her*) is required to agree with the singular antecedent *everyone.*

14. **(E)** The sentence is correct.

15. **(A)** The correct phrase is *In regard to.*

16. **(B)** The adjective *bad* is required after the verb *feel.*

17. **(A)** The verb *is,* a singular form, is incorrect; the correct form is *are* to agree with the plural subject *reasons.*

18. **(C)** *Honest truth* is redundant, since by its very definition *truth* is honest.

19. **(C)** Do not switch from the third person (*person*) to the second person (*you*) in the middle of a sentence.

20. **(D)** The phrase *combined together* is redundant; *together* should be deleted.

21. **(D)** The nominative *whoever* is required as the subject of the verb *need*. Nothing is gained by changing the simple *need* to the more cumbersome *has need of*.

22. **(C)** The antecedent of *that* is the plural *studies*; therefore, the verb must also be plural (*were done*). (A) and (B) use singular verbs. (D) and (E) are ungrammatical.

23. **(E)** The subordinate clause should be introduced by a subordinating conjunction, such as *Because*, and not by the phrase *Due to*.

24. **(B)** The semicolon is incorrect since a comma is required to separate the independent clause from the dependent clause. Choice (E) is incorrect since a comma cannot be employed to separate two independent clauses.

25. **(C)** The first verb (*was riding*) sets the time for the verbs to follow (*came* and *sat*). (A), (B), and (E) shift from past to present tense. (D) incorrectly uses *besides*, which means "in addition to," in place of *beside*, which means close to.

26. **(A)** The sentence is correct. The antecedent of *that* is *trees*, so the verb must be plural.

27. **(B)** In the comparison, the correct phrase is "than any *other* . . . ."

28. **(D)** The collective noun *team* when thought of as a unit takes a singular verb. Since the first verb (*ended*) is past tense, the second must also reflect past time (*was leading*). (A) is a plural verb form. (B), (C), and (E) are all present tense.

29. **(C)** Correct parallel structure requires all of the phrases to begin with *ing* verb forms as in (C) and (E). However, the compound subject requires a plural verb (*were recommended*) which is found only in (C).

30. **(C)** The pronoun *it* is unclear; the verb *shows* requires a more definite subject. Both (C) and (E) provide a suitable subject.

However, the author showed *that*, not *how*, her motivation is greed.

31. **(A)** The sentence is correct.

32. **(E)** The construction *is when* is unidiomatic. Choice (C) is wrong since it is unclear. Choice (E) adds precision and clarity and is the best choice.

33. **(B)** Before the gerund (*refusing*), the possessive *his* is required. (E) confuses *accept*, meaning "to take when offered," with *except*, meaning "to leave out."

34. **(E)** The correct idiom is *sort of*, not *sort of a*. The preposition *except* takes *her* as its object. (D) is grammatically correct, but changes the meaning of the original sentence.

35. **(D)** Versions (A), (B), and (C) all shift from the active to the passive voice. (E) misplaces *carefully*.

36. **(B)** Adding a subject (*he*) to the dependent clause corrects the original dangling modifier. Although (E) provides the necessary subject, it also creates a comma splice.

37. **(C)** Because *have* and *will* are completed by different forms of the verb *to be* (*have been* and *will be*), both forms must appear in the sentence. (E) provides the missing verb form but uses *like* incorrectly.

38. **(D)** The use of *which* creates confusion as to whether the *studios* or the *working writers* ended the strike. (B) creates a comma splice and (E) uses a semicolon incorrectly.

39. **(E)** Since the entire essay concerns the concept that in a free and open society like ours, the citizenry has both the right and the obligation to participate in the election process, sentence (1) presents the main thesis of the essay.

40. **(A)** Choices (C), (D), and (E) omit the concept that these ideas are only *claims*, not statements of fact. Choice (B) omits the claim that the winner is almost predetermined. Therefore, (A) is best.

41. **(B)** Sentence (4) offers the claim that only those with money are selected; sentence (5) claims that poor people are never selected. Thus, sentence (5) is merely a negative restatement of sentence (4) and offers no new information.

42. **(C)** *Whomever* is incorrect usage. The sentence requires a subject pronoun, the subject of the verb *has*. *Whom* and *whomever* are object pronouns. Choice (C) is best since it provides the subject pronoun *whoever*.

43. **(D)** Choices (A), (B), and (C) are incorrect since none corrects the original comma splice error. Choice (E) is wrong because the semicolon is used incorrectly. Choice (D) is best.

44. **(A)** Choice (A) is best since it is both clear and consistent with the tone of the passage.

45. **(B)** As written, the sentence contains two pronouns that lack clear antecedents. Choices (A) and (D) have the same problem. Choices (C) and (E) have comma splice errors. Only (B) correctly eliminates the pronoun confusion.

46. **(D)** Sentence (4) is a fragment. Choices (A), (B), and (C) have the same problem. Both (D) and (E) are complete sentences, but only (D) makes sense in the passage.

47. **(E)** Only choice (E) contains all the essential information from sentences (6), (7), and (8) and places it in the proper tense sequence. The other choices are awkward rephrasings or, as in the case of choice (C), omit material, changing the meaning of the sentences.

48. **(A)** Paragraph two presents an example to illustrate the main position of the writer, that child abuse is terrible.

49. **(A)** The original sentence is awkward and the antecedent of *it* is not clear. The same is true of choice (E). Choice (B) uses *then* incorrectly, and choices (C) and (D) do not make sense.

50. **(B)** Sentence (14) is in the third person (before *they* strike . . . *parents* must be). Sentence (15) starts out in the same third person, but ends up with a second person pronoun (*you*). Choice (B) starts and ends in the third person, thus avoiding the shifts apparent in choices (A), (D), and (E). Choice (C) makes no sense.

51. **(D)** The insertion of *they think* does not alter the fact that *who* is needed as the subject of the verb *may have been contaminated.*

52. **(A)** The idiom is *used to*, not *use to.*

53. **(B)** The intention is to compare *Miguel's looks* with his *brother's looks;* therefore, *brother* should be the possessive *brother's.*

54. **(D)** *Your* should be *one's* to avoid a shift in person from *one* to *you.*

55. **(A)** The subject of the first clause is *advance* (not *glaciers*); therefore, the verb must be singular *(was).*

56. **(C)** *Lower* is the comparative form, used to compare two persons or things. The sentence requires the superlative form *lowest* to compare more than two.

57. **(D)** The subject of the main clause is the singular noun *incidence* which requires a singular verb *(has fallen).*

58. **(C)** The *it* is superfluous.

59. **(B)** The idiom is *influence on* (or *upon*), not *influence to.*

60. **(B)** Substitute the noun *effect*, meaning "result or outcome," for *affect.*

Answer Sheet for Practice Test 4
Part A: Essay Section
Use this space for your essay response.

Part B: Multiple-Choice Section

1 Ⓐ Ⓑ Ⓒ Ⓓ Ⓔ   13 Ⓐ Ⓑ Ⓒ Ⓓ Ⓔ   25 Ⓐ Ⓑ Ⓒ Ⓓ Ⓔ   37 Ⓐ Ⓑ Ⓒ Ⓓ Ⓔ   49 Ⓐ Ⓑ Ⓒ Ⓓ Ⓔ

2 Ⓐ Ⓑ Ⓒ Ⓓ Ⓔ   14 Ⓐ Ⓑ Ⓒ Ⓓ Ⓔ   26 Ⓐ Ⓑ Ⓒ Ⓓ Ⓔ   38 Ⓐ Ⓑ Ⓒ Ⓓ Ⓔ   50 Ⓐ Ⓑ Ⓒ Ⓓ Ⓔ

3 Ⓐ Ⓑ Ⓒ Ⓓ Ⓔ   15 Ⓐ Ⓑ Ⓒ Ⓓ Ⓔ   27 Ⓐ Ⓑ Ⓒ Ⓓ Ⓔ   39 Ⓐ Ⓑ Ⓒ Ⓓ Ⓔ   51 Ⓐ Ⓑ Ⓒ Ⓓ Ⓔ

4 Ⓐ Ⓑ Ⓒ Ⓓ Ⓔ   16 Ⓐ Ⓑ Ⓒ Ⓓ Ⓔ   28 Ⓐ Ⓑ Ⓒ Ⓓ Ⓔ   40 Ⓐ Ⓑ Ⓒ Ⓓ Ⓔ   52 Ⓐ Ⓑ Ⓒ Ⓓ Ⓔ

5 Ⓐ Ⓑ Ⓒ Ⓓ Ⓔ   17 Ⓐ Ⓑ Ⓒ Ⓓ Ⓔ   29 Ⓐ Ⓑ Ⓒ Ⓓ Ⓔ   41 Ⓐ Ⓑ Ⓒ Ⓓ Ⓔ   53 Ⓐ Ⓑ Ⓒ Ⓓ Ⓔ

6 Ⓐ Ⓑ Ⓒ Ⓓ Ⓔ   18 Ⓐ Ⓑ Ⓒ Ⓓ Ⓔ   30 Ⓐ Ⓑ Ⓒ Ⓓ Ⓔ   42 Ⓐ Ⓑ Ⓒ Ⓓ Ⓔ   54 Ⓐ Ⓑ Ⓒ Ⓓ Ⓔ

7 Ⓐ Ⓑ Ⓒ Ⓓ Ⓔ   19 Ⓐ Ⓑ Ⓒ Ⓓ Ⓔ   31 Ⓐ Ⓑ Ⓒ Ⓓ Ⓔ   43 Ⓐ Ⓑ Ⓒ Ⓓ Ⓔ   55 Ⓐ Ⓑ Ⓒ Ⓓ Ⓔ

8 Ⓐ Ⓑ Ⓒ Ⓓ Ⓔ   20 Ⓐ Ⓑ Ⓒ Ⓓ Ⓔ   32 Ⓐ Ⓑ Ⓒ Ⓓ Ⓔ   44 Ⓐ Ⓑ Ⓒ Ⓓ Ⓔ   56 Ⓐ Ⓑ Ⓒ Ⓓ Ⓔ

9 Ⓐ Ⓑ Ⓒ Ⓓ Ⓔ   21 Ⓐ Ⓑ Ⓒ Ⓓ Ⓔ   33 Ⓐ Ⓑ Ⓒ Ⓓ Ⓔ   45 Ⓐ Ⓑ Ⓒ Ⓓ Ⓔ   57 Ⓐ Ⓑ Ⓒ Ⓓ Ⓔ

10 Ⓐ Ⓑ Ⓒ Ⓓ Ⓔ   22 Ⓐ Ⓑ Ⓒ Ⓓ Ⓔ   34 Ⓐ Ⓑ Ⓒ Ⓓ Ⓔ   46 Ⓐ Ⓑ Ⓒ Ⓓ Ⓔ   58 Ⓐ Ⓑ Ⓒ Ⓓ Ⓔ

11 Ⓐ Ⓑ Ⓒ Ⓓ Ⓔ   23 Ⓐ Ⓑ Ⓒ Ⓓ Ⓔ   35 Ⓐ Ⓑ Ⓒ Ⓓ Ⓔ   47 Ⓐ Ⓑ Ⓒ Ⓓ Ⓔ   59 Ⓐ Ⓑ Ⓒ Ⓓ Ⓔ

12 Ⓐ Ⓑ Ⓒ Ⓓ Ⓔ   24 Ⓐ Ⓑ Ⓒ Ⓓ Ⓔ   36 Ⓐ Ⓑ Ⓒ Ⓓ Ⓔ   48 Ⓐ Ⓑ Ⓒ Ⓓ Ⓔ   60 Ⓐ Ⓑ Ⓒ Ⓓ Ⓔ

TEAR HERE

Practice Test 4

Directions: You have 20 minutes in which to plan and write the essay assigned below. Make certain that you do not stray from the topic, that you give specific details as supporting evidence, and that you organize your ideas logically. Remember to proofread carefully to be certain that you have expressed your ideas in standard written English.

Topic: It has been said that "old age is not a defeat, but a victory." And yet it is extremely difficult for many people to meet the expenses brought on by long-term illnesses. The elderly, especially, are often at a loss when it comes to providing for health care for themselves or for family members. For this reason, the federal government should provide additional insurance to assist people during periods of long-term catastrophic illness.

Assignment: Write an essay in which you agree or disagree with this position. Support your opinions with specific examples from your personal experiences, your observations of others, or your reading.

YOU MAY USE THE SPACE BELOW FOR NOTES. BEGIN YOUR ESSAY ON THE ANSWER SHEET PROVIDED.

Part B: Multiple-Choice Section
(40 Minutes)

Directions: Some of the sentences below contain an error in grammar, usage, word choice, or idiom. Other sentences are correct. Parts of each sentence are underlined and lettered. The error, if there is one, is contained in one of the underlined parts of the sentence. Assume that all other parts of the sentence are correct and cannot be changed. For each sentence, select the one underlined part that must be changed to make the sentence correct and mark its letter on your answer sheet. If there is no error in a sentence, mark answer space E. No sentence contains more than one error.

Example	**Sample Answer**

Being that it's such a lovely day, we
  A   B

are having a difficult time
  C

concentrating on our assignment.
  D

No error
  E

Sample Answer
●ⒷⒸⒹⒺ

---

1. She poured over the travel brochure as if
    A   B
she had never seen photographs of snow-
        C
capped mountains before. No error
             D   E

2. At the heart of the New England town
  A
was the common, a public pasture for
        B   C
the citizens' sheep and cattle. No error
      D   E

3. Being a real estate agent it requires
  A   B   C
passing a licensing examination. No error
  D   E

4. These oranges taste more sweetly than
              A   B
any others I've ever tried. No error
    C   D   E

5. In applying for the loan, one is required
  A   B
to supply copies of your federal income
  C   D
tax return. No error
       E

6. Coming from the rain forests, we
  A
never dreamed that the desert could be
  B   C
so beautiful. No error
  D   E

7. On the following day, the blizzard grew
  A   B
even worst, surpassing all previous records.
     C   D
No error
  E

8. All but seven passengers, three crewmen,
     A
and a small dog was lost when the ship
           B   C
sank. No error
  D   E

9. Everybody in the choir except for Meryl
  A   B
and I had sung the hymn previously.
  C D
No error
  E

10. She wrote <u>that</u> they had visited Chartres
          A
and <u>saw</u> the <u>cathedral</u> <u>there.</u> <u>No error</u>
   B   C   D   E

11. Quickly and <u>in a brusque way,</u> the press
             A
agent <u>informed</u> the reporters that the tour
      B
<u>had had</u> <u>to be canceled.</u> <u>No error</u>
  C   D   E

12. Traditionally, the <u>street number</u> of a house
              A
in a Japanese town reflected the relative
antiquity of the building <u>rather than</u>
                B
<u>its location;</u> the oldest house was number
  C
one, the next oldest number two,
<u>and so forth.</u> <u>No error</u>
   D   E

13. Please ask <u>she</u> and the other applicant
        A
<u>to call</u> on Friday <u>to arrange</u> <u>interviews.</u>
 B   C   D
<u>No error</u>
 E

14. One must organize <u>their</u> time efficiently
           A
<u>in order to</u> complete <u>all</u> the assignments
 B   C
<u>promptly.</u> <u>No error</u>
  D   E

15. Though <u>well intentioned,</u> his <u>advise</u> was
      A   B
<u>usually</u> <u>ineffectual.</u> <u>No error</u>
 C   D   E

16. <u>After the fall</u> of the leader, the country
    A
became a <u>theocracy,</u> a state <u>in which</u> the
      B   C
government is <u>not separate of</u> the church.
          D
<u>No error</u>
 E

17. The <u>noise</u> of <u>him</u> typing <u>reverberated</u>
   A   B   C
<u>through</u> the cabin. <u>No error</u>
 D   E

18. In 1901, McKinley was <u>fatally</u> shot, <u>and,</u>
          A   B
<u>at forty-three,</u> Teddy Roosevelt <u>was</u>
 C   D
president. <u>No error</u>
     E

19. *The Front Page*, a play by Ben Hecht and
Charles MacArthur <u>and written</u> in 1928,
          A
<u>was</u> the <u>basis for</u> <u>Howard Hawks' film</u>
 B   C   D
His Girl Friday. <u>No error</u>
      E

20. The reviewer declared <u>how</u> <u>there was</u>
          A   B
a <u>dearth</u> of serious books <u>being published</u>
  C   D
on issues of social importance. <u>No error</u>
              E

GO ON TO THE NEXT PAGE

Directions: The sentences below may contain problems in grammar, usage, word choice, sentence construction, and punctuation. Part or all of each sentence is underlined. Following each sentence you will find five ways of expressing the underlined part. Answer choice (A) always repeats the original underlined section. The other four answer choices are all different. You are to select the lettered answer that produces the most effective sentence. If you think the original sentence is best, choose (A) as your answer. If one of the other choices makes a better sentence, mark your answer sheet for the letter of that choice. Do not choose an answer that changes the meaning of the original sentence.

Example

I have always enjoyed <u>singing as well as to dance.</u>

(A) singing as well as to dance
(B) singing as well as dancing
(C) to sing as well as dancing
(D) singing in addition to dance
(E) to sing in addition to dancing

Sample Answer

Ⓐ ● Ⓒ Ⓓ Ⓔ

---

21. <u>Noticing how close the other car was to him,</u> his hands began to shake and he broke out in a sweat.
    (A) Noticing how close the other car was to him,
    (B) Noticing how closely the other car was following him,
    (C) When he noticed how close the other car was to him,
    (D) After noticing how close the other car was to him,
    (E) He noticed how close the other car was near to him,

22. The money <u>had been split equally between the four gang members.</u>
    (A) had been split equally between the four gang members
    (B) was split equally between the four gang members
    (C) had been split into equal shares between the four gang members
    (D) had been split equally among the four gang members
    (E) had been split equal by the four gang members

23. Hardcover books usually last longer <u>than paperbacks; of course,</u> paperbacks usually are less expensive to purchase.
    (A) than paperbacks; of course,
    (B) then paperbacks of course,
    (C) then paperbacks. Of course,
    (D) than paperbacks, of course,
    (E) than paperbacks, of course

24. In the six months since the truce was declared, <u>several minor skirmishes occurring along the border.</u>
    (A) several minor skirmishes occurring along the border
    (B) several minor skirmishes breaking out along the border
    (C) there have been several minor skirmishes along the border
    (D) along the border there has been several minor skirmishes
    (E) the several skirmishes along the border have been minor

25. I have a fever of 101°, <u>so I have lain</u> in bed all day.
    (A) so I have lain
    (B) so I laid
    (C) but I lay
    (D) so I have laid
    (E) but I lied

26. The desire for public acclaim and recognition is universal, <u>yet it is rarely achieved</u>.
    - (A) yet it is rarely achieved
    - (B) yet its rarely achieved
    - (C) yet it is rarely satisfied
    - (D) however it is rarely achieved
    - (E) yet it is achieved rarely

27. The computer <u>has the capability for processing</u> all the relevant data within a half hour.
    - (A) has the capability for processing
    - (B) has the capacity for processing
    - (C) has the capability in processing
    - (D) can process
    - (E) processes

28. <u>Neither one of the twins has been</u> inoculated against polio.
    - (A) Neither one of the twins has been
    - (B) Neither one nor the other of the twins has been
    - (C) Neither one or the other twin has been
    - (D) Neither one of the twins have been
    - (E) Neither one of the twins been

29. <u>Not only reading in poor light but she warned that sitting</u> too close to the television can strain the eyes.
    - (A) Not only reading in poor light but she warned that sitting
    - (B) Not only reading in poor light she warned, but sitting
    - (C) She warned that not only reading in poor light but also sitting
    - (D) In addition to reading in poor light, she warned that sitting
    - (E) Not only reading in poor light, but she also warned that sitting

30. <u>If I would have realized how much</u> the music disturbed her, I would have turned the volume down.
    - (A) If I would have realized how much
    - (B) If I realize how much
    - (C) Had I realized how much
    - (D) When I realized how much
    - (E) If I would have realized to what extent

31. I prefer <u>him singing his own material</u> to his performances of other people's songs.
    - (A) him singing his own material
    - (B) him when he is singing his own material
    - (C) him to sing his own material
    - (D) him singing his own material himself
    - (E) his singing his own material

32. The geometrical design of the quilt was traditional, but <u>using strikingly modern fabrics</u>.
    - (A) using strikingly modern fabrics
    - (B) strikingly modern fabrics were used
    - (C) using striking modern fabrics
    - (D) making use of strikingly modern fabrics
    - (E) the fabrics used were strikingly modern

33. <u>He handwrote his application sloppily and filled with spelling errors.</u>
    - (A) He handwrote his application sloppily and filled with spelling errors.
    - (B) He sloppily wrote his application by hand and it was filled with spelling errors.
    - (C) His application was sloppily handwritten and filled with spelling errors.
    - (D) He handwrote his application, it was sloppy and filled with spelling errors.
    - (E) His application was handwritten sloppy and filled with spelling errors.

34. Only Congress can declare <u>war officially however</u> the Commander-in-Chief of the armed forces has the power to order a military action without consulting Congress.
    - (A) war officially however
    - (B) war, officially; however,
    - (C) war, officially, however,
    - (D) war. Officially, however,
    - (E) war officially. However

35. <u>For one to accept constructive criticism without getting resentful is a sign that one is mature.</u>
    - (A) For one to accept constructive criticism without getting resentful is a sign that one is mature.
    - (B) It is a sign that one is mature when one accepts constructive criticism without getting resentful.
    - (C) Accepting constructive criticism without one getting resentful is a sign of maturity.
    - (D) A mature sign is to accept constructive criticism without resentment.
    - (E) Accepting constructive criticism without resentment is a sign of maturity.

36. The day was <u>windy and cold and snowed continuously</u>.
    (A) windy and cold and snowed continuously
    (B) windy and cold, and it snowed continuously
    (C) windy, cold, and snowed continuously
    (D) windy and therefore cold and snowy
    (E) windy and cold because it snowed continuously

37. <u>To keep the raccoon was cruel,</u> and letting it go was dangerous.
    (A) To keep the raccoon was cruel,
    (B) To keep the raccoon being cruel,
    (C) Keeping the raccoon being cruel,
    (D) Keeping the raccoon was cruel,
    (E) Keeping the raccoon it was cruel

38. My sister asked me <u>if I knew Jim and will he be at the dance.</u>
    (A) if I knew Jim and will he be at the dance.
    (B) whether I know Jim and would he be at the dance.
    (C) whether I knew Jim and whether he would be at the dance.
    (D) did I know Jim and will he be at the dance?
    (E) if I knew Jim and would he be at the dance?

GO ON TO THE NEXT PAGE

Directions: Questions 39–44 are based on a passage that might be an early draft of a student's essay. Some sentences in this draft need to be revised or rewritten to make them both clear and correct. Read the passage carefully; then answer the questions that follow it. Some questions require decisions about diction, usage, tone, or sentence structure in particular sentences or parts of sentences. Other questions require decisions about organization, development, or appropriateness of language in the essay as a whole. For each question, choose the answer that makes the intended meaning clearer and more precise and that follows the conventions of standard written English.

(1) Advocates of a student dress code maintain that proper attire and proper behavior are interrelated. (2) If a student dresses correctly, they will also behave correctly. (3) At least, that's what is claimed.

(4) I do not believe that this is a valid assumption. (5) I know many young people who come to class in a very informal fashion. (6) They wear sweat suits or cut-off jeans. (7) Sometimes they dress so sloppily that teachers or their peers make remarks to them. (8) And yet their grades are quite acceptable, or often even more than acceptable. (9) I feel that as long as a person performs well academically, the way they dress should be of no concern to others.

(10) I suppose that one day psychologists will conduct studies to test whether or not attire affects behavior. (11) If these studies prove that poor attire results in poor behavior, then school administrators will be justified in trying to establish and enforce a dress code. (12) But until that day comes, dress the way you feel most comfortable.

39. Which of the following is the best way to combine sentences (2) and (3)?
    (A) If you dress well, you will behave well, at least so they say.
    (B) They claim that if a student dresses correctly, they will also behave correctly.
    (C) They claim that students who dress well also behave well.
    (D) As claimed by them, correct dress and correct behavior go hand-in-hand.
    (E) At least they claim that to dress correctly means you will behave correctly.

40. Which of the following best describes the chief purpose of sentence (4)?
    (A) To change the opinion of the reader
    (B) To prepare the reader for a second point of view
    (C) To offer an illustration or example
    (D) To provide a partial summary
    (E) To help the reader evaluate paragraph one

41. Which of the following is the best way to combine sentences (5) and (6)?
    (A) I know many people who come to class dressed very informally in sweats or cut-off jeans.
    (B) I know many students who dress informally, they even wear sweat suits or cut-off jeans.
    (C) Many students I know come to class in sweats or jeans, this is informal dress.
    (D) Students come to class dressed in sweats or other ways.
    (E) If there are students who come to class dressed informally, wearing sweat suits or cut-off jeans.

42. Which of the following best describes the purpose of paragraph two?
    (A) To provide a transition
    (B) To continue the philosophy of the first paragraph
    (C) To summarize the material previously offered
    (D) To present material opposing that already presented
    (E) To offer two diametrically opposing opinions

43. Which of the following is the best revision of the underlined portion of sentence (9) below?

I feel that as long as a person performs well academically, <u>the way they dress should be of no concern to others.</u>

(A) how they dress should be of no concern to others.

(B) the way they dress should not concern others.

(C) their dress should be of no concern to others.

(D) what they wear or how they dress should be their own concern.

(E) the way he dresses should be of no concern to others.

44. Considering the sentences preceding it, which of the following is the best revision of sentence (12)?

(A) But until that day comes, students should dress the way that is most comfortable for them.

(B) But until that day, stop deciding on a dress code for students.

(C) But until that day comes, don't tell students how to dress.

(D) Wait until that day to tell students how to dress.

(E) Until that day, don't attempt to enforce a dress code or regulate school attire.

GO ON TO THE NEXT PAGE

Directions: Questions 45–50 are based on a passage that might be an early draft of a student's essay. Some sentences in this draft need to be revised or rewritten to make them both clear and correct. Read the passage carefully; then answer the questions that follow it. Some questions require decisions about diction, usage, tone, or sentence structure in particular sentences or parts of sentences. Other questions require decisions about organization, development, or appropriateness of language in the essay as a whole. For each question, choose the answer that makes the intended meaning clearer and more precise and that follows the conventions of standard written English.

(1) Everybody is talking about gun control. (2) Some people say that according to the Bill of Rights, every person is allowed to carry a gun. (3) Others say that if you allow guns to be placed in the hands of every citizen, the crime rate will go up.

(4) I think that each person should be thoroughly investigated before they are allowed to own a gun. (5) I know that the rifle associations and all the hunting groups would not agree, but I do. (6) Just think what would happen if each family had a gun. (7) Children and teenagers would begin to experiment with these weapons. (8) At first, it would be fun. (9) But then

they would put these guns to use, to commit armed robberies, petty thievery, murdering, and killing. (10) We would soon turn all our major cities into a replica of Dodge City and there would be chaos and lawlessness.

(11) If a person has a legitimate need to own a gun, then he should get a permit. (12) This would allow the authorities time to investigate the background of the person who wants to own a gun. (13) Don't put guns in the hands of potential criminals, but screen each person carefully. (14) Perhaps this way we will lessen the amount of crimes that plague our cities and also do away with many accidental shootings.

45. Which of the following choices below is the best way of combining sentences (2) and (3)?
(A) There are some people who say that every person is entitled because of the Bill of Rights to possess a gun, others say that the crime rate will go up if guns are placed in the hands of every citizen.
(B) There are those who say that the Bill of Rights entitles every person to bear firearms; others maintain that the crime rate will rise if guns are placed in the hands of every citizen.
(C) Allowing guns in the hands of every citizen, contrary to the Bill of Rights which states that every person should be allowed to bear arms, will cause the crime rate to rise.
(D) Some people say that the Bill of Rights gives each person the ability to bear arms, others say that the crime rate will go up if this happens.
(E) There are some who say that the crime rate will be affected by allowing us to bear arms, while others claim that the Bill of Rights addresses this issue.

46. Which of the following is the best revision of the underlined portion of sentence (4) below?

I think that each person should be thoroughly investigated <u>before they are allowed to own a gun.</u>

(A) prior to their owning a gun.
(B) before a gun is issued to them.
(C) before receiving permission to own a gun.
(D) prior to the receipt of permission for them to own a gun.
(E) before they may possess a gun.

47. Which of the following best describes the purpose of paragraph one?
(A) To state the writer's opinion on the issue
(B) To propose possible solutions to a difficult problem
(C) To cause the reader to alter his opinion
(D) To show two different points of view
(E) To offer two cogent illustrations

48. Which of the following is the best revision of the underlined portion of sentence (9) below?

But then they would put these guns to use, <u>to commit armed robberies, petty thievery, murdering, and killing.</u>

(A) to commit armed robbery, petty theft, and murdering.

(B) committing armed robbery, petty thievering, and for murdering.

(C) to commit robbery, thievery, murder, and killing.

(D) for robbing, thieving, and murder.

(E) to commit armed robberies, petty thievery, and murder.

49. In the context of the sentences preceding and following sentence (13), which of the following is the best revision of sentence (13)?

(A) Don't allow potential criminals to own guns, but let each person be screened carefully.

(B) Guns should not be placed in the hands of potential criminals, each person being carefully screened.

(C) Instead of putting guns in the hands of potential criminals, screen each person carefully.

(D) Guns should not be put in the hands of potential criminals; rather, each person should be screened carefully.

(E) Guns should not be placed in the hand of a potential criminal; but they should be carefully screened.

50. Which of the following is the best revision of the underlined portion of sentence (14) below?

Perhaps this way <u>we will lessen the amount of crimes that plague</u> our cities and also do away with many accidental shootings.

(A) we will lessen the number of crimes that plague

(B) they will shorten the number of crimes which plague

(C) we will decrease the amount of crimes which beset

(D) we will alleviate the amount of crimes that plague

(E) we will lessen the amount of criminal acts that plague

GO ON TO THE NEXT PAGE

Directions: Some of the sentences below contain an error in grammar, usage, word choice, or idiom. Other sentences are correct. Parts of each sentence are underlined and lettered. The error, if there is one, is contained in one of the underlined parts of the sentence. Assume that all other parts of the sentence are correct and cannot be changed. For each sentence, select the one underlined part that must be changed to make the sentence correct and mark its letter on your answer sheet. If there is no error in a sentence, mark answer space E. No sentence contains more than one error.

Example

<u>Being that</u> <u>it's</u> such a lovely day, we
    A   B

<u>are</u> <u>having</u> a difficult time
         C

<u>concentrating</u> on our assignment.
         D

<u>No error</u>
  E

Sample Answer

● Ⓑ Ⓒ Ⓓ Ⓔ

---

51. The <u>acquisition</u> of a new building, along
        A

    with <u>several</u> less expensive issues, <u>are</u> going
         B   C

    to be voted on <u>at</u> the next executive com-
              D

    mittee meeting. <u>No error</u>
              E

52. The <u>college refusing</u> to dismiss the
        A

    <u>controversial</u> professor, despite pressure
      B

    <u>from the community,</u> <u>is</u> an example of
        C   D

    integrity. <u>No error</u>
          E

53. <u>No one</u> among the students <u>was</u> more
    A   B

    <u>disgruntled</u> than <u>her</u> when the assignment
      C   D

    was handed out. <u>No error</u>
              E

54. The argument <u>was that</u> actual or
            A

    <u>potential</u> competition would keep prices
      B

    low and the quality of <u>goods and services</u>
                    C

    <u>would be</u> high. <u>No error</u>
      D   E

55. Michelle, <u>although not</u> the <u>youngest,</u> is
          A   B

    the smallest <u>of any girl</u> in her
              C

    <u>kindergarten class.</u> <u>No error</u>
      D   E

56. Although spring <u>is</u> <u>well advanced,</u>
            A   B

    patches of old snow could <u>still</u> be seen
                 C

    <u>among</u> the evergreens. <u>No error</u>
      D   E

57. <u>Most</u> people spend their evenings
    A

    <u>watching</u> television, an activity which often
      B

    <u>anesthetizes</u> the brain, rather than reading
      C

    good books, an activity which <u>exercises</u> the
                     D

    brain. <u>No error</u>
        E

58. The <u>reason for</u> the <u>postponement of</u>
        A   B

    today's meeting is <u>because of</u> the <u>ten-inch</u>
              C   D

    snowfall. <u>No error</u>
          E

59. A <u>fresh coat</u> of paint, the first in many
       A
   years, <u>improving</u> the appearance of the
                B
   <u>dilapidated</u> house <u>considerably.</u> <u>No error</u>
       C   D   E

60. I <u>had</u> <u>barely</u> returned to my seat when the
      A   B
   <u>third act</u> <u>begun.</u> <u>No error</u>
       C   D   E

End of Practice Test 4

Sample Essay Responses

Essay A

We are all living longer thanks to medical knowledge, and perhaps we should be grateful for this. But I am not at all sure this is true. Sometimes I feel that living longer presents many problems.

For example, I know that my friends grandmother is now in a nursing home where she is suffering a slow death. Each week the family pays huge amounts of money to keep her in the home. Soon all of her savings will be gone and her husband will be reduced to living on welfare if he survives. This is only one case but there are many others.

The goverment should step in and assist. People who have worked all of their lives and have paid taxes should expect some help in their final years of live. Help in the way of additional money would be of great emotional and economic value. We provide social security it is true, but this is not enough to cover unusual medical expenses. We cannot desert these victims of old age when they are ill. We must help.

I urge the goverment to help provide funds to cover home care and to relieve our ill seniors of the worry and dispair that comes from catastrophic illness. We know that the physical pain they bear is great. Lets at least take away some of the economic hurt.

Essay B

The Federal government should definitely provide enough insurance coverage so that families or individuals face with the problem of long-term catastrophic illness will be able to meet the rising cost of health care. Without government assistance, many people today are unable to provide proper care for seriously sick relatives, and as the population of older people increases, the problem will only get worse.

Right now my cousins are faced with a problem that is a good illustration of the need for a better health care program. Their mother has been ill for nearly a year, suffering from heart disease and diabetes. First she was in the hospital, then in a nursing home. Medicare covered a lot of her expenses at first, but not all. Later, the family had to pay from their own savings, and when their funds got low, they took her out of the hospital. Besides, she was not really so happy there, and they missed her too.

At home my cousins have a nurse, which is very expensive. They both work so they need someone to look after mother. But again they are hurting for money and are getting worry about what to do. If they had government coverage, they could keep her at home and take good care of her for as long as it takes.

In conclusion, my observation of this very sad situation proves that the federal government should help people who have long-term illnesses.

Analysis of Essay Responses

Essay A

This is a well-organized four-paragraph response. The writer provides a good introduction which presents the topic and a strong conclusion to summarize the position taken. In addition, in the second paragraph an example is offered to illustrate the problem. The vocabulary and sentence structure are good, as is the somewhat emotional tone.

The few spelling errors (*government, live, despair*) and the omissions of apostrophes (*friends grandmother, lets*) could be corrected through careful revision. The closing sentence, although effective, would be better phrased by avoiding the address to the reader and maintaining a third person approach. A possible revision could be: "The federal government should at least take away some of the economic hurt."

Essay B

This is an interesting and well-written essay. It begins with a strong statement of the author's thesis and employs a two-paragraph personal example to support its view. The writer demonstrates an understanding of the question and an ability to organize a coherent and logical response.

Although the essay is developed in some depth, it would appear that the conclusion is somewhat skimpy. Perhaps the writer might have budgeted the allotted time more effectively to provide for an additional sentence in the final paragraph. In addition, the concluding sentence of paragraph two might have been deleted and more careful proofreading might have eliminated the two ending errors (*face-faced* in paragraph one; *worry-worried* in paragraph three).

Answer Key to Practice Test 4

1.	A	13.	A	25.	A	37.	D	49.	D
2.	E	14.	A	26.	C	38.	C	50.	A
3.	C	15.	B	27.	D	39.	C	51.	C
4.	A	16.	D	28.	A	40.	B	52.	A
5.	B	17.	B	29.	C	41.	A	53.	D
6.	E	18.	E	30.	C	42.	D	54.	D
7.	C	19.	A	31.	E	43.	E	55.	C
8.	B	20.	A	32.	E	44.	A	56.	A
9.	C	21.	C	33.	C	45.	B	57.	E
10.	B	22.	D	34.	D	46.	C	58.	C
11.	A	23.	A	35.	E	47.	D	59.	B
12.	E	24.	C	36.	B	48.	E	60.	D

Explanatory Answers to Practice Test 4

1. **(A)** The correct verb is *to pore over*, meaning "to study carefully."

2. **(E)** The sentence is correct.

3. **(C)** The subject is *being a real estate agent*. The pronoun *it* is superfluous.

4. **(A)** Since *taste* is a verb referring to one of the senses, it should be modified by an adjective *(sweeter)*, not an adverb *(more sweetly)*.

5. **(B)** *You are required* is needed to agree with *your tax return*.

6. **(E)** The sentence is correct.

7. **(C)** To compare weather conditions for two days, use the comparative *worse*.

8. **(B)** When *all* refers to the total number of persons or things in a group, it takes a plural verb: *All . . . were lost.*

9. **(C)** The preposition *except for* takes an objective pronoun: *except for Meryl and me.*

10. **(B)** Since *wrote* is past tense, the events that preceded the writing must be described in the past perfect: *had visited* and *had seen.*

11. **(A)** Use the adverb *brusquely* to parallel the adverb *quickly.*

12. **(E)** The sentence is correct.

13. **(A)** The object of the verb *ask* must be in the objective case; *she*, the nominative case, must be replaced by *her.*

14. **(A)** A singular possessive pronoun *(one's, his, or her)* is required to agree with the singular subject *one.*

15. **(B)** The sentence requires the noun *advice*, not the verb *advise.*

16. **(D)** As an adjective and as a verb, *separate* uses *from*: The government is not separate *from* the church.

17. **(B)** The noise was not of *him* but of *his typing.*

18. **(E)** The sentence is correct.

19. **(A)** The phrase *and written* should simply be *written.*

20. **(A)** The reviewer declared *that* (not *how*) there was a dearth of serious books.

21. **(C)** The sentence should be rephrased so that it does not seem as if *his hands* were *noticing*. Although (E) corrects the misplaced modifier, it creates a run-on sentence.

22. **(D)** The correct word is *among* (not *between*) the four gang members.

23. **(A)** The sentence is correct.

24. **(C)** The original sentence lacks a comlete verb in the main clause. Both (C) and (E) provide a verb that agrees with the subject, but (E) changes the meaning of the original sentence.

25. **(A)** The sentence is correct. *So* establishes the cause-effect relationship; *have lain* is the present perfect form of *to lie.*

26. **(C)** The *it* does not refer to acclaim and recognition, which could be *achieved. It* refers to *desire*, which is either *satisfied* or *not satisfied.*

27. **(D)** The original uses five words where two will do.

28. **(A)** *Neither one* is singular and takes the singular verb form *has been.*

29. **(C)** The original idea poses two problems in parallel structure: (1) The two warnings must branch off grammatically from the subject that *warns.* (2) If the *not only* correlative form is used, it should be balanced by a phrase like *but also.* Only (C) meets both requirements.

30. **(C)** The sentence deals with a condition that is not a fact but a possibility. The verb used to express the condition contrary to fact should be in the subjunctive mood; the verb used to explain the possible conclusion should be in the conditional mood. The first clause should read: *Had I realized* or *If I had realized.*

31. **(E)** If the *material* and the *performances* are his, so is the singing: *his* singing.

32. **(E)** The design and the fabrics are being compared. The verb form should be parallel, as in (E).

33. **(C)** Parallel ideas should be expressed in parallel form. If the application had two faults, they should be expressed in parallel form. (B) contains a faulty antecedent for *it.* (D) contains a comma splice. (E) fails to use commas.

34. **(D)** The original (A) is a run-on sentence. (B) correctly separates the clauses but incorrectly adds a comma before *officially.* (C) creates a comma splice. (E) omits the comma required after *however.* (D) resolves all problems. It assigns *officially* to the President's powers, it puts *however* in the right place, and it uses the punctuation required when such an adverb is tucked inside the sentence.

35. **(E)** The original sentence takes 16 words to say what (E) says in 10 words.

36. **(B)** *Windy* and *cold* can modify *day*, but *snowed continuously* cannot; therefore, (A) and (C) are incorrect. (D) and (E) are illogical. (B) is both correct and logical.

37. **(D)** The most effective means of phrasing this sentence is to use two parallel clauses. Since the subject of the second clause is *letting it go*, the best subject for the first clause is *keeping the raccoon.* The addition of the pronoun *it* in choice (E) makes this version incorrect.

38. **(C)** An indirect question ends with a period, not a question mark, so eliminate choices (D) and (E). Of the remaining choices, only (C) is consistent in the tense of the verbs used (*asked, knew, would be*).

39. **(C)** Choice (A) switches unnecessarily to the second person (*you*). Choice (B) has an agreement problem, using the plural pronoun *they* to refer to the singular noun *student*. Choices (D) and (E) are awkward. Choice (C) is best.

40. **(B)** Sentence (4) states that the material presented in the first paragraph, that a dress code is important, may not be valid. This paves the way for the presentation of another point of view.

41. **(A)** Choices (B) and (C) contain comma-splice errors. Choice (E) is a fragment. Choice (D) is awkward and omits details. Choice (A) is best.

42. **(D)** Paragraph one presents the opinion of those who favor a dress code. Paragraph two presents arguments against a dress code. Since paragraph two offers material opposing that already presented, choice (D) is best.

43. **(E)** The antecedent of *they* appears to be *a person*, but *they* is a plural pronoun and *person* is a singular noun. Choices (A), (B), (C), and (D) do not address this problem. Choice (E) does and is correct.

44. **(A)** Choice (A) is best because it is the only choice which phrases the sentence in the third person, and not in the imperative (command) form.

45. **(B)** Choices (A) and (D) are incorrect since they contain comma-splice errors. Choices (C) and (E) change the facts given in the essay and are, therefore, poor choices. Choice (B) is best.

46. **(C)** The pronoun agreeing with *each person* should be singular. Choices (A), (B), (D), and (E) contain plural pronouns and are, therefore, wrong. Choice (C) is best.

47. **(D)** In the first paragraph, the writer states that there are two camps, one believing in gun control and the other opposed to it. Choice (D) is correct.

48. **(E)** There is a problem with parallel structure in the underlined portion. In addition, *murdering* and *killing* are redundant. Only choice (E) corrects these two problems.

49. **(D)** Sentence (13) is phrased as a direct command and is not in keeping with the tone of the other sentences. (A) and (C) do not correct this and are poor choices. Choice (B) is awkward grammatically, and choice (E) is poor since the antecedent of the plural pronoun *they* is *criminal*, a singular noun.

50. **(A)** Since *crimes* are countable, it is correct to write *number of crimes* and not *amount of crimes*. Choices (C), (D), and (E) do not correct this error. Choice (B) uses *shorten* incorrectly. Choice (A) is best.

51. **(C)** The subject of the sentence is *acquisition*; thus, the verb should be *is*.

52. **(A)** It's not the college that has been singled out as an example, it's the *college's refusing*.

53. **(D)** The word *than* introduces an elliptical clause understood to be *than she (was)*. The subject of this unexpressed (that is, unrepeated) verb *was* has to be in the nominative case (*she*).

54. **(D)** The phrase *would be* is superfluous and interrupts the parallel structure.

55. **(C)** She can't be the smallest *of any girl*, only the smallest *girl*.

56. **(A)** The verb form *could . . . be seen* is in the past tense, so it must be that spring *was* well advanced.

57. **(E)** The sentence is correct.

58. **(C)** Since *reason* already signifies *cause*, *because* is redundant: "The reason for the postponement is the ten-inch snowfall."

59. **(B)** The sentence lacks a complete, independent verb; *improving* is only a participle. As it stands, the sentence needs *improved*, the complete past tense.

60. **(D)** The form *begun* is the past participle (*has begun*, etc.) incorrectly used in place of the past-tense form, *began*.

Answer Sheet for Practice Test 5
Part A: Essay Section

Use this space for your essay response.

Part B: Multiple-Choice Section

1 Ⓐ Ⓑ Ⓒ Ⓓ Ⓔ   13 Ⓐ Ⓑ Ⓒ Ⓓ Ⓔ   25 Ⓐ Ⓑ Ⓒ Ⓓ Ⓔ   37 Ⓐ Ⓑ Ⓒ Ⓓ Ⓔ   49 Ⓐ Ⓑ Ⓒ Ⓓ Ⓔ

2 Ⓐ Ⓑ Ⓒ Ⓓ Ⓔ   14 Ⓐ Ⓑ Ⓒ Ⓓ Ⓔ   26 Ⓐ Ⓑ Ⓒ Ⓓ Ⓔ   38 Ⓐ Ⓑ Ⓒ Ⓓ Ⓔ   50 Ⓐ Ⓑ Ⓒ Ⓓ Ⓔ

3 Ⓐ Ⓑ Ⓒ Ⓓ Ⓔ   15 Ⓐ Ⓑ Ⓒ Ⓓ Ⓔ   27 Ⓐ Ⓑ Ⓒ Ⓓ Ⓔ   39 Ⓐ Ⓑ Ⓒ Ⓓ Ⓔ   51 Ⓐ Ⓑ Ⓒ Ⓓ Ⓔ

4 Ⓐ Ⓑ Ⓒ Ⓓ Ⓔ   16 Ⓐ Ⓑ Ⓒ Ⓓ Ⓔ   28 Ⓐ Ⓑ Ⓒ Ⓓ Ⓔ   40 Ⓐ Ⓑ Ⓒ Ⓓ Ⓔ   52 Ⓐ Ⓑ Ⓒ Ⓓ Ⓔ

5 Ⓐ Ⓑ Ⓒ Ⓓ Ⓔ   17 Ⓐ Ⓑ Ⓒ Ⓓ Ⓔ   29 Ⓐ Ⓑ Ⓒ Ⓓ Ⓔ   41 Ⓐ Ⓑ Ⓒ Ⓓ Ⓔ   53 Ⓐ Ⓑ Ⓒ Ⓓ Ⓔ

6 Ⓐ Ⓑ Ⓒ Ⓓ Ⓔ   18 Ⓐ Ⓑ Ⓒ Ⓓ Ⓔ   30 Ⓐ Ⓑ Ⓒ Ⓓ Ⓔ   42 Ⓐ Ⓑ Ⓒ Ⓓ Ⓔ   54 Ⓐ Ⓑ Ⓒ Ⓓ Ⓔ

7 Ⓐ Ⓑ Ⓒ Ⓓ Ⓔ   19 Ⓐ Ⓑ Ⓒ Ⓓ Ⓔ   31 Ⓐ Ⓑ Ⓒ Ⓓ Ⓔ   43 Ⓐ Ⓑ Ⓒ Ⓓ Ⓔ   55 Ⓐ Ⓑ Ⓒ Ⓓ Ⓔ

8 Ⓐ Ⓑ Ⓒ Ⓓ Ⓔ   20 Ⓐ Ⓑ Ⓒ Ⓓ Ⓔ   32 Ⓐ Ⓑ Ⓒ Ⓓ Ⓔ   44 Ⓐ Ⓑ Ⓒ Ⓓ Ⓔ   56 Ⓐ Ⓑ Ⓒ Ⓓ Ⓔ

9 Ⓐ Ⓑ Ⓒ Ⓓ Ⓔ   21 Ⓐ Ⓑ Ⓒ Ⓓ Ⓔ   33 Ⓐ Ⓑ Ⓒ Ⓓ Ⓔ   45 Ⓐ Ⓑ Ⓒ Ⓓ Ⓔ   57 Ⓐ Ⓑ Ⓒ Ⓓ Ⓔ

10 Ⓐ Ⓑ Ⓒ Ⓓ Ⓔ   22 Ⓐ Ⓑ Ⓒ Ⓓ Ⓔ   34 Ⓐ Ⓑ Ⓒ Ⓓ Ⓔ   46 Ⓐ Ⓑ Ⓒ Ⓓ Ⓔ   58 Ⓐ Ⓑ Ⓒ Ⓓ Ⓔ

11 Ⓐ Ⓑ Ⓒ Ⓓ Ⓔ   23 Ⓐ Ⓑ Ⓒ Ⓓ Ⓔ   35 Ⓐ Ⓑ Ⓒ Ⓓ Ⓔ   47 Ⓐ Ⓑ Ⓒ Ⓓ Ⓔ   59 Ⓐ Ⓑ Ⓒ Ⓓ Ⓔ

12 Ⓐ Ⓑ Ⓒ Ⓓ Ⓔ   24 Ⓐ Ⓑ Ⓒ Ⓓ Ⓔ   36 Ⓐ Ⓑ Ⓒ Ⓓ Ⓔ   48 Ⓐ Ⓑ Ⓒ Ⓓ Ⓔ   60 Ⓐ Ⓑ Ⓒ Ⓓ Ⓔ

TEAR HERE

Practice Test 5

Part A: Essay Section
(20 Minutes)

Directions: You have 20 minutes in which to plan and write the essay assigned below. Make certain that you do not stray from the topic, that you give specific details as supporting evidence, and that you organize your ideas logically. Remember to proofread carefully to be certain that you have expressed your ideas in standard written English.

Topic: "Criminals are not born; they are made." Recently there has been an out-cry against the government's cutting programs designed to help those on a poverty level. There are many who feel that without public assistance, the under-privileged will turn to crime and this will create a great drain on the taxpayer.

Assignment: Write an essay in which you discuss the above statement. Support your opinions with specific examples from your personal experiences, your observations of others, or your reading.

YOU MAY USE THE SPACE BELOW FOR NOTES. BEGIN YOUR ESSAY ON THE ANSWER SHEET PROVIDED.

Part B: Multiple-Choice Section
(40 Minutes)

Directions: Some of the sentences below contain an error in grammar, usage, word choice, or idiom. Other sentences are correct. Parts of each sentence are underlined and lettered. The error, if there is one, is contained in one of the underlined parts of the sentence. Assume that all other parts of the sentence are correct and cannot be changed. For each sentence, select the one underlined part that must be changed to make the sentence correct and mark its letter on your answer sheet. If there is no error in a sentence, mark answer space E. No sentence contains more than one error.

Example	**Sample Answer**
<u>Being that</u> <u>it's</u> such a lovely day, we A B	● Ⓑ Ⓒ Ⓓ Ⓔ
<u>are having</u> a difficult time C	
<u>concentrating</u> on our assignment. D	
<u>No error</u> E	

1. The second speaker was the <u>most amusing</u>
                                        A
    of the two, <u>though</u> he had <u>little</u>
                      B   C
    <u>of substance</u> to add. <u>No error</u>
          D   E

2. Anyone <u>dissatisfied with</u> the board's deci-
                  A
    sion <u>should</u> <u>make</u> <u>their</u> objections
              B   C
    <u>known.</u> <u>No error</u>
        D   E

3. All that <u>he added</u> as extra equipment on
                  A
    the new car <u>was</u> two <u>speakers, a</u> cassette
                      B   C
    <u>deck, and</u> a retractable antenna. <u>No error</u>
        D   E

4. She <u>owned</u> a small glass pyramid
              A
    <u>and a crystal,</u> and <u>claimed</u> <u>that it</u> had a
          B   C   D
    mysterious healing power. <u>No error</u>
                                          E

5. In making rounds, <u>the chief resident</u> in
                              A
    the hospital <u>was always</u> <u>accompanied with</u>
                      B   C
    an <u>intern.</u> <u>No error</u>
          D   E

6. If it is in a <u>person's</u> best interest, <u>then</u>
                      A   B
    <u>she should</u> apply for a stipend as <u>soon as</u>
          C   D
    possible. <u>No error</u>
                      E

7. When the mirror <u>cracked</u> yesterday,
                            A
    <u>they got</u> very nervous <u>about</u> the bad luck
        B   C
    <u>they may be</u> in for. <u>No error</u>
        D   E

8. He <u>tripped</u> on the rock and <u>fell,</u> <u>broke</u> his
              A   B   C
    ankle <u>in the process.</u> <u>No error</u>
                  D   E

9. <u>By changing</u> the combination, the
        A
    locksmith was able <u>to provide</u> us
                              B
    with <u>peace of mind,</u> convenience,
              C
    <u>and feeling safe</u> when we came home.
              D
    <u>No error</u>
        E

10. <u>Having studied</u> your report carefully,
        A

    <u>I am convinced</u> that <u>neither</u> of your solu-
          B   C

    tions <u>are</u> correct. <u>No error</u>
        D   E

11. The <u>fabric, even though</u> it is not
              A

    <u>expensive,</u> <u>feels soft</u> <u>to the touch.</u>
        B   C   D
    <u>No error</u>
      E

12. <u>The major affects</u> of the battle
          A

    <u>were made known</u> to the
            B

    <u>military personnel,</u> but they were not
            C

    revealed <u>to the media.</u> <u>No error</u>
             D   E

13. <u>There was,</u> <u>contrary to</u> what you <u>believe,</u>
        A   B   C

    many complaints <u>about</u> the poor service.
                 D

    <u>No error</u>
      E

14. This chart <u>does appear</u> <u>to be larger</u>
              A   B

    <u>than any chart</u> in the room, although this
        C

    may well be only an <u>optical illusion.</u>
                  D

    <u>No error</u>
      E

15. <u>Even a random sampling</u> of the questions
          A

    <u>reveal</u> that <u>there is</u> an <u>emphasis</u> on
      B   C   D

    correct punctuation. <u>No error</u>
                   E

16. He spoke <u>softly</u> and appealed to the
           A

    audience, <u>using</u> such expressions <u>like</u>
          B   C

    "for the common <u>welfare" and "to</u> help the
                  D

    oppressed and homeless." <u>No error</u>
                      E

17. The leaders of the <u>movement</u> believed
                A

    <u>that</u> persuasion was a more <u>effective</u>
      B   C

    means than <u>to use</u> force. <u>No error</u>
             D   E

18. <u>Thanks</u> <u>in large part</u> to an excellent
        A   B

    <u>score</u> and <u>imaginary</u> staging, the musical
      C   D

    had a successful run. <u>No error</u>
                  E

19. The influence of radio <u>on</u> American life
                 A

    <u>during</u> the Depression years <u>were</u>
      B   C

    profound. <u>No error</u>
       D   E

20. The <u>principal</u> listed the names of the
         A

    students <u>whom</u> he thought <u>ought</u> to be
          B   C

    <u>honored</u> at the assembly. <u>No error</u>
      D   E

GO ON TO THE NEXT PAGE

Directions: The sentences below may contain problems in grammar, usage, word choice, sentence construction, or punctuation. Part or all of each sentence is underlined. Following each sentence you will find five ways of expressing the underlined part. Answer choice (A) always repeats the original underlined section. The other four answer choices are all different. You are to select the lettered answer that produces the most effective sentence. If you think the original sentence is best, choose (A) as your answer. If one of the other choices makes a better sentence, mark your answer sheet for the letter of that choice. Do not choose an answer that changes the meaning of the original sentence.

Example

I have always enjoyed <u>singing as well as to dance</u>.
- (A) singing as well as to dance
- (B) singing as well as dancing
- (C) to sing as well as dancing
- (D) singing in addition to dance
- (E) to sing in addition to dancing

Sample Answer
Ⓐ ● Ⓒ Ⓓ Ⓔ

---

21. In order to achieve the highest rating in the diving competition, <u>it is necessary to enter the water</u> with a minimal splash.
    - (A) it is necessary to enter the water
    - (B) of necessity you must necessarily enter the water
    - (C) the water must, as is necessary, be entered
    - (D) it is entering the water with necessity
    - (E) necessarily you must be entered in the water

22. The ancient Egyptians built structures which still stand after 2,500 <u>years, their accomplishments are a marvel to behold.</u>
    - (A) years, their accomplishments are a marvel to behold.
    - (B) years, their accomplishing marvels that are to be beheld.
    - (C) years; and they have accomplished marvelous beholdings.
    - (D) years; their accomplishments are a marvel to behold.
    - (E) years, beholding their accomplishments is a marvel.

23. The contract that was made between the students and the teacher stated that the students would hand in homework <u>on the day it was scheduled to be.</u>
    - (A) on the day it was scheduled to be.
    - (B) on the scheduled day.
    - (C) in accordance with the planned scheduling.
    - (D) on the scheduled day that it was to be.
    - (E) with the schedule that was handed out.

24. The turnout for the game was very low, <u>but those in attending</u> enjoyed every minute of the contest.
    - (A) but those in attending
    - (B) but those in attendance
    - (C) but those who were in attending
    - (D) but the attendance of those who were there
    - (E) but the people being in attendance

25. People are concerned about the nearby nuclear plant because it employs new technology <u>and that real estate prices will decrease.</u>
    (A) and that real estate prices will decrease.
    (B) and that the price of real estate will decrease.
    (C) and that the decrease will be in real estate.
    (D) and the decrease in real estate will happen.
    (E) and decreases the price of real estate.

26. <u>Several notes were sent by the principal of the school that</u> were concerned with vandalism in the gymnasium.
    (A) Several notes were sent by the principal of the school that
    (B) Several notes written by the principal of the school that
    (C) The principal of the school sent several notes that
    (D) The principal of the school in sending notes that
    (E) Several of the notes sent that

27. Since no one bothered to bring a copy of the <u>directions, so they had no idea</u> how to put the tent together.
    (A) directions, so they had no idea
    (B) directions; they were having no idea
    (C) directions, they had no ideas on
    (D) directions, they had no idea
    (E) directions, their ideas were none on

28. When I mentioned that I was trying to learn a foreign language, <u>the professor recommended that I read comic books written in that language.</u>
    (A) the professor recommended that I read comic books written in that language.
    (B) the professor made a recommendation that I be reading comic books that were written in that language.
    (C) the professor, who was recommended, said to read comic books.
    (D) the professor was recommended because he wrote comic books in that language.
    (E) the professor recommended to me the reading of comic books.

29. The stock market fell over sixty points in <u>one day, this is a sure sign that</u> the economic recovery is not materializing.
    (A) one day, this is a sure sign that
    (B) one day, this sign is sure that
    (C) one day; notwithstanding the surety of the sign
    (D) one day and this was a sure sign when
    (E) one day, and this is a sure sign that

30. A fundamental difference between the two parties is reflected in their attitudes toward affirmative <u>action, one certainly strongly</u> endorses the concept while the other condemns it.
    (A) action, one certainly strongly
    (B) action, the stronger one certainly
    (C) action; one strongly
    (D) action which one, however strongly,
    (E) action, and one certainly strongly

31. Between 10 and 20 percent of the homes in the town <u>are suspected of having</u> a high level of radon contamination.
    (A) are suspected of having
    (B) are suspects in the having of
    (C) are suspicious as they have
    (D) can be suspected of having an ordinary and
    (E) seem to be suspicious in that they have

32. The students disliked the teacher <u>and demonstrating it by</u> not handing in assignments.
    (A) and demonstrating it by
    (B) and demonstrated it by
    (C) and, to demonstrate to the teacher, they were
    (D) and demonstrate it by
    (E) and cause a demonstration when they are

33. Everyone said that John was a natural sales-man; he had a winning smile, an above-average intelligence, <u>and he was always tenaciously persistent.</u>
    (A) and he was always tenaciously persis-tent.
    (B) and he persisted in a tenacious man-ner.
    (C) and, with tenacity, he always persisted.
    (D) and a tenacious persistence.
    (E) and the ability to project his persistent tenacity.

34. Juggling, like any other skill, <u>requires many hours of practice</u> before it becomes easy.
    (A) requires many hours of practice
    (B) requires practice that can be hourless
    (C) requires, among other things, many practice hours
    (D) requires that you practice with it many hours
    (E) requires you to be practicing many hours

35. <u>As whenever the two of them were together they quarreled</u>, we decided to put each one in a different group.
    (A) As whenever the two of them were together they quarreled
    (B) As to the two of them quarreling when they were together
    (C) Since the two of them quarreled when-ever they were together
    (D) Since quarreling was what happened as a result of their togetherness
    (E) Because the two of them quarreled together

36. Having tried to cover too much territory in her brief essay, <u>nothing was analyzed in any detail.</u>
    (A) nothing was analyzed in any detail.
    (B) nothing was analyzed in no detail.
    (C) the analysis was not detailed enough.
    (D) nothing that she analyzed was in detail.
    (E) she failed to analyze anything in detail.

37. If one wishes to be an individualist, <u>you must live with</u> the suspicion and resentment of those who prefer conformity.
    (A) you must live with
    (B) you have to live with
    (C) you must tolerate
    (D) one must live with
    (E) we must live with

38. Stories of huge hailstones have been <u>reported; it is claimed that</u> in Pipestone, Minnesota, in 1911, a 5.5-pound stone fell through the skylight of an office building.
    (A) reported; it is claimed that
    (B) reported, it is claimed that
    (C) reported; they claim that
    (D) reported; it is claimed how
    (E) reported; it is claim that

GO ON TO THE NEXT PAGE

Directions: Questions 39–44 are based on a passage that might be an early draft of a student's essay. Some sentences in this draft need to be revised or rewritten to make them both clear and correct. Read the passage carefully; then answer the questions that follow it. Some questions require decisions about diction, usage, tone, or sentence structure in particular sentences or parts of sentences. Other questions require decisions about organization, development, or appropriateness of language in the essay as a whole. For each question, choose the answer that makes the intended meaning clearer and more precise and that follows the conventions of standard written English.

(1) Prayer has no place in the public schools. (2) Traditionally, we have always had a separation between church and state. (3) Recognizing the dangers of having a state religion, our founding fathers framed our constitution in such a way so as to insure that there would be no one official religion.

(4) Now there are many municipalities that are attempting to change this policy. (5) I recently read that one small town wanted each class in its public school system to start each day with a reading from the Bible. (6) Many residents felt that reading a biblical passage, perhaps a psalm, would set a positive spiritual tone for the students, some objected.

(7) They said that this violated separation between church and state. (8) They pointed out that it was unfair to students who might not believe in the Bible and who were not part of any religious upbringing.

(9) I feel that a wholesome atmosphere can be created in our schools without coating it with religion. (10) It should be free of partisan spirituality which is likely to occur if prayer is introduced into the classroom. (11) You should leave this up to the home and to the parents to decide on the religious training for their children. (12) Schools should stick with academics.

39. Which of the following best describes the main purpose of sentence (1)?
    (A) To clearly and strongly state the writer's opinion on the issue
    (B) To present the problem
    (C) To introduce the idea that this is a controversial issue
    (D) To show a fair-minded and unbiased point of view
    (E) To indicate that a problem exists and must be addressed

40. Which of the following is the best revision of the underlined portion of sentence (3) below?

    Recognizing the dangers of having a state religion, <u>our founding fathers framed our constitution in such a way so as to insure that there would be no one official religion.</u>

    (A) religion. Our founding fathers framed our constitution in such a way as to insure that there would be no one official religion.
    (B) religion; our founding fathers framed our constitution to avoid this.
    (C) religion, our founding fathers fashioned a constitution that would prevent having one official religion.
    (D) religion and framing our constitution in such a way as to insure that there would be no one official religion.
    (E) religion, our constitution was framed in such a way as to avoid this.

41. Which of the following is the best revision of the underlined portion of sentence (6) below?

    Many residents felt that reading a biblical passage, perhaps a psalm, would set a positive spiritual tone for the <u>students, some objected.</u>

    (A) students, some had objections.
    (B) students, some others objected.
    (C) students; however, they objected.
    (D) students. However, some townspeople objected.
    (E) students; however, some were objections.

42. Which of the following is the best way to combine sentences (7) and (8)?
    (A) They said this violated the separation between church and state, and they pointed out that it was unfair to some students.
    (B) They said this violated the separation between church and state, and it was unfair to students who did not believe in religion.
    (C) They said that Bible reading in school violated the separation between church and state and was unfair to those students who did not believe in the Bible or belong to any religious group.
    (D) They said that Bible reading violated the separation between church and state and was unfair to students who might not believe in the Bible or belong to any religious group.
    (E) Saying that this violated separation between church and state and pointing out that it was unfair to students who might not believe in the Bible and who were not part of any religious upbringing.

43. Which of the following is the best revision of the underlined portion of sentence (10) below?

    <u>It should be free of partisan spirituality</u> which is likely to occur if prayer is introduced into the classroom.

    (A) The school should be free of partisan spirituality
    (B) It should be freed from partisan spirituality
    (C) Partisan spirituality should be eliminated
    (D) The school should free partisan spirituality
    (E) It should eliminate partisan spirituality

44. In light of the sentences preceding and following sentence (11), which of the following is the best revision of sentence (11)?
    (A) Parents should leave religious training in the home.
    (B) Religious training is best left up to the parents and home.
    (C) Leave religious training in the home for parents.
    (D) You should let parents decide in the home the religious training for their children.
    (E) Children should receive religious training and parents should decide this in the home.

GO ON TO THE NEXT PAGE

Directions: Questions 45–50 are based on a passage that might be an early draft of a student's essay. Some sentences in this draft need to be revised or rewritten to make them both clear and correct. Read the passage carefully; then answer the questions that follow it. Some questions require decisions about diction, usage, tone, or sentence structure in particular sentences or parts of sentences. Other questions require decisions about organization, development, or appropriateness of language in the essay as a whole. For each question, choose the answer that makes the intended meaning clearer and more precise and that follows the conventions of standard written English.

(1) A few weeks ago I read a short story about a group of people who meet every year to conduct a lottery. (2) But this is no ordinary lottery in which people can win large sums of money. (3) Someone is selected to be stoned to death by their fellow townspeople. (4) One of the authors points, as I interpret them, is that some traditions should not be followed, or at least should be re-evaluated when they no longer make sense. (5) The woman who wrote the tale found a very disturbing way to get the reader's interest.

(6) The story begins on a lovely, peaceful June day. (7) The only hint that something unusual may be about to happen is that children are busily collecting rocks and placing them in neat piles. (8) Then, one by one, people leave their jobs and head for the center of town where they all meet at noon. (9) Everyone is very friendly. (10) Everything is very organized. (11) It is evidently a time-honored ritual. (12) Heads of families pick pieces of paper from a box. (13) One paper has a special mark on it. (14) Whichever family picks the marked paper must have every family member select a piece of paper. (15) Male or female, adult or child doesn't matter. (16) The one who gets the marked paper this time is the victim.

(17) Of course, the "winner" of this lottery is actually a terrible "loser." (18) The author hints at primitive beginnings to the whole thing. (19) Whatever made them do it, no one speaks out forcefully enough against this. (20) The tradition will continue, the story suggests, and only if the young do not throw stones—refuse to participate, in other words—will things change. (21) There are similar things you should think about in your own life.

45. Which of the following is the best revision of sentence (3)?
(A) People are selected to be stoned to death by their fellow townspeople.
(B) Therefore, someone is selected to be stoned to death by his or her fellow townspeople.
(C) Someone is chosen for death by their fellow townspeople.
(D) Instead, someone is selected to be stoned to death by his or her fellow townspeople.
(E) Consequently, someone is selected to be stoned to death by their fellow townspeople.

46. Which of the following is the best revision of the underlined portion of sentence (4) below?
One of the authors points, as I interpret them, is that some traditions should not be followed, or at least should be re-evaluated when they no longer make sense.
(A) One of the authors points in my interpretation,
(B) One of the author's points, as I interpret them

(C) The author's point, as I interpret them,
(D) One of the authors point, as I interpret it,
(E) One of the author's points, as I interpret it,

47. Which of the following is the best way to combine sentences (9)–(12)?
(A) Everyone is very friendly, everything is very organized. It is evidently a time-honored ritual, heads of families pick pieces of paper from a box.
(B) Everyone is very friendly; everything is very organized. In what is evidently a time-honored ritual, heads of families pick pieces of paper from a box.
(C) Everyone is very friendly, everything is very organized. Evidently a time-honored ritual is that heads of families pick pieces of paper from a box.
(D) Everyone is very friendly and organized, in a time-honored ritual of heads of families picking pieces of paper from a box.

(E) In a friendly, organized, time-honored ritual; heads of families pick pieces of paper from a box.

48. Which of the following is the best way to combine sentences (14) and (15)?
   (A) Male or female, adult or child—whichever family picks it must have every family member select a piece of paper.
   (B) Whichever family picks it—male or female, adult or child—must have every family member select a piece of paper.
   (C) Whichever family picks it must have every family member—male or female, adult or child—select a piece of paper.
   (D) Whichever family picks it, must have every family member select a piece of paper—whether male or female, adult or child.
   (E) Male or female, adult or child—the family that picks it must have every member select a piece of paper.

49. Which of the following is the best reason to revise sentences (17)–(19)?
   (A) To eliminate the two sets of quotation marks
   (B) To improve organization
   (C) To use more exact language
   (D) To include the author and title of the story
   (E) To eliminate incorrect punctuation

50. In light of the sentences that precede it, which of the following is the best way to revise sentence (21)?
   (A) There may be similar customs in our own lives that need to be thought about and changed.
   (B) These are but a few of the things that you should think about in your own lives.
   (C) There are many customs like this one that you should think about in your own lives.
   (D) You should think about things like this in your own life.
   (E) Think about this and similar things that affect our lives.

GO ON TO THE NEXT PAGE

Directions: Some of the sentences below contain an error in grammar, usage, word choice, or idiom. Other sentences are correct. Parts of each sentence are underlined and lettered. The error, if there is one, is contained in one of the underlined parts of the sentence. Assume that all other parts of the sentence are correct and cannot be changed. For each sentence, select the one underlined part that must be changed to make the sentence correct and mark its letter on your answer sheet. If there is no error in a sentence, mark answer space E. No sentence contains more than one error.

Example

Being that it's such a lovely day, we
  A   B

are having a difficult time
    C

concentrating on our assignment.
    D

No error
 E

Sample Answer
●Ⓑ©ⒹⒺ

---

51. The office was so overheated that every
        A   B
man present removed their jackets.
    C   D
No error
 E

52. She had never played tennis well on no
    A   B   C
surface but grass. No error
    D   E

53. I had delayed too long by talking on the
         A   B
phone; the shop was close by the time I
             C   D
arrived. No error
    E

54. While it comprises only a small
        A
percentage of the student population, the
    B
club, numbering some 150 members, are
       C   D
very vocal. No error
    E

55. Besides George and her, no one I know
          A   B
seems distressed about the prospect of
    C   D
war. No error
   E

56. The clothes were jumbled altogether in
        A   B
the suitcase; obviously, she had packed
      C
hurriedly. No error
    D   E

57. It's unfair to expect Rob and I to pay
                A
all bills when you're working also.
  B   C   D
No error
 E

58. The previous commander was a personable
                   A
man too concerned with being liked;
    B
as a leader, he was ineffectual. No error
  C   D   E

59. The athlete dove smooth into the lake,
        A   B
creating hardly a ripple on its glassy
      C   D
surface. No error
    E

60. One must be sure of the facts before
        A   B
you make such a serious accusation.
  C   D
No error
 E

End of Practice Test 5

Sample Essay Responses

Essay A

Its true that people should be responsible for themselves and not depend on government agencies for a handout. If we remember a hundred years ago no one helped you if you were poor or without money and yet our country managed.

I remember a film I once saw. It was about a group of kids who grew up in Hell's Kitchen. A slum in New York City. Not all of them turned out to be bad. Although some did become theives and robbers and one even became a murder. But many also grew up to be priests and lawyers and doctors and even cops. They made it by developing character and fighting to better themselves.

So I feel it's really up to each person. If the city or the government gives you money it might make you lazy and not willing to fight harder to overcome bad conditions. Everyone must make his own way in life.

Essay B

Government assistance very often robs the individual of his initiative and his desire to achieve. As a result, many people feel it is a waste of the taxpayer's money to provide handouts for those who are on the poverty level.

I agree that there is a lot of waste and that a good deal of funds designed to help the poor never reach the right person. What we need are programs to provide jobs and to train people to earn a living. Of course, giving out free cheese sounds good. But that only happens once a year or so, and then the poor people are right back to where they started, on the bread line or in the soup kitchens.

I say let's spend our money to wipe out illiteracy, to provide better inexpensive housing, to offer jobs to the needy. Then I feel that fewer will turn to crime because they will have better outlets for their energy.

Analysis of Essay Responses

Essay A

The writer has a sense of organization and development. The use of a film to illustrate the point is valid, and the tone, although informal, is consistent. However, more careful proofreading is necessary to eliminate spelling errors (*Its-It's; theives-thieves; murder-murderer*). In addition, it is preferable to substitute a noun like "people" for the pronoun "you" when the writer is not really referring to the reader (Paragraph one: "If we remember, a hundred years ago, no one helped people who were poor, and yet our country managed." Paragraph three: "If this government gives a person money, he might become lazy and unwilling to fight harder to overcome bad conditions"). Moreover, there are two fragments in the second paragraph: "A slum in New York City" should be connected to the preceding sentence; the fragment beginning with "Although" should be joined with either the sentence that precedes it or with the sentence that follows it.

Essay B

This essay indicates that the writer is capable of performing on a college level. The comments are intelligent and technical aspects (spelling, grammar, punctuation) are sound.

There are two ways by which the essay might be improved. An additional paragraph would be helpful as a transition to clarify the writer's viewpoint, to state clearly that the writer believes that there is a need for a better direction for government assistance. Also, in the concluding paragraph, rather than write, "Let's spend our money . . . ," it would be preferable to state, "money should be spent . . ." or "the government should spend money . . . ."

Answer Key to Practice Test 5

1. **A**	13. **A**	25. **E**	37. **D**	49. **C**
2. **C**	14. **C**	26. **C**	38. **A**	50. **A**
3. **B**	15. **B**	27. **D**	39. **A**	51. **D**
4. **D**	16. **C**	28. **A**	40. **C**	52. **C**
5. **C**	17. **D**	29. **E**	41. **D**	53. **D**
6. **E**	18. **D**	30. **C**	42. **C**	54. **D**
7. **D**	19. **C**	31. **A**	43. **A**	55. **E**
8. **C**	20. **B**	32. **B**	44. **B**	56. **B**
9. **D**	21. **A**	33. **D**	45. **D**	57. **A**
10. **D**	22. **D**	34. **A**	46. **E**	58. **E**
11. **E**	23. **B**	35. **C**	47. **B**	59. **B**
12. **A**	24. **B**	36. **E**	48. **C**	60. **C**

Explanatory Answers to Practice Test 5

1. **(A)** When comparing only two persons or things, use the comparative forms *more* or *-er: more amusing or funnier.*

2. **(C)** A singular pronoun (*his* or *her*) is required to agree with the antecedent *Anyone.*

3. **(B)** The plural verb *were* is required to agree with the compound subject that follows.

4. **(D)** The plural pronoun *they* is required to agree with the plural antecedent, *a small glass pyramid and a crystal.*

5. **(C)** The correct idiomatic phrase is *accompanied by.*

6. **(E)** The sentence is correct.

7. **(D)** For correct sequence of tenses, the verb form *might* is required to follow *cracked* and *got.*

8. **(C)** The participle *breaking* is required to introduce the dependent clause.

9. **(D)** For parallel structure, the noun phrase *a feeling of safety* is required.

10. **(D)** The verb should be changed to *is* to agree with the singular subject *neither.*

11. **(E)** The sentence is correct.

12. **(A)** The correct word is *effects*, meaning *results.*

13. **(A)** The plural verb form *were*, is required to agree with the plural subject, *complaints.*

14. **(C)** In this comparison, the correct phrase is "than any *other* chart."

15. **(B)** The singular subject, *sampling*, requires the third person singular verb form, *reveals.*

16. **(C)** The correct idiomatic phrase is "such . . . *as.* "

17. **(D)** Use parallel forms for comparison: *persuasion* was a more effective means than *force.*

18. **(D)** *Imaginary* means "existing in the imagination." The word needed here is *imaginative*, meaning "creative or original."

19. **(C)** The singular verb *was* is required to agree with the singular subject *influence*.

20. **(B)** The phrase *he thought* is an interpolation that has no influence on the grammar of the sentence. As the subject of the second clause, the correct pronoun is *who*.

21. **(A)** The sentence is correct.

22. **(D)** The sentence contains two independent clauses. If there is not a connective, then the first clause must be followed by a semicolon.

23. **(B)** Choice (B) is more economical and does not end with the dangling infinitive *to be*.

24. **(B)** Although *in attending* might be acceptable in a different context, here the correct word is *attendance*.

25. **(E)** In order to keep the structure parallel, it is necessary to have a present tense verb with an object.

26. **(C)** In the original sentence, it is difficult to be certain whether the school or the notes are concerned with vandalism.

27. **(D)** The word *so* has no function in the sentence.

28. **(A)** The sentence is correct.

29. **(E)** The original sentence would be acceptable if the comma were replaced by a semicolon. It is also acceptable to connect the clauses with *and*.

30. **(C)** The word *certainly* is unnecessary, and the clauses should be joined by a semicolon.

31. **(A)** The sentence is correct.

32. **(B)** Notice that *disliked* is in the past tense. *Demonstrating* is a gerund rather than a verb.

33. **(D)** It is important that the parallelism be maintained. Sometimes it is easier to hear this if you leave a few words out: ". . . he had a . . . smile . . . intelligence . . . and persistence."

34. **(A)** The sentence is correct.

35. **(C)** Besides being least awkward, this choice places the emphasis on the two people quarreling.

36. **(E)** Only (E) meets the requirement that an introductory participle be followed by the subject of both the sentence and the participle.

37. **(D)** The only thing wrong with the original is that it shifts the point of view from the impersonal *one* to the personal *you*. Correct English requires that the same point of view be used throughout.

38. **(A)** The sentence is correct.

39. **(A)** Sentence (1) is a clear and forceful statement of the writer's position on the subject of prayer in the public school.

40. **(C)** Sentence (3) is wordy. Choice (C) offers a better version of the same thought. Choice (A) makes a fragment out of the first part of the sentence. Choice (B) contains an incorrect use of the semicolon. Choice (D) makes the entire sentence a fragment, and choice (E) creates a dangling modifier.

41. **(D)** Sentence (6) has a comma splice error and an ambiguous *some*. Choices (A) and (B) have the same problems. Choice (C) corrects the comma splice, but introduces an ambiguous *they*. Choice (E) does not make sense. Choice (D) corrects both the comma splice and the ambiguity.

42. **(C)** Sentences (7) and (8) contain ambiguous pronouns (*this* and *it*). Choices (A) and (B) have the same problem. Choice (D) changes the intended meaning. It is not *Bible reading* that the townspeople object to, but rather Bible reading *in school*. Choice (E) is a fragment. Choice (C) is best.

43. **(A)** *It* in sentence (10) has no clear antecedent. Choice (A) corrects this error. Either the other choices do not address this error or they change the meaning of the sentence.

44. **(B)** The sentence is best revised by shifting it from the second person to the third person with *religious training* as the subject as in choice (B).

45. **(D)** The subject of the sentence should agree with its pronouns that follow. Singular subjects take singular pronouns. Choices (C) and (E) violate this rule. A transitional word is needed to introduce the sentence. Choice (A) offers no transitional word. Choices (B) and (E) offer the wrong transitional words, *therefore* and *consequently*.

46. **(E)** The word *authors* needs an apostrophe to indicate that it is possessive, not plural. The singular possessive form is *author's* as in choices (B) and (E). However, choice (B) uses the plural pronoun *them* to refer to the singular subject *one*. Choice (E) corrects both problems.

47. **(B)** Choices (A) and (C) contain comma splice errors. Choice (D) is awkward and choice (E) contains an incorrect use of the semicolon. Choice (B) is best.

48. **(C)** *Male or female, adult or child* is best placed next to the noun described, *every family member*. This occurs only in choice (C).

49. **(C)** More specific language is needed. *The whole thing* in sentence (18) is vague and inexact; also, there is no clear reference for *them* or *this* in sentence (19).

50. **(A)** There is no good reason to switch to the second person as in sentence (21). Also the imprecise word *thing* should be changed. Only choice (A) corrects both of these errors.

51. **(D)** Since *every man* is singular, the pronoun referring to it should be *his*, not *their* (*jacket*).

52. **(C)** The combination of *never . . . on no surface* is a double negative. Standard English is *never . . . on any surface.*

53. **(D)** There is a big difference between a shop's being *close* and its being *closed*.

54. **(D)** As a collective noun discussed as a single entity, *club* takes a singular verb: *is* very vocal.

55. **(E)** The sentence is correct.

56. **(B)** *Altogether* means "entirely or utterly." This sentence needs *all together*, implying unity or proximity, or *together*.

57. **(A)** *Rob and I* is a phrase in the nominative case. But the phrase should be in the objective case since it is the object of the verb *expect*: Rob and *me*.

58. **(E)** The sentence is correct.

59. **(B)** The adjective *smooth* should be the adverb *smoothly*, since it modifies the verb *dove*.

60. **(C)** Consistency is important in standard written English; it is either *one must be . . . one makes*, or *you must be . . . you make.*

Answer Sheet for Practice Test 6
Part A: Essay Section

Use this space for your essay response.

Part B: Multiple-Choice Section

1 (A)(B)(C)(D)(E)	13 (A)(B)(C)(D)(E)	25 (A)(B)(C)(D)(E)	37 (A)(B)(C)(D)(E)	49 (A)(B)(C)(D)(E)
2 (A)(B)(C)(D)(E)	14 (A)(B)(C)(D)(E)	26 (A)(B)(C)(D)(E)	38 (A)(B)(C)(D)(E)	50 (A)(B)(C)(D)(E)
3 (A)(B)(C)(D)(E)	15 (A)(B)(C)(D)(E)	27 (A)(B)(C)(D)(E)	39 (A)(B)(C)(D)(E)	51 (A)(B)(C)(D)(E)
4 (A)(B)(C)(D)(E)	16 (A)(B)(C)(D)(E)	28 (A)(B)(C)(D)(E)	40 (A)(B)(C)(D)(E)	52 (A)(B)(C)(D)(E)
5 (A)(B)(C)(D)(E)	17 (A)(B)(C)(D)(E)	29 (A)(B)(C)(D)(E)	41 (A)(B)(C)(D)(E)	53 (A)(B)(C)(D)(E)
6 (A)(B)(C)(D)(E)	18 (A)(B)(C)(D)(E)	30 (A)(B)(C)(D)(E)	42 (A)(B)(C)(D)(E)	54 (A)(B)(C)(D)(E)
7 (A)(B)(C)(D)(E)	19 (A)(B)(C)(D)(E)	31 (A)(B)(C)(D)(E)	43 (A)(B)(C)(D)(E)	55 (A)(B)(C)(D)(E)
8 (A)(B)(C)(D)(E)	20 (A)(B)(C)(D)(E)	32 (A)(B)(C)(D)(E)	44 (A)(B)(C)(D)(E)	56 (A)(B)(C)(D)(E)
9 (A)(B)(C)(D)(E)	21 (A)(B)(C)(D)(E)	33 (A)(B)(C)(D)(E)	45 (A)(B)(C)(D)(E)	57 (A)(B)(C)(D)(E)
10 (A)(B)(C)(D)(E)	22 (A)(B)(C)(D)(E)	34 (A)(B)(C)(D)(E)	46 (A)(B)(C)(D)(E)	58 (A)(B)(C)(D)(E)
11 (A)(B)(C)(D)(E)	23 (A)(B)(C)(D)(E)	35 (A)(B)(C)(D)(E)	47 (A)(B)(C)(D)(E)	59 (A)(B)(C)(D)(E)
12 (A)(B)(C)(D)(E)	24 (A)(B)(C)(D)(E)	36 (A)(B)(C)(D)(E)	48 (A)(B)(C)(D)(E)	60 (A)(B)(C)(D)(E)

TEAR HERE

Practice Test 6

Part A: Essay Section

(20 Minutes)

Directions: You have 20 minutes in which to plan and write the essay assigned below. Make certain that you do not stray from the topic, that you give specific details as supporting evidence, and that you organize your ideas logically. Remember to proofread carefully to be certain that you have expressed your ideas in standard written English.

Topic: Years ago, many people believed in the concept, "My country, right or wrong." But now we are told that patriotism is a thing of the past. Today's generation no longer enjoys displaying the American flag, marching in parades, singing patriotic songs, or praising our country.

Assignment: Write an essay in which you agree or disagree with this statement. Support your opinions with specific examples from your personal experiences, your observations of others, or your reading.

YOU MAY USE THE SPACE BELOW FOR NOTES. BEGIN YOUR ESSAY ON THE ANSWER SHEET PROVIDED.

Part B: Multiple-Choice Section
(40 Minutes)

Directions: Some of the sentences below contain an error in grammar, usage, word choice, or idiom. Other sentences are correct. Parts of each sentence are underlined and lettered. The error, if there is one, is contained in one of the underlined parts of the sentence. Assume that all other parts of the sentence are correct and cannot be changed. For each sentence, select the one underlined part that must be changed to make the sentence correct and mark its letter on your answer sheet. If there is no error in a sentence, mark answer space E. No sentence contains more than one error.

Example

Being that it's such a lovely day, we
  A   B

are having a difficult time
  C

concentrating on our assignment.
  D

No error
  E

Sample Answer
● Ⓑ Ⓒ Ⓓ Ⓔ

---

1. When she graduates college, she will have to
           A   B
decide whether to continue her studies or
        C
seek employment. No error
    D   E

2. Farmers predicted that if the drought
         A   B
lasted another week half the wheat crop
              C
was lost. No error
  D   E

3. When my grandfather comes to visit us,
              A   B
he takes off his shoes and sets in the easy
                C   D
chair all day. No error
       E

4. It is all ready too late for us to do our
  A B   C
Christmas shopping in an uncrowded
             D
atmosphere. No error
      E

5. Lacking the idiomatic vocabulary neces-
  A
sary for true fluency, many students who
             B
study a foreign language in school
are unable to converse comfortably in the
  C   D
language. No error
      E

6. Judging from the beauty of the night, I
          A
believe that we are liable to have good
  B   C   D
weather tomorrow. No error
         E

7. Despite them being abundant, cheap, and
      A   B
rich in protein, mussels are not
  C
a favorite dish of most Americans. No error
  D   E

8. If it is not watered today, one of the
  A
prettiest plants on the windowsill are going
  B   C   D
to die. No error
      E

9. The word *atom* in Greek means "not
divisible" because it was once belief that
  A   B   C
the atom was the smallest possible unit of
               D
matter. No error
      E

10. Before they could <u>adjourn</u> <u>for the day</u>
                          A   B
    they <u>must</u> consider the <u>group's</u> petition.
          C   D
    <u>No error</u>
       E

11. The children <u>who</u> I <u>observed</u> at the theater
                  A   B
    seemed <u>enchanted</u> by the <u>antics</u> of the
            C   D
    puppets. <u>No error</u>
              E

12. Most animals cannot recognize <u>their</u>
                                   A
    reflection in a mirror <u>as themselves</u>; they
                            B
    usually react <u>as if</u> confronted by another
                   C
    member of <u>their species</u>. <u>No error</u>
                D   E

13. Of the two candidates applying for the

    <u>position,</u> we have <u>no doubt</u> that Jim is
     A   B
    <u>likely</u> to be the <u>most favored</u>. <u>No error</u>
     C   D   E

14. There are <u>less</u> workers today in <u>rural areas</u>
               A   B
    <u>than</u> there <u>were</u> a decade ago. <u>No error</u>
     C   D   E

15. She is exactly the <u>kind of person</u> <u>who</u>
                        A   B
    should be chosen for the position of

    <u>discussion leader,</u> since she thinks clearly
     C
    and has a good <u>academic background</u>.
                    D

    <u>No error</u>
       E

16. He <u>looked</u> <u>like</u> he <u>had seen</u> a ghost
        A   B   C
    <u>when</u> his father entered the room.
     D
    <u>No error</u>
       E

17. I really appreciated <u>the fact</u> that you
                          A
    made a special trip <u>just</u> <u>to bring</u> the
                         B   C
    flowers to my mother and <u>I.</u> <u>No error</u>
                              D   E

18. The inhabitants of Pompeii in the

    <u>first century A.D.</u> did not realize that the
     A
    high incidence of earthquakes in the area

    <u>were</u> the warning sign of a <u>much greater</u>
     B   C
    disaster—the <u>eruption</u> of Vesuvius.
                  D

    <u>No error</u>
       E

19. I <u>use</u> to be a pretty good mechanic, but
       A
    lately I <u>haven't</u> had the time to get my
              B
    hands dirty working on my car—or <u>even</u>
                                  C   D
    on my toaster. <u>No error</u>
                    E

20. We were asked, indeed <u>required,</u> to tell the
                          A
    <u>honest truth</u> before the jury or else
     B
    we might <u>well</u> have been accused of
              C
    <u>having committed</u> perjury. <u>No error</u>
     D   E

GO ON TO THE NEXT PAGE

Directions: The sentences below may contain problems in grammar, usage, word choice, sentence construction, or punctuation. Part or all of each sentence is underlined. Following each sentence you will find five ways of expressing the underlined part. Answer choice (A) always repeats the original underlined section. The other four answer choices are all different. You are to select the lettered answer that produces the most effective sentence. If you think the original sentence is best, choose (A) as your answer. If one of the other choices makes a better sentence, mark your answer sheet for the letter of that choice. Do not choose an answer that changes the meaning of the original sentence.

Example

I have always enjoyed <u>singing as well as to dance</u>.
(A) singing as well as to dance
(B) singing as well as dancing
(C) to sing as well as dancing
(D) singing in addition to dance
(E) to sing in addition to dancing

Sample Answer
Ⓐ●ⒸⒹⒺ

---

21. The committee requested that there be input <u>from all the staff before a vote was taken.</u>
    (A) from all the staff before a vote was taken.
    (B) from all the staff taking a vote.
    (C) before the staff took a vote on the input.
    (D) from all the staff before having taken a vote.
    (E) from all the staff who would take a vote.

22. She <u>could not scarcely but be affected</u> by the plight of the homeless.
    (A) could not scarcely but be affected
    (B) could hardly help being effected
    (C) could not help being affected
    (D) could not help being effected
    (E) could not scarcely be affected

23. <u>With regards to examining the union contract, the staff spent several days discussing the various sections and then voted on it.</u>
    (A) With regards to examining the union contract, the staff spent several days discussing the various sections and then voted on it.
    (B) As concerns the contract, the staff spent several days on a discussion which resulted in a vote.
    (C) An examination of the contract resulted in several days of voting and discussing the various sections.
    (D) After several days of discussing the various sections of the union contract, the staff voted on it.
    (E) A vote followed a discussion of the union contract by the staff which examined the sections and followed it with a vote.

24. <u>There are, of course, three possible alternatives that</u> we have in order to reach an equitable solution.
    (A) There are, of course, three possible alternatives that
    (B) There is, of course three possible alternatives that
    (C) There are, of course, three possible choices that
    (D) There are, of course, three possible alternatives which
    (E) There are of course three possible choices that

25. In the dictionary, it indicates how words should be pronounced.
    (A) In the dictionary, it indicates
    (B) In the dictionary, it has
    (C) The dictionary indicates
    (D) There in the dictionary, it indicates
    (E) In the dictionary, it has an indication

26. The actor was apparently unaware or unconcerned by the small audience.
    (A) was apparently unaware or unconcerned by the small audience.
    (B) was apparently unaware or unconcerned, by the small audience.
    (C) was not aware or unconcerned by the small audience.
    (D) seemed to ignore the fact that there was a small audience.
    (E) was apparently unaware of or unconcerned by the small audience.

27. The main pipe broke, and they were without water for a week, which created many problems for them.
    (A) week, which created many problems for them.
    (B) week; this situation created many problems for them.
    (C) week; which situation created many problems for them.
    (D) week, which is creating many problems for them.
    (E) week, this created many problems for them.

28. If we ever have the watch inscribed; we will ask the jewelers to use italic lettering for the quotation.
    (A) watch inscribed; we will ask the jewelers
    (B) watch inscribed; we'll ask the jeweler's
    (C) watch inscribed, we will ask the jewelers
    (D) watch inscribed, we will ask the jewelers'
    (E) watch inscribed, we will ask for the jewelers

29. No one, including Walter and I, have the ability to cash this check for her.
    (A) No one, including Walter and I, have the ability
    (B) No one, including Walter and I, had the ability
    (C) No one, including Walter and me, have the ability
    (D) No one, including Walter and me, has the ability
    (E) No one including Walter and me, has the ability

30. Recognizing the expense of the repairs, the plumbing mishap created a great deal of consternation.
    (A) Recognizing the expense of the repairs,
    (B) Recognizing the expensive repairs,
    (C) Recognizing that the repairs are expensive
    (D) Due to the repairs are going to be expensive
    (E) Recognizing the expense of the repairs, he noted that

31. Seatbelts, while unquestionably a good idea, it's sometimes a nuisance to use them.
    (A) Seatbelts, while unquestionably a good idea, it's sometimes a nuisance to use them.
    (B) Seatbelts, while unquestionably a good idea, are sometimes a nuisance.
    (C) Seatbelts are unquestionably a good idea and also they are sometimes a nuisance.
    (D) Seatbelts, while unquestionably a good idea, but sometimes a nuisance to use.
    (E) Seatbelts, while it's unquestionably a good idea to have them, it's sometimes a nuisance to use them.

32. Your application for a scholarship arriving late, however; it will still be considered by the committee.
    (A) arriving late, however; it will still be considered by the committee.
    (B) arrived late, however the committee will consider it still.
    (C) arrived late; however, the committee will still consider it.
    (D) will be considered by the committee which arrived late.
    (E) arriving late and is being considered by the committee.

33. When I travel, I most always enjoy seeing sights that differ from the typical tourist traps.
    (A) I most always enjoy seeing sights that differ from the typical tourist traps.
    (B) I almost always enjoy to see sights other than the typical tourist traps.
    (C) I most always enjoy seeing sights that are different than the typical tourist traps.
    (D) I almost always enjoy seeing sights that are different than the typical tourist traps.
    (E) I almost always enjoy seeing sights other than the typical tourist traps.

34. Unless treated and rewarmed, hypothermia causes death.
    (A) hypothermia causes death.
    (B) death results from hypothermia.
    (C) hypothermia kills.
    (D) the victim of hypothermia will die.
    (E) hypothermia will cause death.

35. First choose a recipe; then you should make a list of the ingredients needed.
    (A) then you should make a list of the ingredients needed.
    (B) then a list can be made of the ingredients needed.
    (C) then you can make a list of the ingredients needed.
    (D) then you should list the ingredients needed.
    (E) then make a list of the ingredients needed.

36. Living in the city for the first time, the traffic noise, she found, disrupted her sleep.
    (A) the traffic noise, she found, disrupted her sleep.
    (B) she found that the traffic noise disrupted her sleep.
    (C) she found out how the traffic noise disrupted her sleep.
    (D) her sleep, she found, was disrupted by the traffic noise.
    (E) her sleep disrupted, she found, by traffic noise.

37. Elgin called to find out will you lend him your bicycle.
    (A) will you lend him your bicycle.
    (B) will you lend him your bicycle?
    (C) did you lend him your bicycle.
    (D) will your bicycle be lent to him?
    (E) whether you will lend him your bicycle.

38. Making new friends, the obstacle of shyness must be overcome.
    (A) Making new friends, the obstacle of shyness must be overcome.
    (B) To make new friends, we must overcome our shyness.
    (C) In order to make new friends, the obstacle of shyness must be overcome.
    (D) Making new friends overcomes the obstacle of shyness.
    (E) To make new friends, there must be an overcoming of shyness.

GO ON TO THE NEXT PAGE

Directions: Questions 39–44 are based on a passage that might be an early draft of a student's essay. Some sentences in this draft need to be revised or rewritten to make them both clear and correct. Read the passage carefully; then answer the questions that follow it. Some questions require decisions about diction, usage, tone, or sentence structure in particular sentences or parts of sentences. Other questions require decisions about organization, development, or appropriateness of language in the essay as a whole. For each question, choose the answer that makes the intended meaning clearer and more precise and that follows the conventions of standard written English.

(1) Hopefully the government of the United States will soon make sure that all their citizens are able to have good, affordable health care. (2) If legislation is enacted and national coverage is assured, we will truly be ready to enter a new age in America. (3) It will be one in which all people—rich or poor, working or unemployed—will be provided for when they are ill.

(4) The significance of a national health care plan cannot be overstated. (5) Recently, for instance, my aunt and uncle were involved in an automobile accident. (6) Although their injuries were pretty serious, yet after some emergency treatment they didn't get a lot of medical attention. (7) Due to the fact that they didn't have much coverage. (8) So doctors and hospital staff didn't want to treat them. (9) It's hard to believe that good, hard-working people like my relatives, now they are being neglected by society.

(10) And this is only one example of a situation in which people without adequate protection are mistreated by the medical profession, there are many other stories that could be told. (11) For this reason, that's why I sincerely hope that our government will soon provide for all those needy people, like my aunt and uncle, who presently lack adequate health care coverage.

39. Which of the following is the best revision of the underlined portion of sentence (1) below?

    <u>Hopefully the government of the United States will soon make sure that all their citizens are able to have</u> good, affordable health care.

    (A) Hopefully the government of the United States will soon provide all citizens with
    (B) It is hoped that the government of the United States will soon make sure that all its citizens are able to have
    (C) Hopefully the government of the United States will soon make sure that all citizens would be able to have
    (D) I hope that the government of the United States will soon make sure that all its citizens will be able to have
    (E) I hope that the government of the United States soon makes sure that all their citizens would be able to have

40. Which of the following is the best way to combine sentences (2) and (3)?
    (A) If legislation is enacted and national coverage is assured, we will truly be ready to enter a new age in America, being one in which all people, rich or poor, will be provided for when they are ill.
    (B) If legislation is enacted and national coverage is assured, we will truly be able to enter a new age, one in which all Americans—rich or poor, working or unemployed—will be provided for when they are ill.
    (C) If legislation is enacted and national coverage is assured, we will truly be ready to enter a new age in America, it will be one in which all people, rich or poor, working or unemployed, will be provided for when they are ill.
    (D) If legislation is enacted then all people, no matter what their abilities will be provided for by their government at all times.
    (E) If we enact legislation and assure national coverage, we will be able to enter a new age in America; in which all—rich or poor, working or unemployed—will be provided for when they are ill.

41. Which of the following is the best way to revise sentences (6), (7), and (8)?
    (A) Although their injuries were serious, after some emergency treatment, they received very little medical attention. Since they did not have much coverage, doctors and hospital staff did not want to treat them.
    (B) Although their injuries were serious, yet after some emergency treatment, they didn't get a lot of medical attention. Due to the fact they didn't have much coverage, doctors and hospital staff didn't want to treat them.
    (C) Their injuries were pretty serious although after some emergency treatment they didn't get a lot medical attention, due to the fact that they didn't have much coverage. So doctors and hospital staff didn't want to treat them.
    (D) Their injuries were pretty serious, yet after some emergency treatment they did not get much medical attention. Due to the fact that they did not have much coverage, so doctor and hospitals did not want to treat them.
    (E) Although their injuries were serious, after some emergency treatment, they didn't get a lot of attention because of the fact that they didn't have much coverage so doctors and hospital staff didn't want to treat them.

42. Which of the following is the best revision of the underlined portion of sentence (9) below?

    It's hard to believe that good, hard-working people like my relatives, now they are being neglected by society.

    (A) relatives. Now they are being neglected by society.
    (B) relatives and being neglected by society now.
    (C) relatives are now being neglected by society.
    (D) relatives and now they are being neglected by society.
    (E) relatives have neglected society.

43. Which of the following is the reason sentence (10) should be revised?
    (A) To provide another example
    (B) To correct an error in usage
    (C) To correct a sentence structure error
    (D) To correct an error in verb agreement
    (E) To correct a pronoun reference error

44. Which of the following is the best revision of the underlined portion of sentence (11) below?

    For this reason, that's why I sincerely hope that our government will soon provide for all those needy people, like my aunt and uncle, who presently lack adequate health care coverage.

    (A) Because this is why
    (B) For this reason it is why
    (C) Because of this reason is why
    (D) This reason is why
    (E) This is why

GO ON TO THE NEXT PAGE

Directions: Questions 45–50 are based on a passage that might be an early draft of a student's essay. Some sentences in this draft need to be revised or rewritten to make them both clear and correct. Read the passage carefully; then answer the questions that follow it. Some questions require decisions about diction, usage, tone, or sentence structure in particular sentences or parts of sentences. Other questions require decisions about organization, development, or appropriateness of language in the essay as a whole. For each question, choose the answer that makes the intended meaning clearer and more precise and that follows the conventions of standard written English.

(1) When my family came to the United States to live, we spoke no English. (2) My parents luckily got a job and my sister and I were very young and we did what many other immigrant children did. (3) We learned English in public school and learned our native language and culture at home with our family. (4) It was not long before we all realized that success in the United States would depend on our ability to be fluent in English.

(5) Because of my own case I think that bilingual education is not as good as English in school, native language at home. (6) But I know of other people who found a bilingual education to be just what they needed, in fact it was essential to their progress since their English was so limited. (7) However, some people I knew did drop out of school later on. (8) Some of them had been labeled learning-disabled. (9) It was really just a language problem. (10) And some of my friends' parents felt that their children's bilingual education was ineffective or harmful, while others felt it was very good for them.

(11) As a result, I cannot decide for certain whether English is being taught better to foreigners today than it was in the past. (12) But I think that I would like to see small groups of non-native speakers taught in English by caring, well-trained professionals. (13) Then I would like them to be moved into regular classrooms as soon as possible. (14) In that way, I think they would be best served by a school system that has not always done justice to their needs. (15) Perhaps that would be one way to solve the problem of how to help them to succeed in school and in their life in the United States.

45. Which of the following is the best way to revise sentence (2)?
    (A) My parents luckily got a job. My sister and I were young. We did what many other immigrated children did.
    (B) My parents luckily got a job and my sister and I were very young so we did what many other immigrants did.
    (C) My parents got jobs, luckily; my very young sister and I did what many others did.
    (D) Luckily, my parents got jobs. My sister and I, who were very young, did what many other immigrant children did.
    (E) Luckily, my parents got jobs and my sister and I were very young. We did what many other immigrant children did.

46. Which of the following is the best way to revise sentence (5)?
    (A) Because of my own experience, I think that a bilingual education is not so good as learning English in school and the family's native language at home.
    (B) In my own case, bilingual education is not so good as English in school and native language at home.
    (C) I think that because of my own experience, English in school, native language at home is better than bilingual education.
    (D) As a result of my own case, I think that bilingual education is not as good as students who learn English in school and their native language at home.
    (E) Because of my own case, I consider bilingual education less effective than learning English in school and their native language at home.

47. Which of the following is the best revision of the underlined portion of sentence (6) below?

But I know of other people who found a bilingual education to be just what they <u>needed, in fact it was essential</u> to their progress since their English was so limited.

(A) needed; in fact it being essential
(B) needed, being that it was essential
(C) needed; in fact it was essential
(D) needed; essential as it was in fact
(E) needed. In fact essential

48. Which of the following is the best way to combine sentences (8) and (9)?
(A) Although it was really just a language problem; some had been labeled learning-disabled.
(B) Some of them were labeled learning-disabled, it was really just a language problem.
(C) Some of them had been labeled learning-disabled, even though what they really had was a language problem.
(D) Some of them were learning-disabled with a language problem.
(E) Some of them had a language problem that made them learning-disabled.

49. Which of the following is the best revision of sentence (10)?
(A) Some of my friends' parents felt that their children's bilingual education was ineffective or harmful, while others felt it was very good for them.
(B) Some felt that their child's bilingual education was ineffective or harmful, but other of my friends' parents felt it was very good for them.
(C) Though some of my friends' parents felt it was very good for them, some felt that bilingual education was ineffective or harmful.
(D) Although some of my friends' parents felt it was very good, some felt that their children's bilingual education was ineffective or harmful.
(E) Ineffective or harmful though it may have been to some, others of my friends' parents felt that their children's bilingual education has been very good.

50. Which of the following would be the best way to improve the last paragraph?
(A) To incorporate transitional words or phrases
(B) To eliminate the specious argument presented
(C) To present a more personal point of view
(D) To adopt a less sympathetic tone
(E) To be more exact and concise in wording

GO ON TO THE NEXT PAGE

Directions: Some of the sentences below contain an error in grammar, usage, word choice, or idiom. Other sentences are correct. Parts of each sentence are underlined and lettered. The error, if there is one, is contained in one of the underlined parts of the sentence. Assume that all other parts of the sentence are correct and cannot be changed. For each sentence, select the one underlined part that must be changed to make the sentence correct and mark its letter on your answer sheet. If there is no error in a sentence, mark answer space E. No sentence contains more than one error.

Example	**Sample Answer**

Being that it's such a lovely day, we
　　A　　　B

are having a difficult time
　C

concentrating on our assignment.
　D

No error
　E

Sample Answer
●ⒷⒸⒹⒺ

51. Neither the dilemma nor the solution
　　　　　A　　　B
are as simple as that editorial would lead
C　　　　　　　　　　　　　D
one to believe. No error
　　　　　E

52. Few freshmen these days are as ingenuous
　　　　　　　A　　　B
as him that first year. No error
C　　D　　　　　E

53. Even though you can see the results of an
　　　　　　　A
earthquake on television, we cannot fully
　　　　B　　　　　C
understand its destructive capabilities

unless you see it in person. No error
D　　　　　　　　　E

54. There is talk that the Congress will soon enact
　　　A　　　　　　　　B
legislation that would attempt to slow the
　　　　　　　　C
raising trade deficit which the U.S. is cur-
D
rently experiencing. No error
　　　　　E

55. Listening to another student's question, I
　　A
frequently discover that they are confused
　　　　　　　　　　B
about the same points that I am. No error
C　　　　　　　　　D　　　E

56. The anthology was comprised of modern
　　　　　　A
American poems and included a varied
　　　　　　　B　　　　　C
selection of lesser known works by Stevens
　　　　　　D
and Williams. No error
　　　　　E

57. It is not I to whom you ought to complain.
　　　　A　　B　　　　C　　　D
No error
　E

58. We planned to canvas the neighborhood,
　　　　　　A
going door to door to get signatures on
B　　　C　　　　　　　　　D
the petition. No error
　　　　E

59. The conditions of the contract by which
　　　　　　　　　　　A
the strike has been settled has not yet been
　　　　　B　　　　　　C
made public. No error
D　　　　　E

60. Myths are often marked by anthropomor-
　　　　　　A
phism, the concept where animals and
　　　　　　　　B
inanimate forces are invested with human
　C　　　　　D
characteristics. No error
　　　　　E

End of Practice Test 6

Sample Essay Responses

Essay A

   We are still patriotic. Holidays like July 4th and Veterans' Day are still very special. I know that my entire family gets together for a big meal or a picnic and we really count our blessings and are greatful that we live in a fine country like America.

   My parents were born in Europe and they tell me that they didn't have the freedom that we have here. They worried about being taken prisoner. And were forced to serve in the army and fight and even get kill. So they appreciate living in the United State and even if sometimes we take things for granted deep down we love our country and are patriotic.

   I think that everyone should learn about what it is like to live in a country where there is no freedom. And no liberty to be able to worship where you want and to be able to vote and to have free speech. Then we would all be even more patriotic here in our country, the United State of America.

Essay B

   Patriotism has many faces. I think that I am still patriotic even though I do things in a different way than my parents and grandparents did.

   Maybe I don't march in parades and wave a flag. But I still get a wonderful feeling when I see the Statue of Liberty. Maybe I don't sing patriotic songs, but I still am proud that I live in a country that allows me to have free speech and the freedom to worship if that's what I believe. Maybe I don't repeat patriotic sayings that my parents memorized, but I still am thrilled that in my country I can disagree with the government and not be thrown into jail.

   I am patriotic and I show it when I vote, when I study about my country, and when I do all I can to make my country better so that my children will continue to be patriotic in their way.

Analysis of Essay Responses

Essay A

This writer appears sincere and consistent, has a sense of organization, and knows how to write an introduction and suitable conclusion. In addition, the illustration in the developmental paragraphs is drawn from the writer's own background and is both interesting and appropriate. Unfortunately, the errors in spelling (*greatful*), the omission of final letters (*kill, State*), and the fragments (paragraph two, sentence three; paragraph three, sentence two) detract somewhat from the value of the presentation.

Essay B

This essay is well thought out, clear, and well written. The writer possesses a fine style and is creative in language and approach. The point of view is consistent, and each paragraph is logical and connected to the central idea. The repetition of the word "maybe" as an initial word in the second paragraph provides a neat balance, as do the several specific illustrations. In sum, the essay clearly indicates that the writer is capable of doing college-level writing.

Answer Key for Practice Test 6

1.	A	13.	D	25.	C	37.	E	49.	D
2.	D	14.	A	26.	E	38.	B	50.	E
3.	C	15.	E	27.	B	39.	D	51.	C
4.	B	16.	B	28.	C	40.	B	52.	C
5.	E	17.	D	29.	D	41.	A	53.	C
6.	C	18.	B	30.	E	42.	C	54.	D
7.	A	19.	A	31.	B	43.	C	55.	B
8.	D	20.	B	32.	C	44.	E	56.	A
9.	C	21.	A	33.	E	45.	D	57.	E
10.	C	22.	C	34.	D	46.	A	58.	A
11.	A	23.	D	35.	E	47.	C	59.	C
12.	E	24.	C	36.	B	48.	C	60.	B

Explanatory Answers to Practice Test 6

1. **(A)** The correct idiom is *graduates from college.*

2. **(D)** The conditional sense of the sentence requires *would be.*

3. **(C)** The standard form is *sits.*

4. **(B)** The correct word is *already.*

5. **(E)** The sentence is correct.

6. **(C)** *Liable* is used here incorrectly. The word needed here is *likely.*

7. **(A)** A gerund (*being*) is modified by a possessive pronoun (*their*).

8. **(D)** The subject *one* requires a singular verb, *is.*

9. **(C)** The sentence requires the past-tense verb *believed*, not the noun *belief.*

10. **(C)** The verb form *could adjourn* establishes the action as past tense. Therefore the second clause must also be in the past tense: not *must* consider but *had to* consider.

11. **(A)** As the object of *I observed, who* must be in the objective case: *whom.*

12. **(E)** The sentence is correct.

13. **(D)** The comparative *more* is required since *two* people are mentioned.

14. **(A)** The correct word is *fewer* because *workers* are countable.

15. **(E)** The sentence is correct.

16. **(B)** The correct phrase is *as if* to introduce the clause.

17. **(D)** The object of the preposition *to* should be *me.*

18. **(B)** The singular subject *incidence* requires a singular verb, *was.*

19. **(A)** The correct word is *used.*

20. **(B)** The word *honest* is redundant.

21. **(A)** The sentence is correct.

22. **(C)** The double negative (*could not scarcely*) is incorrect. *Affected* (meaning "influenced") is correct.

23. **(D)** *With regards to* is unacceptable for *in regard to*. (B) is awkward and wordy, (C) is illogical, and (E) is repetitious. (D) offers the best expression of the thought.

24. **(C)** *Choices* is used for three or more items, *alternatives* for two; the *commas* separating *of course* are correct.

25. **(C)** There is no antecedent for the pronoun *it*; the subject of *indicates* should be *dictionary* as in (C).

26. **(E)** *Unaware* should be followed by the preposition *of.* Choice (D) alters the sense of the sentence.

27. **(B)** The original sentence (A) is awkward, since *which* seems to refer to *week*, rather than to the *situation*, which created the problem. (D) and (C) have the same problem, and (C) uses the semicolon incorrectly. (E) is a comma splice.

28. **(C)** A dependent clause introduced by a subordinating conjunction is separated from the main clause by a comma. Choice (D) is incorrect since *jewelers* is not possessive and does not require an apostrophe; choice (E) is awkward because of the preposition *for* following *ask*.

29. **(D)** The preposition *including* takes the objective case, *me*. Choice (C) is incorrect since the correct singular verb *has* (the subject is *no one*) is changed to the plural *have*. Choice (E) omits the comma after *one*.

30. **(E)** As the sentence stands there is a dangling participle (*recognizing*) so that the meaning conveyed is that the plumbing mishaps recognized the expense of the repairs. A subject must be added in the main clause.

31. **(B)** The original includes the superfluous pronoun *it* and leaves *seatbelts* without a verb. (D) and (E) do nothing to correct these problems. (C) provides the verb needed to make a complete sentence, but it is awkward and wordy. (B) is both correct and concise.

32. **(C)** When used as a conjunctive adverb, *however* is preceded by a semicolon and followed by a comma. Additionally, a semicolon is used to join closely related *independent* clauses. (B) is a comma splice,

(E) is a fragment, and (D) changes the meaning of the original sentence.

33. **(E)** The correct expressions are *almost always* (not *most always*) and *different from* (not *different than*).

34. **(D)** The *victim* is the one who must be treated and rewarmed. Only (D) correctly places the subject next to the phrase that modifies it.

35. **(E)** The original sentence shifts needlessly from the imperative (*choose*) to the indicative mood (*you should make*). Choices (C) and (D) do the same. (B) shifts subjects (from *you* to *a list*). (E) is consistent in both subject and mood.

36. **(B)** The original sentence says, in effect, that the *traffic noise* is living in the city. (B) provides the correct subject for the introductory phrase and the rest of the sentence. (C) uses *how* when logic calls for *that*. (D) says that her sleep is living in the city. (E) creates a series of introductory phrases with no main clause.

37. **(E)** There is a word missing in (A). The second clause (*will you . . . bicycle*), which is the object of *find out*, lacks a conjunction to link it to the main clause (*Elgin . . . out*). Only (E) provides this link in an indirect question.

38. **(B)** The original (A) and choices (C) and (E) all begin with a dangling modifier. An obstacle cannot make friends; nor can *there*. (A) and (C) also shift, without reason, from active to passive voice; (E) uses an equally awkward construction. (B) is correct; the introductory modifier relates, with the very next word, to a plausible subject (*we*), and the main clause is in the active voice.

39. **(D)** To start the sentence with the adverb *hopefully* is poor since hopefully does not modify government. Therefore, choices (A) and (C) are weak. Choice (B) is vague, and choice (E) has a problem of reference (*their* should be *its*). Choice (D) is best because the entire essay is written from the first person point of view, and the pronoun is correct.

40. **(B)** Choice (A) is weak since the phrase *being one* is poor. Choice (C) contains a comma splice error following *America*. Choice (D) does not convey the sense of the original sentence. Choice (E) is poor since the semicolon following *America* is incorrect punctuation.

41. **(A)** The only choice that is clear and grammatically sound, with proper punctuation and good word choice, is (A).

42. **(C)** Choice (A) makes a fragment of the first part of the sentence, and (B) makes a fragment of the entire sentence. Choice (D), like the original sentence, includes the extra pronoun *they*. Choice (E) changes the meaning.

43. **(C)** The error in sentence (10) is a comma splice error. A comma cannot separate two main clauses. A period or a semicolon should be used after *profession*. This type of error is an error in sentence structure.

44. **(E)** The underlined portion is redundant, as are choices (A), (B), (C), and (D).

45. **(D)** What is required is a grammatically sound and precisely worded revision. The adverb *luckily* is best placed at the beginning of the sentence. Choice (D) is best.

46. **(A)** The only choice that is not awkward and does not misrepresent the material given is choice (A).

47. **(C)** A comma cannot join two independent clauses as in sentence (6). Choice (C) corrects this error by replacing the comma with a semicolon. In choices (A) and (D), the words following the semicolon do not form an independent clause. The use of *being that* in choice (B) is incorrect. Choice (E) creates a fragment.

48. **(C)** The word *it* in sentence (9) has no clear reference. Choices (A) and (B) have the same problem. In addition, choice (A) has a fragment, and choice (B) has a comma splice error. Choices (D) and (E) change the intended meaning. Choice (C) correctly eliminates the vague *it* and makes it clear that these students had a language problem, not a learning disability.

49. **(D)** Choices (A), (B), and (C) are poor since the antecedent of the pronoun *them* is not clear. Choice (E) is wrong since the sentence is awkwardly phrased. Choice (D) is best.

50. **(E)** The use of the pronouns *they* and *them* in sentences (13), (14), and (15) is not always clear. One is not certain to whom the pronoun refers. Often, a precise noun would be a better choice.

51. **(C)** The subject is singular (either *dilemma* or *solution*) and so the verb should be *is*, not *are*.

52. **(C)** The verb is understood, so the phrase should read, "ingenuous *as he (was)* that first year."

53. **(C)** The same person should be maintained. When writing, one should not switch from *you* to *we* without good reason.

54. **(D)** The adjective *rising* is correct.

55. **(B)** It is one student's question; hence, *he is* or *she is* (not *they are*) confused.

56. **(A)** *Is (or was) comprised of* is incorrect. *Comprised* means "embraced, included;" it is not a synonym for *composed*.

57. **(E)** The sentence is correct.

58. **(A)** Canvas is the name of a coarse fabric. This sentence requires the verb *to canvass*, meaning "to go through (an area) to solicit votes, orders, or opinions."

59. **(C)** The subject of the main clause is *conditions*, a plural noun taking a plural verb (*have not*). The subject of the subordinate clause is the *strike*, which properly takes the singular verb *has been settled*.

60. **(B)** A *concept* is not a *place* to be referred to as *where*. A concept is an idea, which we can refer to by using such expressions as *according to which, by which*.